THE INITIALS
IN THE HEART

Other books by Laurence Whistler

ON HIS ENGRAVINGS
The Engraved Glass of Laurence Whistler (1952)
Engraved Glass 1952–1958 (1959)
Pictures on Glass (1972)
The Image on the Glass (1975)
Scenes and Signs on Glass (1985)

POETRY
The World's Room: Collected Poems (1949)
The View from This Window (1956)
Audible Silence (1961)
To Celebrate Her Living (1967)

ON REX WHISTLER
Rex Whistler, His Life and His Drawings (1948)
The Work of Rex Whistler (with Ronald Fuller) (1969)
¡OHO! (1947) *AHA* (1978) (verses to Rex Whistler's
Reversible Faces)
The Laughter and the Urn: The Life of Rex Whistler (1985)

ON ARCHITECTURE
Sir John Vanbrugh, Architect and Dramatist (1938)
The Imagination of Vanbrugh and His Fellow Artists (1954)

THE INITIALS
IN THE HEART

A Celebration of Love

Laurence Whistler

WITH
ADDITIONAL POEMS
by Jill Furse

Weidenfeld and Nicolson
London

This edition published in 1987 by
George Weidenfeld & Nicolson Limited
91 Clapham High Street
London SW4 7TA

ISBN 0 297 79020 X

Printed in Great Britain by
Butler & Tanner Ltd
Frome and London

FOR TESSA

Where the lost truth, being treasured, remains true,
There now, inextricably dear, are you.

Little Place
Lyme Regis

I

The best thing my poetry ever did for me was to bring about the story of this book. But that is enough to compensate in advance for the inevitable death-bed recognition of failure.

To be a poet! Not relinquishing this hope, from the age of fifteen or so until now when I was twenty-four, I published in November 1936 a third book of verse called *The Emperor Heart*, and at my elder brother Rex's suggestion sent a copy to the novelist Edith Olivier at Wilton, that well-read, vivacious, slightly eccentric person who was his closest friend, though perhaps twice his age, and who lived in the Daye House, the converted dairy at one side of the park. Staying with her when it arrived was a young actress, then twenty-one, whose career of great promise on the London stage had been interrupted by illness—paratyphoid, it was said. Edith Olivier had known her from infancy; for she was the grand-daughter of Sir Henry Newbolt at Netherhampton House near-by. In fact almost her earliest memory, from the age of one, was of sliding on a tray along the snowy road beside the wall of Wilton Park. Now she had arrived to convalesce in the little Italianate house just inside the wall, as Edith's journal records. "Jill Furse came before dinner. She has lost her six months' contract to play Shakespeare's *young* heroines at the Old Vic. She still looks very ill." It was her first major disappointment.

Then she was gone, summed up in those not-too-indulgent pages as "lovely to see, perfect manners, very intelligent, sensitive, and great fun." My poems had arrived before she left, and Edith had read them aloud, she told me, "straight through from end to end with a very delightful, sympathetic and poetic guest." Name not given, and effect not mentioned. But she had perceived some effect; for she presently proposed that we should meet, all four, in her house.

Accordingly Rex and I drove to the Daye House in February 1937, where on Sunday morning Jill Furse was to arrive by train for an actress's week-end of one night. (She was playing by then in *Because We Must* at Wyndham's.) Rex, who had met her once already, went to Salisbury station alone. Probably this was said to be less intimidating for her. In reality Edith liked first meetings to take place in her own house. Waiting in the Long Room, I heard the shutting of the car door with the slight uneasiness evoked by that typical sound—an inclination to withdraw from a new encounter that comes of shyness. Devoid of preconceptions, I went out on to the stone path.

My first impressions of people are never overwhelming or reliable. Nor were Jill's, she was to tell me later—a thing seldom admitted by women. I had, gradually, these impressions. A lovely girl of refinement and simplicity, and natural poise; slim, tallish, with a clear musical voice, gentle rather than soft. Both spiritual and spirited. Yet also reticent. Not at all the conventional actress; though that I did not expect her to be. Distinct features, and the skin finely drawn across them. A sensitive mouth. A small straight nose, very faintly raised at the tip and with flared nostrils. A high intelligent forehead left uncovered by the hair— very beautiful hair that flowed away medium-dark but with auburn high-lights. It was a face at that time more childish than it appears in this book. Meeting her first at a theatre, Rex had wanted to paint her (though he never did), being taken by something that he called her "primness." It seems an odd word for her, in retrospect. He must have meant a touch of the demure, of the Victorian, which intrigued him. If his noun is accepted, it needs to be qualified as a physical primness, not a moral one—intriguing just because it was contradicted by a strong suggestion of warmth, an immediate response to anything beautiful or anything funny— by a trustfulness that perhaps had already made her suffer. Such qualities are hardly prim. She did look sad, as though she found

8

life piteous, without pitying herself. She was both tentative in approach and socially quite at ease. Somewhat "mute, mild and mansuete," she nevertheless had "danger" or "daungier"—in the mediaeval sense of compelling deference. She parried the teasing jokes of customary Edith, she fenced with the unfamiliar Whistler interest, more formidable because doubled in brothers. But she ventured shyly, if at all, on jokes herself. She made no deliberate attempt whatever to attract, concerned with things of the mind, and content to be whatever she was, though she did not appear to set conscious value on that. These impressions, I say, came slowly—not all on the first day.

It was St Valentine's Day. (Had Edith arranged even this?) The snowdrops would be out where she remembered them from childhood in the park. My sharpest picture is of standing at a bedroom window—how an incident framed by a window gains meaning, as if removed from the merely fugitive!—to watch her running out of the house and down the track to where they grew. Spontaneous and virginal, her hair bobbing in the wind. Quite unknown. Not "mysterious" in the usual sense, but remote and warm as sunrise on far-off mountains—unexplored as a spiral nebula. Whose was she? Nobody's, perhaps.

The next day occurred one of those little decisions that determine lives. Rex offered me his car, an open Swallow Special, precursor of the Jaguar, to drive her back to London. He was tired, he insisted, and would really prefer to rest and go later by train. (He left, I find, within an hour or so.) It could have been a suggestion of Edith's; but he was of all men I have known the most generous. He needed no prompting. Thus it came to me gratis and unearned from the very beginning.

Not that the drive was eventful, but it established her as my friend more than his. Had he wished otherwise I should have stood no chance. No doubt I should have tried to compete; and, competitive, should not have made myself any more personable. Admiring him as I did, I should have withdrawn without spite at the first clear mark of her preferring him. How could she not?

His reputation would have meant little to her, and his (comparative) wealth nothing—apart from the opportunities for pleasure that only money can create. But considering his looks, charm, character, and gifts, to say nothing of his concern with the theatre, the two might have seemed ideally matched. In point of fact he was involved elsewhere—as often, doubly so, and rather wretchedly; and perhaps he could not have been ideally matched with anyone. For myself this was not love at first sight, and the spirit of perception did not say so clearly to me, "Your blessing has now appeared." But a mutual response had been felt, and I was quick to take chances. She agreed to lunch with me the next day, and on the next again there was supper at the Café Royal, à quatre with Rex and one of his girls, after seeing Jill in her play.

That she was born to act had been foretold in a most striking way when she was seven. The poet Ralph Hodgson came to tea and declared that she had genius, nothing less. When I reminded him of that, years later, he replied, "Heavenly little elf!—as I write this I shut my eyes and here she is, tripping in and out from behind my chair again, each time in an entirely different character—doing anger, pity, sorrow, merriment. . . . It required no especial insight on my part to make that confident prediction: I knew I was watching a consummate artist in advance of time." None of that reached her ears, of course, or was taken very seriously at the time: there was no professional acting in her ancestry. Her own later version was this: "I very soon found out that when I made faces grown-up people laughed, and I definitely held performances." At ten she was taken to the single performance in London of the fairy play Crossings by Walter de la Mare. In this Ellen Terry appeared for the last time on any stage—appeared twice, but only for a moment, as the ghost of the old lady. She did not speak; she smiled—at Ann, the child with whom Jill perhaps identified herself. It was while watching this farewell that Jill first recognized her calling.

A year later Sir Henry Newbolt was describing family charades to a friend. "The quietness and the certainty of her conversa-

tions were marvellous. She said afterwards, 'Oh yes, I did *love* it
—I felt as if I were in a dream'—which sounds rather as though
she had been really acting." [1]

She was fifteen when Ralph Hodgson returned from Japan.
Inviting him to tea, her mother gave news of the family, saying
that Jill did want to act, and recalling that he had seen in her the
promise of talent. "Ah, Jill has no *talent* for the stage," he replied
with conviction undiminished after eight years. "What I saw was
something beyond talent. You'll know all about it when you
open *The Times* on the morning of a day in the autumn of
19—. I forget the exact date, but it is all right. Let her keep her
health and avoid elopements." The two conditions. Twin in-
junctions from a fairy godfather.

He came—as Jill recorded on the first page of the diary she
had been given for Christmas. It had a lock and key and would
become a familiar sight in the family, always locked, but with the
key left dangling. She thought this an excellent arrangement; for
everyone would know that it was private; and the key would not
be lost.

> Mr. Hodgson came to tea. . . . He talked about everything
> under the sun, breaking off to tell me I looked—then he said
> he'd better not tell me how I looked but he would one day.
> He said I must go straight to the top and be a great actress as
> that was my "spiritual home."

Unwaveringly she held to this one ambition. Soon she was in
Switzerland, at St George's School, learning to be a fluent speaker
and writer of French, while the life and the landscape gave happiness. Then, at seventeen, she became a drama student of Elsie
Fogerty's at the Albert Hall. This was a worrying time; for
though it was seen that she was gifted, and though she was un-
shakeable in purpose, her confidence was only too easily shaken.
She appeared to fellow-students, and often to herself, so unlike
what an actress is supposed to be.

[1] *Later Life and Letters*, 1942, p. 348.

At about this time Norman Marshall had bought the small private theatre in Villiers Street called the Gate, and reopened it to give the kind of plays that West End managements never gave; and at least seven of them to a season. No long runs, no stars, equal salaries and those very small—it was an intimate affair. But the audience was said to be the most intelligent in London, as the theatre was certainly the most exciting. The second season, of 1935, included a new play from the French of Jean-Jacques Bernard called *National 6*, simultaneously produced in Paris. Marshall says:

> I found the leading part extremely difficult to cast. It needed an actress who was youthful and unsophisticated without being girlish and ingenuous. Most young English actresses are, on the stage, either too old or too young for their years. They lack the genuine simplicity of youth because they have either tried to grow up too fast or refused to grow up at all. After interviewing dozens of young women the only hope seemed to be to find a girl of the right type who had never been on the stage before. At Miss Fogerty's School I found Jill Furse. She was at once recognized by the critics as an actress of rare and exquisite quality.[1]

Elsie Fogerty thought he was making a mistake. "There's no bellows there!" she told him, thumping her chest. She did not mean simply carrying-power; for she had stationed herself at some remotest point in the Albert Hall and heard Jill speaking every word on the stage, a test that defeated many students. Doubtless she found her altogether too reserved. By contraries Jill may have found that rather fruity and Edwardian example inhibiting.

"It was only after the first night," Norman Marshall says, "that I learned that she had, during rehearsals, gone through agonies of doubt about her ability to do the part. She showed no signs of her nervousness. She always seemed so calm and businesslike."

"The most promising of first performances," wrote W. A.

[1] Norman Marshall, *The Other Theatre*, 1947, p. 111.

Darlington in the *Daily Telegraph*. "If she can keep the delicate sensitiveness of her touch she may go far." The *New Statesman* critic declared: "At present she is neither a great nor even a good actress, but her ethereal charm comes from a personality of the true magnetism from which great acting sometimes springs." One press-cutting arrived from her earliest backer in Japan, simply endorsed, "Good report. Quite content. R.H."

Of course she was longing to play Shakespeare; and Michael Macowan saw her in the play and tried to cast her for Perdita at the Old Vic. But Lilian Baylis did not think her equal to so large a theatre. Her second play was therefore *Whiteoaks* at the Little Theatre, with Stephen Haggard in the cast, on which the *New Statesman* commented, "That lovely actress Jill Furse had too little to do." Miss Baylis and Tyrone Guthrie were now satisfied. Within a week or so came the breathtaking offer of the young Shakespeare heroines, Miranda, Beatrice, and the rest. And the contract was signed. And then illness ruined all. Later Desdemona was offered, and she began to grow long hair. But the production was shelved.

So now in February 1937 here she was in *Because We Must*, another mediocre play, with Vivien Leigh. Mr Darlington still approved. To him her performance was "just about the best thing in the evening." So thought I, distinguishing between criticism and incipient involvement, on that evening when with Rex and his girl I went to see her. But it was a pity that I missed her, next month at the Gate, as Lily in *Out of Sight*, the daughter of the clerk who has gone to prison, a part that required the pathos she could give it. During this run she wrote in her diary:

When I played on Saturday I nearly broke down and cried. —I have wondered since if that was why Lily was so good that night. I thought at the time it was because ——— was there. But it happened again last night and again I gave a very good performance. I must try one night crying properly and see what happens.

13

She had not been ready for Shakespeare last year. She recognized that. But now she was brimming with expectancy.

> I wonder what's going to happen next. I want a marvellous part now—it would be such fun. Desdemona, Desdemona, Desdemona. How she haunts me and tantalises me.

A few notes in her copy of the play suggest that she would have made of that heroine a playful, even teasing, innocent; not a woebegone of purity.

Fundamentally the reason I missed *Out of Sight* was poverty. My father's building business, once lucrative, had dwindled to nothing by the time he retired. At Balliol I was generously supported by the College, but I did little work there, and had no ambition whatever but in verse. Coming down with a second, I took a second-rate job in Church Assembly, rashly telling a friend that "a year's future is all one ever wants to see." I quickly found that I was sunk without trace beneath the feet in the tube lift, morning and evening, for ever . . . That is, for five months. For I was rescued in 1935 by the astonishing award of the King's Gold Medal for Poetry, the first and most publicized; or rather I was rescued by Kenneth Rae, my original publisher, who now commissioned a life of Vanbrugh, chosen because his architecture excited me. Sweet rescue it was. But scholarly biography does not pay—at least when undertaken by a novice who cannot write prose as fast as some poets write verse. £50 down, in exchange for £3 a week: it meant giving up my London room, and working mostly at my parents' house in north Buckinghamshire. Fortunately I had begun to engrave glass with a diamond, teaching myself, since there was no one to learn from. But this, with the frequent versifying, meant that Vanbrugh was still very much of a labour when Jill and I met.

Neither was happy. She ought to have been happy with so promising a future and so many friends. She did not falter, but she had innate misgivings—about herself. Her unconfidence had been worsened by the slow fading out of a relationship in which she had trusted, her first true affair of the heart. Writing her diary after the play, she fell into the slightly stilted cynicism of youthfulness. "He liked me tonight. I'm afraid it must have been the spring—or my new hat. It would be rash to impute it to anything more lasting. I must see Rex and Laurie again. I've been re-reading Laurie's poetry." Any implication in the sequence of ideas was quite unconscious, but the entry shows that she was ready for new friendship, though not for new trust.

I was unhappy, without need of external cause. Too timid and self-conscious, and too poor—I had had no cheque-book—to make anything of Oxford until it was nearly too late to begin, I had seen a little gaiety in my last year, but had come down without one new permanent friend of my own age. I had nothing to recall of that time but two love-affairs and two books of verse, all outgrown. No companionship was like Rex's; but in the presence of others he inhibited me and I felt like his shadow. Consequently in that brilliant world which he longed to introduce me to, I made small headway. Not that this worried me: the reputation I coveted was in the twilight world of poetry. Yet in poetry I was bewildered. I had been sped on my way—and failed to "arrive." I had failed with the younger reviewers, and the medal only earned me their rancour. I feared that the older men rejoiced to back me as a young traditionalist, out of step with the disturbing new movement. Which they did, and I was. With my assumption, never examined, that "traditional" must be a synonym for "conventional" I was often silenced completely. Then that dejected me still more. For then I supposed that if I had any talent I should know it—and was like some Calvinist horribly not-conscious of being one of the Elect. And still there were those other times when I could not think my rapture in the use of words to be wholly spurious. Thus I alternated between advance and repulse, like an obstinate snail bumped by a windy leaf. I remember as a moment of sun the news of de la Mare's approval, passed on by Jill who had known him from her childhood; but even he was not young in years.

I, too, had innate unconfidence; and this prevented my believing that I could do anything at all unless I had, by sleight, or by accident as it seemed, already done it. My uncertainty extended beyond verse to the very citadel of self, or rather radiated from there. I did not know what I believed. I did not know who I was. Often I did not *like* living, which is not the same thing as wishing it to stop. I was saved from cynicism only by the glad appetites of youth and the never-extinguished craving to create. My emotional life, once happy, had arrived at an end distressingly drawn out. At twenty-five—to be a little portentous, but appropriately so—I was like a shaky civilization not asking for a new religion to transform it.

Thus Jill in London, and I in the country. We could meet only when I came up for architectural research in museum and library, and to make use of Rex's flat. She too lived at home. Very few established actresses of twenty-two would be content with this, but she was more at peace with her family, and superficially less grown-up than is normal. She had been ill too often to be eager for independence of the outward sort; and inwardly she had it, as I presently perceived. In April we began to meet about five times a month, mostly for lunch in modest Soho restaurants; rarely in one more expensive. I noticed that while she relished the good living other friends could provide, she took it for an occasional luxury. Pleased with *vin ordinaire* as with a vintage wine, she chose inexpensive dishes without a hint of motive, making poverty seem ours, not mine. It was courteous, but more than courtesy, this early mark of an unspoilt simplicity. We had the same love-hate towards London, it appeared. We began to make excursions of escape: as once to Oxford, to lie in the fritillaries beside a punt in Port Meadow. Late that night I said that I was entirely at her feet. She was pleased, and did not believe me; for this was only a half-truth, as the conventional phrase made evident. It was a pity to have spoken prematurely. It did not matter.

Through such days I discovered the strength of her character, and what I would call the clarity of her spirit. It sprang from a fusion of humility and sure ideals. She did not seem to have intellectual convictions; at least she did not have rigid opinions. Strong opinions she had, and expressed them with zeal, but as like as not would break off with "Well, I don't know . . .", having instantly seen how an opposite case could be argued. Her mind was open. Her certainties were of the heart and imagination.

Through such days, too, I discovered her sense of humour, in some of its variety. It could be childish. It could also be deliciously indecent, belying that demure appearance. Indelicate, however, it hardly was, so nimbly did she confine it at that time to the broken sentence, the dropped glance, or the eloquent silence, never permitting more than was appropriate to our degree of intimacy; and that was not great. . . . Indistinct days of some progress to no distinct end.

And then I began to understand the sadness that lay beneath laughter and enthusiasm. Early childhood, it appeared, had promised something glorious of life which the adult world would never now fulfil. It could not be helped; for such was growing-up. Recently, supporting her pessimism, there had been the last and worst disappointment of love; but no one was to blame. This failure she revealed to me, after a while. Meanwhile the locked book was receiving similar reflections. She wanted to go abroad, to unknown countries like Provence and Italy, but preferably alone. "I think I'm growing to need people less. I'm always happy by myself as long as I have books or lovely things to look at. One should be self-supporting inside if one can be—I'm sure God means us to be." Another day it was London spring across the black little garden walls, sharply recalling Netherhampton. "Will one never look forward again?" Nothing, she wrote in her diary, would ever matter like the impact of beauty in childhood, not even her career—"nor any one person any more."

She did not want to be hurt any more. New companionship she wanted, but not self-surrender. My case was altogether different, if not opposite. Nothing but possession would assuage me, and the lack of it was very hard to bear at times. My mind leapt ahead to it, and, finding no assurance, recoiled into frivolity. Though never intentionally cruel, she would jib and side-step, laugh and parry to the end of time, I thought. I adopted a frivolous pose to provoke. "Have you heard any Chinese music?" —I put the needle on a badly warped dance record. "How fascinating!"—She was touchingly easy to take in. But there was an ache like a hollow tooth in this teasing. I longed to be somewhere beyond it with her, somewhere hardly imaginable, where the necessary laughter sprang unanimous out of intimacy, and did not involve her in "playing back" to a joke, did not call for the mock-pout and charming mime of injury: "I think you're horrid!" But thus it was. And "Chinese music?" became a question in her guarded glance, until it fell out of currency for ever.

It was more than a pose, it was a persona I adopted. Immature as I was, there were times when I was dreadfully afraid that I was no one. I had to be someone in her eyes, even if someone who had been what she would not approve of. She would not condemn, I knew. She was realistic about people, and very gentle in her natural wisdom. Unconsciously despairing, then, of any future together, I let her form the impression that I had been rather a "rake," as she presently put it. This was not only absurd but manifestly so, because any genuine rake in my situation would be at pains to camouflage himself; but this did not strike her unsophisticated mind. My experience of love, in fact, had been as honest as Rex's, and narrower. Really I made out a very poor case for myself, fabricating by innuendo to my own disadvantage.

She was brought up with the same Christian notions of marriage as we were, and her view of love was exalted. Marriage was a sacrament, the most beautiful and difficult form of loving, only to be attempted by those who were prepared for sacrifices. She had put down in her diary, at nineteen, a conversation with a fellow-student who used to confide in her, much to her surprise.

People can be classed as natural penitents or confessors, and Jill had notably the three marks of a confessor: warm understanding —discretion—and no itch to be told. Your confessor can have anyone's story at will; never tries to; and often must. Anyone's, that is, except another confessor's. I mention this only because I was one myself, in a much smaller way; and thus we did not rush to unburden our histories, but rather revealed them in hints, and step by step, more easily talking of ideas and sensations. This fellow-student, then, had a new mistress, with whom he had nothing in common but sex. "I wonder why I don't behave like that," she had asked herself, "and whether if I live among these people it will be harder. It all seems so sordid and the spoiling of something rare that belongs to one man only, and it doesn't matter whether you know him yet or not. A. said it was ridiculous to be faithful to a woman you've never met. But then it isn't being faithful to the woman that counts but to the eternal that she brings in her. Perhaps this is all rubbish and I should have lived with someone if I hadn't lacked the curiosity or had been brought up differently. The trouble is it seems to matter so little." She must have been aware of the notion that "experience"—which always means sexual experience in this context— would be good for her art, but she wisely thought that it would not, unless it mattered. About ideals in general she was now telling herself "They should be pure—and livable. Like a long unending range of peaks, impossibly lovely, but scaleable all the same."

Throughout our first spring, then, Rex, who was approaching thirty-two, could have been a formidable rival had he chosen to be. In May she recorded:

I had lunch with Rex at the Jardin des Gourmets and that was *lovely*. He is a darling, one of the most attractive and fascinating people in the world. But he has a sad face and his hair is going grey. He works much too hard and has I believe been always fond of people who wouldn't marry him. He's a more trustworthy person than Laurie I think and has far more fundamental goodness in his face. In lots of ways they're very alike—the same voice and hands and the same freakish sense of humour. I should love to know him really well. But then I always fall for sad people. I always think they are the kind I should like to marry and make happy for ever after. I feel I could give something that they've never had before. But I expect it is only a fancy like all my hopes and ideals.

As for Laurie, I'm much too fond of him without either trusting or being in love with him. I love his mind—one side of it, and we fit extraordinarily well. We're much too like each other, though.

"Too like." It is not the usual obstacle; and surely it could only intrude for potential lovers each of whom was dissatisfied with himself. We were already half-conscious of something we shared with each other as never with anyone else. Does not everyone feel that he looks out from some inmost cell—or gazebo—of personality, to a vision of existence that is utterly private and in-communicable? Well, we sensed that our secret visions over-lapped, notwithstanding our outward differences. She thought it inauspicious; that I needed someone quite different from her, and she from me; that there has to be a sense of "otherness" in love, as of strangers grown intimate. I thought this wrong, but could not prove it. The truth that physical love, when happy, provides through the opposition of sex all the "otherness" one could wish for, and permeates the whole of ordinary life, like roads winding up to and down from a glittering hill-city—this truth was unguessed by her. How one could simply trust love to thrillingly impose on similarity the huge distinction of sheer gender was not envisaged.

On the other hand small similarities were only helpful. For example, neither of us smoked—but smokers never conceive that the flavour of stale nicotine in a kiss can be disenchanting. Then her eyesight matched mine. She could compete with me for the tiniest marks on a glass, and for the faint pricking of an obelisk twenty-five miles away. We saw the world clear and liked clarity, liked it more than the mistiness preferred by most painters. Yet to say this is no truer than saying that one likes darkness—as indeed we did. No one likes total darkness. What the eye feeds on must always be light—and in darkness the mystery, solace or excitement of diminished light. Total clarity also would be disagreeable. It is the softening of the sharpest daylight into blue remoteness that appeals. We discovered an equal relish for the remote, and one day she would think of writing an Ode to Distance.

For she wrote verses, in both English and French, and began to show them to me, with much diffidence. They issued from the single mood of reflective sadness.

> *Tonight there was a woman come to stare*
> *From the opposite window, parting the firelit lace*
> *Of curtains on the vacant square;*
> *Fingers on glass, eyes upon nothing there,*
> *And hardly light on that indifferent face.*
>
> *I never saw a woman more alone—*
> *A statue to empty lives that grow, obscure:*
> *Sad when their narrow day is gone*
> *That there was no love said or done,*
> *Knowing their sadness only will endure.*

She had been passionately fond of poetry from the earliest years, encouraged and educated by her grandfather, Newbolt, that catholic appreciator. And it was, after all, poetry of a sort, her own sort, that had brought and kept us together, as she was to remind me, years later. "I remember the shock, almost physical and almost prophetical, that went through me when old E O read *The Emperor Heart*. I suppose that to the part of me which recognized you in that moment in Edith's room, all this was *known* —had happened and was still happening. Otherwise it would not have made such a tremendous impression." Another time she wished that a soldier-friend at the war could have had with his mistress "an intellectual contact to hold on to in letters. It was always that which kept me with L before I learnt to love him." And once when I teased her for being biased in my favour, she replied, "But I loved and admired your poetry *long* before I loved or admired you, so I've never seen quite where the prejudice came in!" Thus she disproved that faint verse never won fair lady.

One day as we ate together, after her return from abroad that summer, I quoted Hawksmoor's recommendation of a design he had made. "What I have sent you is Authentic, and what is According to the ye antients, and what is Historicall, and good Architecture, Convenient, Lasting, Decent, and Beautifull." A fairly wide range of virtues—I suggested that we might mark each other out of ten. The result shows what each of us thought, or thought it best for the other to think:

	Convenient	Lasting	Decent	Beautiful
L on J:	5	10	7	10
J on L:	10	0	0	6

I got full marks for Convenient, because, with theatrical business and a more social day than mine, she was always cancelling or altering our arrangements, and I never complained; for she was never capricious. The biggest error was my nought for Lasting, had she only guessed. And for that my fatuous persona was to blame. I almost knew that mark was wrong.

II

Returning from a holiday abroad with a sense of roots torn in both countries, she felt that she belonged to the seventeenth century, was irremediably old-fashioned, hated the speed of the present. She was still there, in the little Swiss courtyard, where the wistaria had moved against the wooden gallery. She daydreamed with her diary.

> If I planned my life now, setting my stage life apart, I should like a husband whose career was vitally important—to me if to no one else!—who loved me enough to forgive my failings and not enough to spoil me, who loved only a few of the things I loved, I couldn't hope for all.

She pictured the home they would have (some other Netherhampton, of course), the children, the ilex, and the river. She recognized that really her longing was for early childhood, in an adult world that now seemed glamourless and alarming. Thus in a poem:

> *With every rapture that I sing*
> *The childish tears will blind me.*
> *In every room I look into*
> *A door has closed behind me.*

But she did not mean to remain an escapist. "I'm not really afraid, at least I don't think so." The purpose was there. The mountains were climbable. Then with a complete change of mood—"I have found Donne and am happy. He fascinates and repels me, and any man who does that is dangerous." The next day, convinced by the frankly carnal Elegy XIX, she denied the repulsion, finding only "a glorious comprehension of both physical and spiritual." In such hours she grew; for growth is not continuous.

There were hours, though, when she was wretched from "a mixture of no work, Laurie, and the unsettledness of myself." Ralph Hodgson would have thought our friendship precisely the kind she should avoid. Not that "elopement" was likely, for we made no progress: fell back, even. Still, we could not relinquish each other. A day at Stowe together, where I had been at school, filled her mind with the beauty of round grey temples in a gauze of rain. We were not happy face to face, as it were; but when we looked at good things side by side, it seemed by their expression that we ought to be. "I wish I didn't make you sad, my dear—it's so wrong and such a pity. I always get so much pleasure from seeing you." And to herself: "There is so much in him that I love and so much that I distrust and fear. He has been so very kind to me, and I don't think knowing me has made him more unhappy than he was already."

Depressed by failure, tormented by sex, I padded moodily like a caged animal, or did turns for relief. I seemed cynical, and felt merely discontented, aimless. Reading Freud for the first time, she wrote, "It's a great pity to reduce everything to sex and deny that there is a life of the spirit." I agreed. "You probably won't agree with me as I know your philosophy of life is very, very different from mine." It had not been very different once, and was becoming less so, under her influence. She took a private vow to live for her acting,

work harder, and worry less about what is happening to me personally. Until I fall really in love and marry I must dedicate myself. I know that, fundamentally, I think about the theatre in the right, truly artistic and humble way. But one is led superficially into becoming faintly vain and self-expressionist. Today I want to dedicate myself to the highest things—to doing all that I can to the glory of God. And God help me not to be selfish.

The "marvellous part" she wanted was not forthcoming, and perhaps she was being pigeon-holed under "pathos." After *Out of Sight* she had appeared in *Lord Adrian*, also at the Gate. Perhaps the big parts would not come her way until her personality had been enriched by happiness. How to be enriched, though, and still heed Hodgson's warning not to jeopardize her whole career? In September she went into *Victoria Regina* at the Lyric, taking over the minor part of Lady Jane.

By winter's end three events had occurred. My family home had been sold, since Buckinghamshire was too cold for my father in failing health; and I was delivered of *Vanbrugh*, with relief; and I had taken a small flat in London. Years later, casting back in memory, she sent me a poem written, she said, "because I thought how odd it was that while you were at Oxford and I in Switzerland we couldn't *know* that we were moving all our days towards each other. That even then I was like an unlit candle in the shadows of your room."

My new room was on the first floor of Constable's House, No. 76 Charlotte Street, and had once been the drawing-room of the painter I loved most in those days. On the mantelpiece I put the human skull I had acquired while at Oxford, called Truepenny. For £7 a month I had this room and the small one behind it, and Rex furnished them for me in the Regency style, with striped curtains, and gave me a set of coloured eighteenth-century prints of Rome which for years made me suppose that city to be spaciously laid out, like Belgravia. Somewhere he found me a self-portrait of Constable as a young man at his easel, in features very like the pencil portrait of 1806: one day it may well be accepted as authentic. He designed the curved wooden frame, with padded upholstery striped green and buff, which by day turned my bed into a capacious sofa at one end of the room. Then he gave me a little oil painting he had made of Eros and Psyche, she kneeling naked, her face lifted to the hands of the winged boy who bent towards her. This I placed above the bed.

When Jill came to see me the first day, we leant on the sill,

25

looking down into Charlotte Street, still more or less Georgian, and less squalid than now, pondering my new stretch of living with that sense of "time enough" which only young people have. Spring was actual above the houses opposite, London's flat dandelion spring of down clouds over parapets, and yellow light on stock bricks. Summer seemed lengthy, but still notional. From far away to the left, out of Oxford Street, by way of Percy Street or Rathbone Place, in a high crescendo of voices, the news-boys came baying a special edition. Hitler had been speaking on Czechoslovakia.

Nothing followed from the move but pleasanter days for me, though I made hardly any new friends in that quarter of artists. When Tambimuttu, the poets' compère, rang the bell in friendly inquiry, I gave him but an awkward welcome, partly because I had gone down in my socks, for some reason. I wrote, and I engraved—thirteen glasses this year, earning perhaps £130. It seems odd that I could share so much of life with my £1800-a-year brother up the road, but then his generosity was always reducing the effective difference. I liked the long twilight of my open window, warm-scented with grime and exhaust, a twilight drawn to a thread by the sketchy tinkling of a distant barrel-organ.

Jill had returned to the Gate for *Elizabeth La Femme Sans Homme*, followed by *The Masque of Kings*, Maxwell Anderson's play on the Mayerling tragedy. In this she played Marie Vetsera, Prince Rudolph's seventeen-year-old mistress. "Miss Jill Furse, with a radiantly virginal air, played an unvirginal character with a delicacy fetching in itself, but fatal to the character," said one critic, though others were better pleased. Then she was away to Switzerland, Paris, and the Riviera, where she danced and lived well for a week, met Maurice Chevalier, the Oliviers and other stage friends, and resisted an invitation to go to Cornwall with a member of the Crazy Gang.

We were supposed to be uncommitted; and yet, in Cambridge for the first time, at the exact moment when we stepped from sunlight into the chill glory of King's Chapel, the organ burst out into Bach's Toccata and Fugue in D Minor, and, by the sheer gooseflesh thrill of it, turned our entry into a coronation. In love, when the notion of providence replaces the notion of coincidence, the committal has occurred. But we had hardly acknowledged that, and were still groping. For example, neither was particularly jealous by nature, though she more than I. When she was jealous I hated it: so that when I was jealous I concealed it. Yet jealousy too well hidden is not flattering to a woman. Then, I made it a point of honour to earn my ten for Convenient, only to find that she began to take it for granted. Irritated to be supposed a kind of spaniel, and exasperated by her long reserve, I lay on the sofa with her one day and took her character to pieces, indifferent to the consequences, which, with most girls, would have been injured pride and a quarrel. She defended herself, but with a look of quiet interest; and years later claimed it as the hour in which I won her respect. But neither of us knew what was needed, or what would result from any action. We were still taking risks of losing one another.

On my way to Clovelly that August I was invited to spend one night at the Furses' holiday home, called Venton, a farm on her grandfather's estate somewhere to the south of Torrington. From the wayside station the car took me deep into an unknown part of North Devon that had always seemed, from my annual Clovelly point of view, obscurely "mid" and sadly unmaritime; and now seemed each minute more indispensable and gay, with the glorious blue wave of Dartmoor, new to me, flowing along on the left, over wind-skewed beech hedges. At the end of a rough lane, near a group of elms, I found an ancient farm of rough stone and white cob, under a long thatched roof that rose to an engaging hump about the middle, with rather the effect of a crouched animal, but a friendly one.

I had first met Jill's parents at the Coronation of the year before, on a stand in the Mall, when I had scored a good mark for entertaining the youngest children, Nicolas and Theresa, and a bad one for making Jill giggle with a joke about the ritual—weak, but harmless, I had wrongly supposed. Perhaps my judgement had been warped by my love for Sir Edwin Lutyens, who never ceased from far worse flippancies. This lapse had been overlooked, possibly: anyway I was received without the least constraint, whatever was thought, by a family that loved one another with a refreshing lack of the aggressive or, at best, subtly exclusive "family manner" which commonly results from a strong bond. I took instantly to them all and to their way of life in this house, which for me perfectly combined a measure of style with pastoral simplicity—a painted panel in the Queen Anne parlour, with old string-and-bobbin latches to the bedroom doors. The farmer's family lived under the same roof-tree, at one end of Venton beyond a door left unlocked, and that itself was characteristic of the easy simplicity. It seemed to me a delectable way of life: farm-house meals on a bench in the stone-flagged kitchen, raw home-brewed cider and Devonshire cream—and all the day and all the night of deep country.

I woke to a second day of dazzling light. Jill showed me the farm, and led me out through the high-banked fields to where they fled steeply into a narrow valley, from the bottom of which rolled up higher again on the other side the huge August boskage of a hanging wood. Somewhere, to the west, there was a river— but for another visit. Here, down the floor of the wood, flowed a stream, meandering half out-of-sight among hart's-tongue ferns and mossy roots. Then I twisted my ankle.

Apt and singing pain! There is nothing like a small physical pain for a solvent to the affections. I sat and cooled the bulge on tender instructions in flowing crystal. I relinquished the satisfactory lump to fingertips that bound and knotted the handkerchief with deftly feminine solicitude. I made light of it, and the most of it. I rejoiced to have it hot and gleeful in her hands. For how could there be anything but rare pleasure in all this for the pair of us? I now had a footing in the Eastern Brook. It had hastened to take a hand in the story.

An hour before the car was due, she suddenly asked me to engrave the family names on the guest-room window-pane. Across a landscape where a distant church tower stood up beside a round bit of Dartmoor's blue, I wrote:

Ralph and Celia Furse
Jill, Patrick, Nicolas and Theresa

and then the date—*August 17th 1938*. As I did so, she, silent beside me, said something that made me glance at her. It was not already in my mind, and yet it seemed that I had said it myself. That instant I knew beyond doubt that she really did look at life with my eyes, a thing never known or hoped for. One day she would write:

> Seeing things the same . . . that is our most perfect gift of all. Do you remember the first time you came to Venton and stood engraving on the window of what would be our room, and I said something. . . . That and your ankle were I suppose what made me love you. But I can never imagine why I took so long!

In my thanking letter I asked her mother if I might return—just to finish the engraving. But it could not be managed. In twenty-four hours we had advanced measurably, and it may have been thought wise, for the moment, to part the speeding guest. Our letters had a new tone. "Today it's pouring with rain, as it was before you came, and I have to go and look at the window-pane against dark clouds to make sure that it wasn't a dream. . . . Having you here has made everything more valuable. We are so very bound together in some ways. Don't let us lose each other."

I did not return to London but to Salisbury, where my father and mother had settled in the Walton Canonry, No. 69 in the Close. Red-brick-pilastered, it stood in a cul-de-sac beyond the west front of the Cathedral, with a long garden running down to the Avon and the water-meadows beyond. Rex had taken a lease, and was enraptured by the prospect, for he hoped one day to bring a bride to the house. As for ourselves, there could be no going back now, though we hardly perceived it. For the slow unfolding of two slow-paced lives nothing lacked but the expectation of peace; and that had dwindled to nothing.

"I don't think I'm a coward in any physical sense, for myself," Jill wrote in the mounting tension. She went up to rehearse, but the play was put off, and on the day when war seemed certain she returned to Devon. We travelled together from London as far as Salisbury, tranquil and at one. Chamberlain, however, was at Munich; so next day a telegram recalled her to London. I came to Salisbury platform and handed her a rose. At Waterloo the old lady in her compartment broke the silence of English reserve to exclaim, "You *are* a lovely girl!" Such was our Munich crisis.

"I should like to write a poem about that journey to Salisbury," she said. "It's strange having everything given back after such a complete renunciation." We were closer, if not clearer in mind.

I wish I could give you the things you need. I think I shall learn. What I said today about your work and the need for sacrificing to it is something that worries me often—both for you and for myself. And I can't bear to think that other people have helped you to write. It's that that makes me sad when I'm with you. Suddenly it comes over me and everything seems clouded with ghosts. But you must bear with me. What we have is so precious that surely there must be a future for it. If we believe in ourselves (or rather in each other, as neither of us will ever believe in himself!) we can save it out of the chaos of the modern world . . . Even if things go all against us, remember that as long as you live and I live there is someone who knows and loves you for what you are.

I've been suddenly changed in these last few weeks. I've told you things I've never told anyone before and have found that you understand them as if it were one person and not two. I'm writing this on the awful pink couch in my dressing room. I love you so much.—I've never written that before— it looks strange, scribbled in pencil—but as it's recorded in the stars as well, I expect this doesn't matter.

Her new play was *Goodness, How Sad!* at the Vaudeville, an entertaining light comedy by Robert Morley. In this she played Carol, the heroine, and it was a bigger, if not a better, part than any she had had. Her acting had always been distinguished for emotional integrity, and perhaps the events of the summer had given it substance; for all the critics were pleased, and several looked ahead. "A good omen for a brilliant career." "Jill Furse looks like making herself famous." "She is an actress headed for the top."

If I went to America in the Spring to make money, would you wait for me? How long would you wait? Would you wait alone? Questions to be answered in the affirmative or not at all. I wonder if it *would* be possible to combine marriage and a career—how much would you mind if I did?—supposing we did marry. But anyway it's all out of the question for a year or so, I imagine. I hope I shall like '39—it has a friendly and encouraging sound.

Few people really understood that war must come. One hoped for a miracle—a second one, and more honourable.

It was shaping to be that rare thing in the south, a snowy Christmas, and our walks about London were heightened with white. From her stage-door off the Strand I escorted her up the short hill, bright-eyed in a flying scarf of breath, to supper in the warmth of Rule's, there to glance with interest at Charles Morgan, then dramatic critic. So home by tube to the Victorian silences of Holland Park, and the leaves in lamplight over the last corner, each with an exact white outline to trace with a meditative finger. But on the night before Christmas Eve I brought to her dressing-room a Siamese kitten, which was named Vanbrugh and would presently turn into a devil. "Sir John sleeps round my neck and I love him nearly as much as I love you. It's a bit frightening to find oneself feeling as deeply as this." He entered symbolically into the first happy dream she had had of us.

You came down a huge flight of stairs poised in the air with no base and no top. We met in the middle and you kissed me and we stood leaning over the parapet and looking down on a tiny harbour rather like Clovelly, and on the quay there was a lion walking up and down among the lobster pots. We were ridiculously happy and the sun was warm and the world looked distant and hazy.

It still looked distant on New Year's Day when she arrived at the Close for her first visit to my family. But soon "world events" were pressing again like a cancer on the nerve of personal living; and there is no other living.

Her life now had a strain of its own, for she was acting at night and filming by day. Her success as Carol had led quickly to two contracts, and first to a small part in *Goodbye Mr Chips* with Robert Donat and Greer Garson. An assistant director was Pen Tennyson, a gay and brilliant extrovert who had been my friend at Balliol—who would today be famous if he had not disappeared on a flight in the war. Promoted to director, he at once engaged Jill for a film about boxing, called *There Ain't No Justice*. She played the hero's sweetheart, a milk-bar girl. At one point she had to hold a crying baby; but it refused to cry. Tennyson was merciless.

> They smacked it and washed its face hard with a scrubby towel (which it hates), and it would cry till I picked it up, and then smile at me through its tears and murmur, "Oh golly!" I nearly cried most of the time, but not the baby.

The climax, directed by the veteran Bombardier Wells, and constantly rehearsed, was a realistic free-fight all round the ring. A mutual attachment soon formed between Jill and the toughs who crowded the set, and were much concerned for her safety. On the film's release she was thought by the *Sunday Times* to be "the answer to some of our industry's worries." But the cinema was no rival to the stage.

She was sometimes ill, and often haunted by the sense of time running out, yet uncertain of action. (The Germans marched into Prague.) "Did you pray for me in the Cathedral this morning?

I need someone to pray for me a little now and then when they can spare the time. I don't think I make a very good attempt at living, and after all it's the most important thing in this life—far more important than the actual things we do." But what was living likely to involve? "It's funny—writing this I can hardly remember you—not your face at all—and your hands only a little." Sir Thomas Browne observes that "whom we truly love we forget their lookes . . . and it is no wonder, for they are our selves, and our affections make their lookes our owne." There is then a degree of identification which makes it easier to picture almost anyone more clearly than the beloved. Was she experiencing this already; or still some deep reluctance?

For her birthday, April 3rd, I engraved a goblet, adapting two lines from a poem of hers, to make them speak of incorruptibility in a deliquescent world, and so of herself:

> *Like swans that illustrate illustrious waters,*
> *Breasting the warm air with a shield of snow.*

Next day, she left *Goodness, How Sad!*, and I travelled with her family to Venton for a ten days' visit over Easter.

This Devon was becoming for me, privately, the landscape of home. I am a Hampshireman on my father's side, with a mother devoted to that county from childhood, though I have never lived in it myself. Hampshire is debatable West Country, but at least it is Wessex. Hardy links it with Devon as "Upper Wessex" with "Lower," and I am glad of this, for my compass-needle has always swung west. Jill was anciently of Devon as a Furse, but with a mixed ancestry where Irish and French Huguenot seem most clearly to account for other sides of her character. The Halsdon estate was a Furse inheritance, bounded on the west for about two miles by the Torridge.

Accordingly this country answered an ideal—indeed more for me than for her, whose affection hitherto was chiefly for Wiltshire, the country round Netherhampton. She showed it to me exactly as she would have shown me her remote valley of gentians and waterfalls high on a mountain in Switzerland. I saw that her pleasure in my pleasure was pure. In it there was no trace of the smell of ownership.

The Furse children were spirited. The elder pair, Jill and Patrick, understood one another and clowned together infectiously. She mixed, I thought, a robust Furse vitality with an accurate delicacy of perception that might be Newbolt. The younger pair, Nicolas and Theresa, were full of wild or deep adventures—Theresa especially absorbed in the life of the woods and fields. I loved the whole family, their individualism and wood-smoke, their hard beds and their eager minds, their fowls and flowers and hilarity, their courtesy and their dogs, their wild daffodils and religion. I may have been a stranger to them: they were never strangers to me. I felt a marked kinship with my own family, in tone of living and believing, and this is not common; for sex, the ironist, delights to pick true partners from the most diverse backgrounds, as if to chuckle at their laboured adjustments.

Among the children of both families it was accepted that art was supreme and great work must be achieved by us all. "I wonder what you'll be like when you're famous—if I'll know you by then," Jill had just written in dejection. "Perhaps we'll meet in other people's drawing-rooms—both stars in our own right." Art was life, and the very mode of her faith, though other forms of eminence might be interesting. "I like reading about saints without any Catholic treacle," she would say, later on, of Vita Sackville-West's book on Teresa of Avila, a saint whose brilliant and amusing goodness delighted her. . . . But Pat would paint, Theresa would write, and in all their arts they had support from their parents. So did I from mine, though my only ancestor of artistic eminence was Paul Storr the silversmith, my great-great-grandfather. I was never under extreme pressure at home to earn my living in another way, and yet for years I could not earn it in this. To Whistlers and Furses, of Jill's generation and mine, parents were truly the background, or more properly the ground, the fertile seed-bed. "That's what you're *for!*" Jill would protest, when some demand on her mother's energy or time met with demur. She frankly exploited her, but because of their love for one another it did not seem to matter. She had a theory of gems and matrixes—that creative talent often skips a generation, whose mission is to guard and transmit it to the next; but she applied this theory only backwards, never to her own children. Thus two generations back she had a poet,[1] a sculptor,[2] and a painter.[3] Now there were her brothers, Theresa, and herself, all aflame with enterprise. "And look at you in between!" she once cheerfully exclaimed to her distinguished father and her gifted mother. That was going too far. She was put in her place.

Year by year adventurous young men were being hand-picked for the Colonial Service by her father, as Director of Recruitment. Sound and likely though they were, they were not much encouraged to meet his daughter, it was said, for fear of one carrying her afar; though it is hard to see her mixing sun-downers on some Buganda verandah. She chose her own young men, and a miscellany we were—not all of us adventurous in the best way, or sound and likely in any. But she was free, with the freedom from moral coercion that prevailed in her wise family; and thus I was accepted with more than kindness—with a gradual affection.

So in this blossoming farm, whose life was according to my notion of living, whose views were my views, whose window I now engraved at her father's suggestion with the Furse coat-of-arms, I rejoiced. It broke a silence—had me writing again—sent me back to a narrative poem I had abandoned two years before, the story of the Shunammite woman transposed into the English countryside, and told in Chaucerian rhyme-royal: than which anything less likely to succeed in the 1930s would be hard to imagine. Jill at once proposed, and her parents gave consent, that in May I should return to write by myself, looked after by the farmer's wife.

[1] Sir Henry Newbolt.   [2] John Henry Furse, her other grandfather.
[3] Charles Wellington Furse, her great-uncle. A great-great-uncle was William Cory.

On a day when the dictators were more than normally disturbing we travelled to London, for rehearsals of the next play. This was *The Intruder* at Wyndham's, a translation of *Asmodée* by François Mauriac. The producer was her friend Norman Marshall, who had discovered her. He described to me afterwards how "she instinctively husbanded her energies except when she was actually rehearsing. So she gave the impression of being very quiet and reserved. Her method was painstaking. Except in her first part, I don't think she had any doubts about being able to understand and experience the emotions of a part, so she took immense care over the technical details." In quality of writing *The Intruder* was much the best play she was ever in. A straightforward young Englishman (Peter Coke) comes to stay *au pair* at a French country house and unintentionally arouses complex emotions, pure and corrupt, in all around him. He falls in love with Emmanuele, who wants to be a nun, and she gradually with him. Then jealousy consumes her widowed mother, also the tutor, who himself makes a pass at the girl; but against corruption she is armed by the wisdom of innocence. The conclusion leaves the younger pair with a prospect of happiness; and the older—with each other.

It was not an easy play for a first-night audience, the theme being spiritual, and some of them talked and tittered, mostly at the reptile tutor (Eric Portman). Perhaps Jill was uneasy about it for an opposite reason, sensing the evil, yet feeling the issues too imprecise—at least when expounded by an English cast—and therefore subtly unpleasant. But she was delighted with Emmanuele, a character from the hand of a master, and thus not confined to the usual clichés of dramatic invention. In this young girl of pure and tender passion, who learns to replace one kind of ecstasy by another in the imagination of her heart, she had a rôle as congenial as she could wish, and made a most lovely and convincing thing of it. She did not mind the first-night disturbances, if I remember right; and next day the critics united in such approval of her playing as she had not known. "Perhaps the real triumph is for Jill Furse, who gives so true a picture of young love. Her acting is extraordinarily moving and tender." Agate said that it could not possibly be bettered—"the pathos of the opening bud." Playgoers, said another, "will remember for a long time the love scenes, as natural and beautiful as anything in Turgenev".

This was the eighth time that Norman Marshall had produced her. It is rare, as he says, for a producer so to guide and watch:

> I don't think I have had any more rewarding experience than that of watching her genius begin to unfold. Her reputation grew with every part she played. As a person she had a withdrawn quality; she was never quite of the world about her; certainly not of the world of the theatre. It was this air of withdrawal into a world of her own that gave her acting its clear rarefied quality. It also made her difficult to produce. The producer's task was to help and encourage her to project her personality without losing anything of her own peculiar individuality.[1]

I was soon back at Venton, as she had arranged, and any other year it would have been perfection—this beauty of spring, and this solitude, tempered by occasional meetings with the friendly farmer and his wife. But a week in London had intervened, when I had watched her as Emmanuele. For the first time in her life she had the taste of great success, and wanted to share it with me. She wrote: "Sometimes when I think about you and me I feel as if all the doors in the world had suddenly been flung open for the sun." And the doors of the world were coldly shutting. "There's only one thing more I'd ask of life and that is for us to have a child—but perhaps one shouldn't ask for more."

She had planned my solitude, even paid for my keep, with advance payment on a glass, but from the moment I entered my retreat she could not resist teasing. "Everyone who comes to see this play is either drunk or amorous—or both—what is there in

[1] Norman Marshall, *The Other Theatre*, 1947, p. 112.

this part that does it, do you think?" I could have told her: she was Venus' nun. "I had one who was both, in my room last night." On a visit to her brother at Oxford she was treated like royalty by undergraduates.

> I've had a *very* gay week—I can't go straight home after Emmy—she's too strung up—so I go out to supper every night in a fascinating new dress. I must say it's tremendous fun—I've never been fêted before. *So far* I've done nothing you'd disapprove of! The play seems to be steadily picking up—I still hate it—but I must be wrong. Periodically I get very bad-tempered at your not being here—but I'm having a lovely time really. And we were seeing too much of each other, I think.

And in that perverse mood which resembles deliberate working on a sultry tooth, she supposed that I should never be in London again for more than a few days, that there would be a crisis in September, and if there were not, that she would go to Hollywood. But she would end less disruptively: "If knowing me has helped you to write again, I think it's the thing I'm proudest of in my life."

In my periods of despair she had a reassuring tenderness that I knew now could never be exhausted. In one she had written this acrostic on my name:

> *Lean your dark head on my breast*
> *And let these arms entreat you rest,*
> *Until their warm horizon seems*
> *Recorded in your sliding dreams.*
> *Enter this gentle place and keep*
> *No wish beyond a mortal sleep,*
> *Content to lie no more alone,*
> *Empty of grief and all your weeping done.*

Now she was reversing the image:

I want to put my face down in your hands and forget everything—the uncertainty and doubting. Oh, how I *wish* you were here, you'll never know how much and I shan't tell you. It's you who should be saying that and not me, but I know how nice and contented you are, out of the way of my moods. Poor darling—I lead you a dance sometimes, don't I? I'm afraid my heights and depths of happiness and despair are more violent than yours—it's the only thing we seem unalike in. I shall expect you in a fortnight tomorrow—*not* before—and then we'll see what we will see.

I played Emmy suddenly for the first time yesterday. She came alive—and it's the most exciting thing in the world.

I had expostulated that it was cruel to make me jealous, and to sharpen that sense of "music in another room" which I had had all my life.

Your letter this morning is quite the loveliest that anyone ever received since the world began. Dearest, I don't want to make you jealous. I wouldn't dream of trying to. You *know* I wouldn't. I'm too proud of your trust in me. As for being so attractive, that's *entirely* your fault; and when you are away I have to deal with the consequences myself. It's a little difficult! I had dinner with Tenny [Pen Tennyson] last night and he said that *he* wouldn't be able to leave me!

I must quote you a bit out of the *New English Weekly*. "The character of Emmanuele, as flower-like and as stern in innocence in English as in French, holds the play together and draws all the escaping realities into its own strong net. Jill Furse plays this part with a simplicity so moving as to lift *The Intruder* from our home-counties atmosphere into the upper blue; she almost compels us to cry out at the play's end, 'Non angli sed angeli.'" Having indulged in that burst of quite unjustifiable conceit I'm sending you fifty-one kisses in earnest of all the others waiting for you when and if you ever grace this benighted city again. I can assure you that I don't feel at *all* like an angel.

I'm so gloriously happy that I think I shall go up like a rocket and burst into a cloud of gold stars. Come back soon, you're missing so much and so much.

The barrage had become insupportable. I cut down my stay from three weeks to two and returned with the poem unfinished, but with fifty-one stanzas achieved, for what they were worth; which now is nothing, in balance with the days we might have had together.

On June 15th she resumed her private record, after a year.

How I wish I'd kept a diary all these months—ever since I fell in love with L suddenly after nearly two years of being so sure I wouldn't. I've learnt so many things, ecstasy, peace and real understanding with someone who is more like me than I am myself. I never dreamed it would be as overwhelming as this. I do believe we are fated for each other. We meet in every way—mind, imagination, tenderness, passion—he's cleverer than I am—we're equally sensitive—he's steadier really and wiser. If only the outward clouds would lift a little and if he could make a little money we could marry.

It's all very difficult; these days of unrest are haunted always with fear. But I've been so happy. Loving him has seemed like the sun coming out and everything seems to come with it, success and a little fame and still more a real "beginning" in my acting—a warmth and depth that were missing, a certainty that one day I might really be good. The other day Bertie Scott said, "You will be one of the greatest of our time, Jill."

But I care for L's work more, and long for his success and recognition more than I ever did for my own.

Such was her generosity. For this was true.

Herbert Scott, known as Bertie, was a likable Irishman and

energetic teacher of genius, who had first been brought over from Belfast by Tyrone Guthrie to take charge of Flora Robson's voice in a crisis. Soon many of the leading players were his pupils. Jill no doubt went to him for help in "projecting" herself—personality through voice. She was attached to him.

But, for ourselves, viewed together—nine months of wasted time. Or, if not wasted, not tasted as they might have been. Nothing was possible before Munich, for sure. But that reprieve was granted; and slow we had been to exploit it—or so it would seem. It was not that we were barred from marriage by the bourgeois notion of a respectable living-standard: we could have swept that aside, given certainty. Certainty we had lacked. Marriage seemed exceedingly doubtful—as well it might for Jill. Often the old unconfidence had paralysed one of us, infecting the other. I remember her saying pensively, and perhaps it was not long before this time: "We might hurt each other so much it just wouldn't be true." On the whole she had been the happier of the two. Possession is nine parts of love, and though there is a charm in the tenth which comes first, it is a charm more appealing, perhaps, to the feminine mind. In a later year she would write,

> Sometimes I try to go back and tell like a story the very beginning—Edith reading *The Emperor Heart* in her sunny room—seeing you for the first time, your profile against the dark wood of the outside of that room—and how your eyes followed me all that week-end. And the day in Oxford and how you asked if you might kiss me. Do you remember that? I don't suppose so! Many times in Rex's car—talking, kisses and tears and frustration, and the rain fingering the roof and a light glimmering among the dials on the dashboard. Yes, I wish we could have it over again. There's something in those bitter-sweet days of beginning that is haunting now and beautiful—green like the little figs over the wall in the lamplight.

Certainly for us the discovery of love had been what she said in a poem written soon afterwards.

41

But there is grief at all nativities,
The birth of love is anguished and obscure,
And its hot flame in growing travail burns
All our first dreams, our childish furniture.

Till we come naked to the brilliant hour
Of earthly beauty, when in passion's name
Flesh too must fall and be consumed with fire
Like a white tree of thorn in flame.

And she meant by that deliberately confused image the sensation of being burnt away and still remaining in blossom.

III

We seemed on that particular day to be back where we were before separation. It was June 18th 1939, and Sunday. Still despairing of any future to enjoy each other and be blessed, we lay under the trees in the Park in final desolation, supposing nothing else was to be done. Well might Emmy have preferred the gaieties of her success to the company of this dejected and dejecting familiar. But in talk, as always, we grew better. Then it came on to rain, and the sound of the band sauntered over the water, dismal and mellifluous with all the accumulated Sunday afternoons of feckless couples—foretelling, in our case, the tea with a yawning family; and then the restaurant; and then the film; but nothing beyond that. For later, in this last and most bleak of warm midsummer evenings, we arrived at Constable's House; and there, presently, occurred a reversal of mood and mind. Out of inertia another world began of unknown joy. Easy to say that the decision was simply to go forward into marriage, that the difficulties were all suddenly found to be of our own contrivance. No doubt they were. But to such as us the prime resolution of two lifetimes was momentous.

On arriving I had switched out the lights, lit the sconces over the bed-sofa—that little dark Eros and Psyche between them—and taken two more candles to the chimneypiece across the room. There came a time in the exchange of certainty that was our conversation when this even penumbra grew unsettled, began to shake and curiously brighten. A flame on the mantelpiece, burning low, had arrived at the corner of a sheet of paper, which evidently had fallen forward against the wax. It was the drawing of a temple I had designed, and now a ripple of fire was flowing unevenly downwards across it—in the first surprise it was as if the

43

room had quietly ignited of its own accord. The drawing had become symbolic of the hour, and for a moment I hesitated between saving the symbol, and letting it consume away like our misery.

The candles were burnt out, or very low, when I telephoned for a taxi, and took her back across an altered London at its emptiest hour, between the pleasing flats, unlit; down the edge of an unrecognized Park. Somewhere beyond Notting Hill Gate we dismissed it, and walked the rest of the way. At the last corner of deserted roads we stopped under the street lamp, as so often before, and looked up at the sky, with the mumble of sleeping London all round the horizon. Streaks of grey were in the clouds to the east, and in vague lucency it was nearing daybreak. Gratitude for a resolution brimmed from those leafy cross-roads. More light and light it grew. She said, looking up at the lime leaves, "I'm so happy, I should like to die this moment."

I spoke to her on the telephone a few hours later, so that bright daylight should know the compact of the recent night. A new life had begun. "I've given everything into your keeping," she wrote, "and I trust you as I have never trusted anyone in the world. It has taken me a long time because I come to things very slowly, really. You can have no conception how exquisitely happy you make me. I'd give my whole life to make you happy and repay you." And later:

I wonder if I shall ever discipline my feelings enough to keep any relationship from shipwreck. I do think I can, with you. I'm going to try to be more gay, and less of a chameleon. I'm sorry I'm so mercurial, it must be rather unsettling for you. All the emotions inside me are so much stronger and wilder than they appear to outsiders, because for years—since I was sixteen—I have fought and struggled to cage and control them. But things unused atrophy, and that surely must be wrong. I believe that is the true reason I wanted to act from the age of seven. I don't and never have believed in your

44

theories of inhibitions. [Discarded theories of my Freud-and-bitters past.] I've wanted to use everything I know is inside me and I realised that the theatre is the only way.

The new life had begun with the last week of *The Intruder*. Now other plays were in the offing, and now, at last, nothing was needed but time. Given time, not much, she could use her gift fully, and as well she could earn money for us both. Should I mind? "The money means nothing to me," she said, "as long as you're not going to feel bad about it. You must remember that apart from you I have simple tastes." Given time, rather more, I should make a fair living out of glass; for I was on the edge of a reputation in this minor art of my reviving. Given only time, the common expectation of the young, inconceivable happiness lay ahead. But time was the one good we lacked.

They say I'm going to be a great actress. But I never shall be. This has been my year and now it's over and I'm ready for the future. We are all in a tragedy and it's got to be played till the final curtain. Few young people have had such incredible happiness, luck, and success as I've had in the last year. The news continues much the same but I can't feel hopeful. I did so want to have a few months with L before it came. But there's nothing now to regret and we love each other completely. Oh God if only this cup might pass from us.

She jotted down the rough sketch of a poem:

> *We keep a lovely, desperate peace*
> *That a mad stranger in the foreign sun*
> *May with rapacious dreams destroy*
> *And we wake to a war begun.*
>
> *Almost one hopes the guns will speak,*
> *Answer, and make an end of this;*
> *The long anxiety, the fretted hope,*
> *That quickens fever in a haunted kiss.*

These were verses from the background of her mind, like a love-poem of my own called "In Time of Suspense." In the foreground there was no constraint, and one thing alone greatly disturbed: her brother Nicolas had polio. From this, however, he recovered quickly and entirely.

Now in the evenings there was leisure. She was a beautiful dancer. Spinning in the Viennese waltz, the gardenia above her ear, always proximate, stirred softly this way and that, this way and that, in the rhythm of her turning head, dancing in tune like a medium of buoyancy, until the Osterley ballroom dissolved into horizontals of gold, white, and colourful dresses. The gardenia I used to bring to her dressing-room on first nights, so exciting in its blend of purity with heady fragrance, had become the flower of her secret personality, more felicitous in that it would be thought by the world too exotic for her emblem.

There was this leisureliness in the summer evenings because she was no longer watching the clock for the summons to become Emmy—leaving suddenly nothing but a trace of scent in the dark little hall of Constable's House. The note of Rex's horn brought us both to the window to invite him to a cup of tea. Time passed, and again the little toots on the horn. "Come up and have some tea!"—"You can't still be having tea! You're like a pair of old Russians." He and Raimund von Hofmannsthal had given a party in his Fitzroy Square flat. It was "for lovers only," perhaps twelve pairs of us, and none but lovely girls. We danced to a two-piece "band," and by way of cabaret listened to the primitive syrupy Pan-pipes of Faniker Luca, from the Palladium. Such, in an England still at peace, was our portion of banquets, Dorick music, midnight revel.

We went down to Venton in August with some of the family, and carried our felicity into a landscape that was equally formed to amplify and conceal it. Between the valleys of the stream and the river, the deep and the deeper, the Halsdon ridge rose to a green brow with a wood on top, a landmark for miles. We began to know it as the Top of the World, the hyperbolical family name

for a humbler knoll of my boyhood. From here extended westwards a view which I came to know like a face and love like a
third person. It was a large view, though not large by the standards of mountain country—a semicircle of hilly distance that
flowed from fluent Dartmoor about fifteen miles to the south,
along the last high ground towards Cornwall, over flat tops and
leafy knobs, grooved lanes roughly pointed towards hamlets,
scattered white farms, and minute church-towers on skylines,
round to Torrington spire, dead north; unexpected; a far sharp
thought in a spireless composition.

Towards that point the river dwindled in perspective, through
a shaggy serpentine channel, hardly glimpsed. Engulfed immediately below us, it was quite unseen—but deeply understood
—in the wide sweeps of its valley, whose funnelling walls were
largely covered with woods cascading out of sight. From the
pastures above they looked like overgrown amphitheatres of prodigious size, especially when a low sun put half into shadow, em-
phasizing the swerve of the fringed lip.

To many it might seem a very pleasant sample of pastoral England, hardly more. To me it was perfection; for it was secret and
candid at once, wind-swept yet rich. To me it was inevitable
that her beauty should have this for home, that such a girl should
spring from such a countryside, and bless it more and more as
her birthright. She was fond of its people, deeply fond of
some, and they of her. It was a part of our strange, late
Providence that felicity should come to fruit no otherwise than
here.

So here, while the sun was still rising, we may have idled on
the top of our world; but soon we dropped down through
slender oaks, light-flashing with cobwebs, down by zig-zag
bends, and out on to the open floor of a valley so solitary that I
have often swum and run, worked and picnicked, naked all day.
It is a valley of the salmon and the otter—Tarka passed through
it on his travels—and of the buzzard, lazily pivoting high above,
with stretched wings that are marbled when they catch the sun,

and all but transparent when it shines clear through them. Here I saw my first heron get up, uneasy as a heavy ghost, and here Jill's quick eyes would catch before mine the whizzing jewel of the kingfisher, the genius of the place, the mild-faced fervent little god, interrupter of talk, needle of enterprise, drawing a long blue thread through doubled happiness. It twists about, this divine river, more frequently than its floor, so that wide level spaces are formed, now on this side, now on that, called Marshes still, though long-since pastureland. For us they had the air of a classical legend. This valley, self-contained, yet with that sense of mission that comes from a river carried through and beyond, seemed special and other. If no place so green could be Greek, all the same it had a Grecian note, a note of Poussin perhaps, and the feel of noble purpose, foreign to the ploughland and pastures up above, but implied in these passages of soft vivid turf threaded on and on beside an alder-fringed river. We could imagine naked youths at play—those Spartan boys who are teased by girls in Degas's painting. Or a horseman might bound from the shadows, draw rein, signal, and vanish behind willows. We could well see how a javelin would float up high, and travel, dilatory, across the hanging oak-woods. Even, in the sharp outbuildings of the old farm opposite, called Greatwood, we could fancy that we caught a hint of temple pediments.

Midway in Manna Marsh the Torridge received its small tributary, the Mere, under a great tutelary ash that gripped the very corner of confluence like a fist, the knuckles washed clean by the torrents of winter. Here one might see the kingfisher speed on, or swerve aside, blue-pencilling the course of one or other. Then, at the head of the long cursus of that marsh, two tall oak-trees stood out in the middle, very close to one another, interlocked like lovers in a metamorphosis from Ovid. Almost one could envy their state, safe from history in a beaming quiet. For these were Philemon and Baucis, faithful guardians of the temple, whom the god allowed to grow old side by side and to die simultaneously, turning into trees.

Mutua, dum licuit, reddebant dicta "vale" que
"O coniunx" dixere simul, simul abdita texit
Ora frutex.

The games Jill liked were casual. She had never had the inclination or the continuous health to master the advanced and organized sort. Thus she liked racing the paper boats I made, and was a
good hand at multiple ducks-and-drakes across the water, with a
flat stone sucked smooth as a sweet by the current. One did not
have to pretend any longer not to be what one was.

But we would move on to the most remote and beautiful of the
marshes, and there presently below a cliff on the shore we would
build a fire out of twigs that whistled like a bird. Hung from a
stake, the kettle would not come to the boil, and then came to it
suddenly and furiously over flames transparent as water in the
sun. Incomparable simplicities of food were laid out, for the
moment came when to eat and drink was the reason for existing.
Soon in sharp evening light the sweep of the woods above us assumed that faint air of onlooking—massed heads of an amphi-
theatre, ranked shade above shade. And the personal valley
seemed then to applaud and protect.

Brief entries in her diary account for three days. The invasion
of Poland. No news; but no hope. Then the old-fashioned, digni-
fied Declaration of War, the last that may ever be made. "The
year is over, our lovely *annus mirabilis*—the only year in my life
that has really mattered." War came in a shower of Sunday rain
beyond the parlour windows. From listening with the family to
Chamberlain on the wireless, we walked out to the summerhouse
between wet cabbages across the lane. Now we could earn nothing; now all the theatres were closing; and who now would order
an engraved glass? Evidently it was the moment to be married.
We thought we had enough to support us until I joined up. For I
should try to play whatever part was assigned to me.

One continued to fetch *The Times* from a hole in a tree at the
top of Venton Lane, and to read about Poland, ignorant of the

agony begun. In Britain the descent into war was strangely un-eventful. That was common experience. We ourselves were exceptional only in this—that it coincided with greater hap-piness than either of us had known. When you can say, "This I was born for," it matters curiously little how long you will en-joy it; for the meaning of life, once revealed, is not conditional. Or if these were the conditions—numbered days, ending in separation or worse—we could accept them. We would guard the temple while we could. Thus we went on with the same life, and arranged to be married at once, by special licence in Salisbury Cathedral. Borrowing a car for a brief honeymoon, I drove there on the 11th, setting down Jill and her mother and sister at the house of a friend.

Her great-uncle Mike Furse, the Bishop of St Albans, was to marry us with the help of the Dean, and on the morning of Sep-tember 12th, in a little room somewhere above a tea-shop, we did battle with him over one word. Stressing that the vow was ab-solute, he wanted her not to say "obey," because it is unrealistic in our time. She wanted to say it, and did; for not to say it seemed to make it conspicuous in absence, and was almost a reservation of independence. Too spirited to be in danger of subjection, she held sincerely that in the last resort a wife ought to submit to her husband, and in one of our few quarrels would ex-claim, "Why did I promise to obey you at Salisbury!" For my part I was not masterful: I am a natural equalitarian, even anarchist, one who resents being ruled and has no fondness for ruling. We both sensed already that felicity is only to be kept in subtle balance by two equals, willing one another's good; as Chaucer beautifully expounded in the Franklin's Tale. Love is not to be constrained by mastery.

The drawing-rooms in the Close were made ready for the re-ception, and after lunch, in a heightened air of excitement, I walked over to the Cathedral with Rex, who was to be my best man. We found its long, light aquatint of an interior almost empty, for this quietest of cathedral weddings. From the front pew, glancing

50

round, we could easily survey them all: a number of Furses, a few Whistlers, Margaret Newbolt, David and Rachel Cecil, Siegfried and Hester Sassoon. I was nervous, but manageably. It seemed a long while before Jill and her father appeared far off, making the journey of the nave with deliberation. She was not in white, nor veiled. Her long dress, pale grey, was covered with upward-opening hands and the doves they had just released. Her narrow grey gloves, edged in lace, hung from her wrists during the service, like the little hands on the ends of sunrays in Egyptian wall-sculpture. Her small bouquet of myrtles and roses with jasmine was equally formal and compact. So she moved forward, a grey band in her hair, the hair falling clear of that open forehead, in large waves to the collar. A little keyed-up within, she seemed ecstatic, yet serenely pensive, as if in some warm trance.[1] When she arrived, and I moved out beside her, we smiled at one another. It may seem natural enough, yet it was a critical moment, for she had feared that I might not, out of nervousness. From there we were borne away into the ritual, saying and doing all, in obedience to the towering bishop; and in the intervals prayed in ardent snatches. At least I did: she perhaps was more collected. It was like a charade and a coronation at once, we being children marshalled through a ritual game, and royalty beside whom no one was of consequence; for in truth it is the lovers themselves who celebrate the sacrament of marriage, and the priest is no more than their assistant. Now it was both strange and moving to address by name the person one loved and already knew better than anyone else, and formally say what one actually meant. The word "death," our death, passed between us twice. Anywhere else that would have been inopportune. But couples are made by the Church to face the ending of their time together before it has fully begun. Death kneels between them, the merest shadow admittedly, not dreadful with ridiculous grimace and spider hands, but folding his bleak sticks somewhat apologetically

[1] Edith Olivier wrote of her appearance, at that moment, in *Night Thoughts of a Country Landlady*, 1943, p. 45.

on the sensuous cushions. And we accepted him and were nearer at that moment than ever again to the funeral only one of us could attend. There were also, no less, the sentences about life everlasting. All implications were in her mind, exalted beyond ordinary happiness, as she recorded, and moving on through this enormous and shared dream. Advancing to the High Altar we had the episcopal blessing brought down, to speak for myself, with a palpable weight that almost bent the neck. I remember hoping that it was tempered for her, while aware of that charitable authoritative ardour that was resolved to "let me have it" at some pressure.

It had not occurred to me that the main west doors would be open for us until we saw them so, a long way off, and through them a panel of bright afternoon, a microcosm of new world. This also had the symbolic quality of dreaming: the sharp and grave perspective of arches—light sliding under a groined roof—the bright square of world—and the complete emptiness of the nave down which we paced to a Handel overture, with hands linked, free now to whisper, but still obedient to that compelling ceremoniousness behind us. At the door we glanced back automatically— quite the wrong thing to do, no doubt. That, too, seemed symbolic to Theresa at the chancel steps, and like a farewell. No car awaited us, it was only a short walk across the Close. No photographer asked us to pose: one had offered himself and been refused. On the whole I am content that no photograph remains.

Champagne and a health. A minute wedding-cake, made in the Furse village. We drove away from the crowded steps, past the sunlit front of the Cathedral, the doors now shut, along the river and out of the town; and so past the Netherhampton turn which also led to our first meeting; on then through valleys unknown. The September sun shone in its thoughtful way. The colours in cottage gardens clashed yellow, mauve, and scarlet with the immemorial advertisements on walls, Goldflake and golden rod, Lyon-bright tea, the hirsute tar against an azure

52

ocean. The war itself seemed easy as barred clouds in a warm Old Master light, and driving westwards like our destiny. Nothing of hauntedness, nothing of apprehension, in the light of this day. Over orchard hedges the loaded apple-trees swung round like planetariums. Nondescript houses and hoardings at the start of a village, a can on a doorstep, the mereness of grasses nodding on a wall—all had the elated foreignness of things seen along the road in a going to the sea in childhood, a passing particularity, an unlamented transience; and all were held in a mood beyond the range of childhood, because tellable in words, or, what was more telling, shareable without them. And we, sauntering westwards, pulled by the sun in the windscreen. Figures crossing, recrossing, swinging in a meadow, were rolling marbles, chips of value. At tea-time in Glastonbury a little girl passed us in the street with hands raised, and forefingers, for some reason, pointed horizontally at one another. Going by, she kept looking narrowly at the gap between the tips. It seemed as though all creation could be detonated in that eternally-appointed spark-gap.

At about twilight we reached the Quantocks and so arrived at the Old School House, Aisholt, lent to us for a six-day honeymoon by Jill's grandmother, Margaret Newbolt. It was a cottage at the bottom of a hollow, end-on to the lane, with very small casements under heavy-lidded thatch. The sky may have shadowed over by this time, for the interior seemed very dark and low, and smelt of civilized living in the country, with a fire in the grate, dark shiny furniture, and blobs of candlelight. It moved Jill that a spinster cousin had come and gone, putting out the flowers and the wine, and herself making the bridal bed. The old servant was a connoisseur of honeymoon couples. She greeted us, the one with affection, the other with quiet interest; and soon we sat down to a supper of hock and chicken.

In the earliest pallor of day some bird uttered beyond the square of little window. Having woken at the same moment, as we should so often, we reviewed the situation. That this was permitted! The sensation was of exhilarating freedom, not of

53

bonds—of freedom from that codified morality, whose approbation need never be considered again. Very properly, we were not called by Lizzie, and acquired merit by not coming down to breakfast until eleven. It was a drenching day, making yesterday seem all the luckier, and we kept reverting to it with gratitude, reliving the service, and retrospectively preening ourselves in the presence of so much regard—indulging in other words that sense of felicitation which is not very wrong in lovers, when indulged in privacy.

The afternoon broke into moist sunlight. In Bridgwater I bought for not many shillings an old green glass bottle with a clear glass stopper and rope handle, to become my wedding present. After supper I began to work on this, while the recipient was using the same lamplight to send a good report to her mother, and was thinking, to her diary, "all the dark days in each direction have faded and vanished away." She did not see it as a makeshift wedding, a hasty, private, diminished, economical wedding; with marriage from the wrong family home, no bridesmaids, very few presents, and the briefest of honeymoons. Nor did it seem odd for the bridegroom to have brought along the tools of his trade. Work was only pleasure, after all. Consequently it was not immoral. It had been intrinsic to our relationship from the beginning; nor was there anything pleasanter than this novelty of shared ordinariness.

With an equal passion for desultory sight-seeing—and the more desultory the better—we poked about the hills; stood looking down at gables through sliding columns of rain; stood becalmed in some church with greenish windows and a feeling of godly love. Of all places we should ever visit, old country churches were the most congenial and generative: in their week-day emptiness, I mean, more than at service-time. The sense of the past was in them, and in their monuments, and in their dry, mute, reasonable, Anglican smell. Of course our craving for escape into peace and security found answer there, but more than that the sense of timelessness was in them. They were points where past and present were fused into a unified notion of existence, and, fertilizing the imagination, were budding-points of the future. As we lay in the heather, picnicking, the blunt jar of blasting came now and again from some quarry, a harmless reverberation. One plane went over, the first of the war.

On the third morning we drove into Taunton, where, after a search of several antique shops, we came at last on a Georgian ring with a little rosette of paste and emerald chips, set in greenish gold, "very pale and underwater-looking, like a ring for Undine," as she said, desiring it at sight. The price was £1. It was typical that we should choose it together, and that it was old. Of course I could not have afforded any tolerable new one, but she liked old things for their craftsmanship; also for their history, known or unknown. That this ring came out of a dusty tray and had been worn by other fingers was no drawback at all. It was instantly rebegotten in her looking, to be reborn in her careful polishing, or "nourishing," to use her own word. It had this unobtrusive dimension of age; yet it was brand-new at that moment when I stopped the car, somewhere in a country lane, and slipped it on to her finger, my engagement ring—a little late, according to the world's custom.

IV

To be carriage-folk for a week had been a luxury. Now we were to be tethered, carless, in an unknown place. For our honeymoon had been extended by the lease of a cottage on the coast near Berrynarbor, and for as long as we could afford the small rent. We found Goosewell Cottages on a slanting country road, an isolated terrace of little Georgian houses, all stuccoed white, or else hung with slates, and with plain slate roofs. Solitary, and with the Bristol Channel behind them, they looked like coastguard cottages; only the shore was well down out of sight and perhaps half a mile away. Southwards across the road the bank rose steeply to a rabbity sort of meadow, backed by a long belt of woodland. Our home was in the house last-but-one from the right-hand end, No. 8. It had a diminutive front garden with bushes of box and choisia, and with a pair of wooden seats across the corners, facing the lane, among virginia stock, valerian and tobacco plants. The door was in the middle, with a window each side and another pair above.

We let the car go and began to take stock. There were six rooms, to our surprise, all admittedly minute, and all pleasantly furnished, a sitting-room and dining-room each side of the steep stair, a dressing-room and bedroom at the top. The paintwork was the same good green throughout, and for light there was nothing but oil lamps and candles, which suited us entirely. The narrow bedroom ran the full width from front to back, if "full" is the word, having one window to the road and one to the sea, and a well-sprung divan bed below each. With difficulty I persuaded Jill to take the seaward bed, and we knelt on it, looking out. A humped coastline interrupted the great grey ruler of waters in various places, with the swelling immediately ahead of us a wooded one. From in front of that a field of purple cabbages ran back to the abandoned kitchen garden just below us. Then, by leaning out, we could see where the waters disappeared behind the Little Hangman, a high pyramid that seemed to be the outpost of Exmoor. It was all windswept, austere, casual, unpretty—very different from Aisholt, cosy and ramblered in its combe; and much better. There we had been transitory guests of the furniture and watchful servant, but here we were alone for the first time in our own home, so that combe and upland became symbols of restraint and freedom respectively. And it is odd that in the country, no less than in London, you can continue to feel quite alone in a house sandwiched between two others, with a neighbour only like a tree, or less noticeable. Actually no one lived in the end house next to ours, and the front garden was squalid with an iron bedstead and other rubbish. In the field adjoining it there was a 1917 Crossley, open to the skies. None of this mattered at all. The old touring car seemed romantic—a memento of the other war. As for our home, it was Penultima Thule, the best we should ever have, except one.

No doubt if we had thought of it as really home the squalor in the next garden would have been a blemish, and that it wasn't shows that we didn't. But this was not manifest then. We simply did not think in terms of real or pretence, permanent or provisional. We were living in a present almost datelessly detached from a disagreeable future and inadequate past. In the morning we awoke to the presence, or the present rather, of a new day, and would greet the ocean and the weather with the same delight, however they looked. Any weather was good weather: bright or rainy was only like a gay or serious turn to a good conversation. I fetched the letters. If there was a parcel I favoured unpicking the string, in order to savour possibilities. She collected the string, but was more impetuous. "Couldn't we cut it, and use it for something smaller?" Wedding presents were a surprise, so little had they entered into our reckoning. Three tables, a rug, a lamp, a breadboard and knife, a brooch, and the first refusal of a

Dachshund were about the sum—apart from those intermittent cheques which enabled us to extend our lease, a few weeks at a time. We never took up the Dachshund. We wanted a black Border Collie to accompany our walks, and flounce the long field-banks of Devon with a white furbelow.

Breakfast was laid for us by a friendly person who came in to cook and clean at 7*d.* an hour. Jill could barely cook at all, and was alarmed by a frying-pan. With illness and the theatre she had been excused learning; nor was it obligatory for girls of her station, in those days of increasingly dear but still plentiful servants. Although she meant to learn now, she made little progress beyond scrambled eggs, for there were always better things to do. She did take pains with her accounts, against all inclination, because of our poverty. "I didn't know a joint cost 8*s.* 6*d.*!" she told her mother. "However, I made it last a week and it was very good." She had never dealt with a servant of her own, and I, not ignorant of London charwomen, had to instruct her in removing some little friction that worried her. Cut off from the world of her success, reading the theatre news and the *Picturegoer* with avidity, never nibbling her fingers but sometimes brusquely deciding not to, she was surrendered to the new life, but still almost as a child might be, unoccupied else. And perhaps it was childish to say at twenty-four, as she once did, to my distress, when I had made the new life seem momentarily formidable, that she wanted her mother. I never thought it so—partly because I was childish myself; also by reason of the view of life we so exactly shared. In this the early years hold the sense of detached wonder and the absolutely mint response from which, later on, art may draw nourishment. It seems that imaginative people tend to "derive" from childhood or infancy; practical people from boyhood or girlhood; and both can be partially "left behind." Thus men of action are often permanently schoolboys, and artists often permanently infants. Childhood may be intensely happy, unhappy, or boring, the intensity is what matters, and hers had been all three. She had, like me, been full of imagined horrors, and yet she had often wished herself back into its lights. Even so, the early years had tantalized. Part of our felicity was in finding the half-caught significances of childhood made lucid, its doubts and humiliations mutually condoned; in finding childhood itself caught up and redeemed in this far greater mode of being. Nevertheless it would have worried me had I thought this incompatible with essential maturity. I was free to enjoy her in the rôle of little girl, from time to time, precisely because it was a game, and I knew she was not one. It was a game that showed her "derivation," so to speak. I knew that she could face life far better than many who appeared more adult, but wanted her certainty, and the resilience it permitted. I knew, beyond doubt, that she could accept whatever the years would be giving—would be giving shortly—but not yet.

The belt of trees along our landward crest concealed one of those ornamental drives that were made on this coast in the last century, like the Hobby Drive at Clovelly. It followed a twisting course downhill for about two miles, crossing our road by a bridge, and ever descending to a Gothic castle near the sea, but it was now scribbled over or narrowed by undergrowth, and seemed like all such forgotten tracks to be romantically far older than it was. Beyond it stretched mere upland Devon, a country of rough-walled fields, of plover and gull, and of remote, chain-rattling collies. We planned to penetrate this for miles; for she loved rambling as much as I, and seemed built for it, with that easy stride. But here the paradox of her make-up was evident. You could say that she looked frail, and was really strong—she possessed a good punch for a slight girl, and in childhood had knocked down a boy in the lane for calling her "Carrots." Or you could say that she appeared strong and was really frail—her superlative vitality was literally ephemeral, a day's combustion. Our first expedition was to Ilfracombe, a tramp perhaps as long as from Fiesole to Florence, and comparable—so heightened were the minutes spent in the empty café, beside the empty slopping harbour, and elsewhere. But next day she was laid low with a severe pain. So later expeditions of any length were by bus, and our radius afoot narrowed in. Then the remote began sooner, that was all. Thus Bowden's Farm, and even Hill Barton, though quite close, have far-away names to me, with a touch of the enhancing glaze of distance.

In tawny warmth beneath the weak blue skies of October I used to take pencil and paper to a hollow in the fields, that way, and there in a hot corner under a broken wall I wrote for her the dedicatory poem to my next book; also one about seven buzzards I had watched on a hill-top, building the invisible staircase they mounted, spiral above spiral. She meanwhile might be clacketing away at versions of other poems. With scrupulously worked-out spacing she made a stylish typescript of the book, but having no fondness for the machine, always wanted to spare me the din of it, typing by herself. Then she would bring out a picnic lunch to me under the wall. Upright on her haunches, eating a sandwich with both hands, back very straight, she looked something like a red squirrel. She would gaze about her at the hills and sigh with rapture. The shadow was there, but almost necessary. "I never thought a war which I have dreaded all my life could be the actual means to my happiness," she wrote; "though perhaps one should not say that yet."

Strolling in the old drive at sundown we had the yellow sun through branches like a wild-leaded stained-glass window; and then the oblique rays threw patches of theatrical brilliance, spots and bars over the mossed gravel—circles of plush light that seemed to be floating in the twilight, detached. In those pointedly advancing nightfalls of autumn we would walk to catch the last Tennysonian gleam in the western sky beyond Lundy—or vast moonrise like a back-drop to the church in the valley, rising tall and ink-black from its well of late warmth. One night, when we were pottering about the mounds of the rough meadow opposite, a shape, vaguish-white, came hurtling down on us from higher up, with muted thunder. I turned on it, shouting and waving, and thus earned a good mark. It was nothing but an old nosey white horse, who pulled up to stare about him at darkness, under blond lashes, puffing out cones of velvet warmth. He became our most audible neighbour.

And so home to supper by the fire, and the long evening of contentment, while I finished her wedding-present glass, to her reading aloud. Sharing the oil-lamp on the edge of the table, she read *Pilgrim's Progress*, an allegory of great significance to us— her voice pensive, even a little sad in tone, but full of expression. ". . . which led him into a field full of dark mountains, where he stumbled and fell, and rose no more." The picture we formed of that mysterious field, and the isolated figure traversing it, was something like a Blake illustration to Thornton's Virgil. It belonged to a category of inexplicable magic that began to have relevance, not fully understood. All the while the sea-wind called low in cracks, or rain touched the window, or the moon got up to suggest a last saunter before bedtime. We loved the night, as I have said. By day people's eyes are commonly used on a level, or below it. In hot sunlight they may be downcast under a shading hand, as if they went in awe of the ferocious god. But those who step out into a fine night stand naturally with faces lifted to heaven, and feel refreshed merely by doing so.

It was a miracle—drawn out through time. That we, of all people, should have slipped into this life so effortlessly! In becoming each other's we did not for a moment have to cease being ourselves. In the wonder of it we hardly gave weight to the cause—these two and a half slow, painful years through which we had negotiated all perils, such as loving, not a person, but the idea of a person, or even, fatally, the idea of loving. I knew her for what she was. And who I was she knew; but she was wise and loved me nevertheless. When at last we set out, we were already there; and joy was more like a recognition than a discovery. "Had we but world enough and time" this delay would have been ideal. It may have been indispensable, even as things were.

Admittedly there were practical disadvantages to being in tune —as when answering letters. Never had she accumulated so many; some of her answers, unfinished, lay about for weeks. "It has—all my shortcomings have—infuriated my family," she told a friend, "and the bliss of having married somebody who is just as bad himself and finds it very funny in me is indescribable." If ever conscience disturbed me enough to collect pen and correspondence out of various rooms, I would find that she had companionably settled to the same task, overspreading the one small table from the other side, to the confusion of our papers. She claimed that she lost more things by being tidy than untidy, and certainly any drawer or suitcase of hers seemed to contain a broad sample of her possessions, so that putting away was not obviously helpful. Yet she could not fairly be called untidy-minded. She was supposed to be too electric to wear a watch: she never had one. Time, so often, did not matter. When it did, she had a remarkable sense of it. She was never once late for the theatre. Capable of intense concentration in things of importance, she postponed dealing with the rest. Like myself she found it wearisome to attempt anything even mildly virtuous out of a pure sense of duty. She had to contrive to see it as enjoyable, an act of the heart. The notion that it would be more meritorious if unpleasant was repugnant to her, seeming to reflect a moral self-concern. Active good was a function of relationship—I and you —whether "you" were divine or human. Duty was a substitute (necessary, of course) for imagination. It was depressingly abstract and bodiless. But then, what more could be expected of the stern daughter of a *voice?*

There Ain't No Justice had been chosen for showing to the troops, and she now had a small fan-mail from camps around the world, and from America. Amusing and sometimes touching, these letters were enjoyable to answer. In Ilfracombe we went to a film, and emerged into a dusk charged by its amorous unreality, the sweet ugly dusk of an abandoned resort. And "in Ilfracombe," she wrote of that outing, "I ran into Marius Goring, a very good actor, and we had a talk on the theatre as if we'd known each other all our lives! But each had seen the other and we felt like exiles—terribly exiled. However, L came out of Smith's and took me home and I wasn't so sure I minded being an exile after all."

The theatre—whose assumed death had made it easy to marry —was returning to life. She declined a revival of *Goodness, How Sad!* at Kew. That was nothing. The pull, though, was strong at once, and was the cause of our one quarrel. Two latent anxieties peeped out and inflated each other, the actress fearful of being lost in marriage, the husband fearful that its unity would not extend to her career. Yet I very much wanted her to act; nor could I ever think it intrinsically damaging to marriage—quite the reverse. I pleased her by saying that a woman's place was in the home or on the stage. And this we really thought—that no other life can be led by a woman for long, without slightly distorting or detracting from her nature. So it was reaffirmed that she should act presently, but not yet. All was well. And I had forgotten the debate when I went to London to surrender my flat, she to Venton. But generosity made her see herself in the wrong, as it invariably would.

I am so very glad that we have had these few days apart. It made me realise that all I had argued during that afternoon was wrong—hopelessly wrong. Because when you went on in the train it was not you who went but half myself. And here I'm a visitor in a place and position that were once my place and position and aren't any longer. Forgive me and don't be too hard on me. I love you enough to alter anything in my life or my desires. I have felt ever since our last and rather stormy talk that I had spoilt something for you, and this has saddened me terribly. I do know and understand that what you said about a unit is right.

We knew by now that the great maw of conscription would not swallow the men of my age until far into the following spring. To volunteer did not hasten the process, or very little: volunteers were not needed. However, as I did not relish being forked into the ranks of the infantry, I volunteered at the outbreak for a signals unit. But I lacked the qualifications. During the winter I tried for a commission in the Tower Hamlets, and for some other service, but was too old. It seemed best not to worry—wise to catch the flying, once-only joy, and await the event. Thus conscription gave an easy conscience. But had the year been 1914, and every man posed with the same choice, I could not have lived blithe like this, for month after month, putting off the war.

Her brother Pat was about to be called, and "the war really starts at that point," she wrote. He was gone by the time we paid a brief visit to Venton, there to taste the novel pleasure of being guests in her own home, as she said—of being appraised and approved, and set apart, with subtle deference to our unity. It was like playing the solo parts in a double concerto; and if I prefer the concerto to the symphony as a musical form, it is because I hear in it a metaphor of heaven. It stands for the joy that must always be the joy of one particular instrument, or of two-like-one, though obedient to a general harmony and contributing to it. Only, in heaven each instrument would rejoice to be simultaneously solo in its own concerto and orchestral in numberless others; whereas here the particular is always shutting itself up in the exclusive.

We returned to Goosewell, and soon felt the darkening-in of November around us. We walked on the damp hills under a reeling cloudscape. Gales troubled the seaward window. (Sometimes the Bristol Channel was all dotted with the creeping ships of a convoy.) Long files of rain marched for hours down the empty road. Sometimes a night of huge rain might make a weather to sleep in. Sometimes she was in bed for a day, patient of continuous pain, and relishing the indulgence of it. Clearer than anything, I see my landward view from the bedroom window: a tree of some sort, the drops sidling on the telephone wires, the rough grass shrugging them off opposite—all the fluttering green-white continuum of a long wet morning. Twelve weeks in that little house, put by. . . . On the final night it suddenly struck us that the bedroom could be more convivially arranged. This meant moving the furniture and replacing it next morning, but it did not seem a whimsical thing to do, or a waste of time, when any night, like any day, was the first of its kind.

The first Christmas of the war, so unexpectedly like a Christmas of the peace, only better, we spent in Salisbury Close. Our plan was that Jill should return to the stage or the film studios for the winter, and in the spring, with riches in the bank, we should rent Goosewell again. Then we should begin a family. But her medical advice in Devon had been misleading, not for the last time. Those pains had been traced to what is called a backward displacement of the womb, and until it had been righted, said the woman at the clinic, conception would be almost impossible. In December Jill conceived, and there was now a danger of miscarriage.

Riches were beyond our getting. Now work must be confined to a little acting for the B.B.C.—as when one night her Miranda came over on the air. Luckily I had glasses to engrave after all, and one very large, to a design by my brother, for which I should be paid £50, a sum that only he could have asked. "Someone has made a smash-hit first appearance which has very stupidly depressed me!" Jill wrote. "She does sound really good though, which is exciting." In London she went to a stage party, and found there

the same pleasure and sadness that one has in going back to a school. I felt as if I'd grown, on another stage, into a fuller life. I am much too happy to pine for anything, but I long and long to work and to put into it all our happiness together. However, if that goes into our child! . . .

My mother and father had handed over to us the big bedroom facing the Close. Paper bells were put up, and gay clothes lay about, her untidiness and mine for ever a source of mutual absolution. Her sandwiches from some forgotten train-journey emerged on the window-sill when we left, curled up like last year's sandshoes. There was a musical box, a wireless, and a gramophone—amenities never missed at the cottage—and there was much playing of the Flanagan and Allen songs, "Run, rabbit, run," "Any umberellas," etc. Rex said the room was like a Fun Fair, and this was rather apt, for it was a place of enjoyment, but temporary and rootless. So also may be a hotel bedroom. But it was not quite that. It was not an oasis, not a refuge; for there was nothing positively alien to escape from. My father pottered about, remote and pathetic: he would have liked and admired Jill at any time. My mother all her life needed one man to support her, and, being so supported, was strong like a vine. Her first concern was for my father; but for support she turned increasingly to my brother. This enabled her to be quite unpossessive towards me, and I never myself felt that she loved me any less than him. She deferred to Jill in everything concerning me, and a courtesy of affection arose between them, made easy no doubt by what they so markedly shared, a light touch on life and a "new every morning" response to it. At a party she would ask Jill to pour out behind the silver urn, withdrawing from the position of hostess. I could see that she was basking a little in an unfamiliar pleasure, having found in her the daughter of the house she had lacked for twenty years, since my sister went abroad.

Still, it was not contenting, and was never intended to last three months. Jill felt herself "mewed up," neither acting nor home-making, only expecting, and that was not enough. She did want a child a great deal, and fortunately all went well, though she was very sick at first. But she was not one who could plunge and lose herself in the maternal instinct. One night we listened to the voice of her dead grandfather in a recording of "Drake's Drum." The final "long ago" of the poem, musical and sad, seemed to refer to himself; and she wept. "I *wish* you had known him." She felt much more Newbolt than Furse at this time, and to forget homesickness for the theatre began to put down her many memories of early days at Netherhampton, memories that were overwhelmingly of sensuous beauty and of atmosphere. It had been

a childhood that began in one war and finished in another. For however childish one may remain, marriage is an adult state, and the prospect of watching over another childhood makes one's own suddenly much further away.

V

It seemed like a notable spring already in the hard yellow start of it, with crocuses for that extremely early Easter, and with the last white "Alleluia" winging down the Early English nave. Perhaps it had begun on the day when Jill returned across the Close like Persephone with swags of daffodils. The sickness had gone by then, and she felt and would continue to feel very well.

In April the house would be let and the family scattered. Goosewell had been our constant objective, but Goosewell we should never see again. For now Evie Furse, her step-grandmother, was offering us a cottage rent-free on the Halsdon estate. Jill knew it of course, and in childhood must have gone there with messages to the gardener.

We walked out from Venton and looked down on it with altered eyes. It stood in the valley of the Eastern Brook, on the narrow floor of that valley, a big white cottage with wooden casements under a thatched roof, half hidden from us there by the ashes and willows that told the course of the stream. Set back to the left there was a smaller white cottage, more leaf-bound, the home of Puddicombe, now manservant to Jill's invalid grandfather and formerly his groom. Behind both houses towered up the Eastern Wood with its great variety of forest trees planted by William Cory, deciduous and conifer, and among them certain slender cherries, stippled over with blossom. In front of our house was the steep little garden, still neat if now tending to wild; the stream at its foot; then a hedge; and then the green cheek of Venstave, the field down which we hurried.

The walls were of cob in the traditional manner of the county: that is, of mud plastered over and whitewashed, uneven as a home-iced cake. The windows were put in a bit at random, as they might be in a modern painting. The back was a windowless blank to the immediate steepness of the overhanging wood. Somewhere at the right-hand end must once have revolved the great wheel, driven by water taken from the stream higher up: the leat, now full of dead leaves and primroses, could be traced along the side of the wood. For this was Halsdon Mill, on the ancient track between Venton and Halsdon, last of the mill-houses that had served them, no doubt, since both were Saxon farms.

The door opened directly into the kitchen. Here was an old cast-iron range, surprisingly framed by an early Georgian chimneypiece of wood, with cornice-shelf and bolection mould-ing, a little crooked. Through a door in the right-hand corner we climbed directly into a narrow bedroom. But the speciality of the place was the third bedroom, approached only through the other two, a spacious room lit at front and side, and shadowy without seeming blind, in its candid wavy walls and low cracked ceiling. It was all stripped bare, yet imbued with the sense of other lives: at once well-handled and virgin—like her engagement ring. But how to furnish it?

We did actually possess furniture. Up in London there was her modern "bedroom suite" in light waxed oak. She had insisted on buying this with her twenty-first birthday present from her father, in the belief that an actress had to live in such a room, and as a gesture of enfranchisement. There it remained, to her shame —and to my relief, recollecting my own wilful follies. It would look ridiculous in the cottage, and anyway we could not afford to move furniture from London, or from Salisbury where my own was now stored. From there, however, I brought a green stair-carpet. Beds, tables and chairs, linen and crockery were borrowed, and we fitted a few curtains and stocked the larder.

Having loaded smaller chattels into a Swiss cart with the help of Nicolas and Theresa, we all set off down the lane with suitcases, like refugees uncharacteristically high-spirited. On the slant of

Venstave the Swiss cart overturned at speed, and Truepenny, the skull from Constable's House, rolled down the slope. We stood it in the narrow window of the staircase bedroom, only one-pane-wide. Climbing the now-luxurious stair you came upon it, *memento mori*, flanked by an explosion of jugged lilac, and backed by the green hill. Descending that hill you could see the cranium against the slip of shadow, like a wan full-stop. I think this shows that we were not superstitious, in the timorous sense. In the trustful we rather were. Three was a lucky number—while thirteen was indifferent. Almost all the great events of both our lives had been and would be connected with the number three or its multiples. But this would be more convincing if I did not have to say "almost."

Now began such a time as neither of us had known or imagined, a time that made Goosewell seem "early" and confined, both by narrowness of autumn and narrowness of scope. Now it was spring, and a spring of exceptional brilliance. The West Country was prinked and lit with blossom, our hollow full of wild flowers. Waking in the big room, we at once grew aware of the birds, a noise thick, passionate, and vehement, in that tree-surrounded house. And then there came to us an audible undercurrent from the foot of the garden, a *continuo* rustle too liquid and musical for the wind in the trees, and with a suggestion of voices that one could not quite catch. At the window the book of April lay open once more—and the image is not over-fanciful for that particular view. Venstave rose so high that the upper hedge could not be seen by someone standing at the back of the room. From there the window-oblong was all green, or grey with dew at this hour. Suppose then a figure, farmer or postman, "walked o'er the dew of yon high eastward hill." He crossed it slantwise and with deliberate pace, whether up or down, on account of the steepness. Out there, isolated on the page of green, he seemed curiously emphatic and like an illustration to *Pilgrim's Progress*, eloquent of "setting out on a journey."

There seemed to be a pointedness in many sights of the valley.

Not only was the hill the very type of the high, the green, and the smooth—the very clouds building above the top hedge seemed roundier and whiter than elsewhere, the blue between them of a paintbox potency, the stream at the foot the paradigm of a stream. It flowed, our west-running brook, into sight and hearing round a little shaded peninsula which we called the island, where there was a broken-down seat among primroses and wood-anemones, and then forward to the garden's foot, overhung by the slant finger of an ash.

Yet Halsdon Mill did not entirely answer to the picturesque painter's idea of a cottage, less still to the modern calendar-artist's. It was not a gabled *cottage orné*, or self-consciously pretty, but quite work-a-day, a little mill-house built as economically as it could be. Also there were features that the calendar-artist would never observe. East of the garden was the Ram Meadow. This contained no obstinate tup, but a small yellow-brick shed for the machinery that pumped the stream-water up to Halsdon. Its rhythmical jangle could be heard in the garden now and then, harmlessly scored into the general music of the valley, and scarcely more monotonous than the chaffinches. Then, down-stream beyond the wooden bridge, some of the richest wild flowers grew in a deserted orchard that was now a rubbish heap. We deplored it naturally, conscious even so that wild daffodils never have more poignancy than when they dance in a bottomless slop-pail.

The house never seemed shut in. The hill in front never oppressed, even in dark weather. It was too responsive to the changing lights. This waking each day was like *The Prelude*—

While yet our hearts are young, while yet we breathe
Nothing but happiness, living in some place,
Deep Vale, or anywhere, the home of both.

And it is the word "anywhere" that moves us chiefly in this passage. For it is exactly when "anywhere" would do, that the ideal "here" has full value.

Under the boots of Hutchings, our friend the postman, the pebble path along the front sounded hollow as a well-covering. We opened the post in bed to bellows of laughter or cries of desolation, as Jill read of her friends' war-time antics or of good parts going elsewhere. She then made a quick toilet, concentrating on her face. Never a great one for washing, she seemed to have as a gift the freshness that generally requires heavy maintenance. As for the natural waves of her hair, they only required combing—and she would not have relished her inclusion in *The Changing Face of Beauty*, 1957, as an exemplar of the Permanent Wave. With straight back she would lean to her looking-glass, to print in a moue one lip from the other, and star her lashes with the side of a finger brushed upwards. And so downstairs—to make excellent coffee in an open saucepan, over a wood fire preferably, for breakfast outdoors. Here was a revolution!

Our monotonous fare in the Close had something to do with it. On the offer of the cottage she had decided to learn a skill that had seemed hateful before; and she now gave herself to it with quiet, passionate absorption. She read her cookery book in bed as if it were some enthralling novel. She bent over table and stove, staring into pots and dishes as though to mesmerize them into the right answers. She herself could give no answers to remarks she had not heard, or she said the opposite of what she meant. She went about the house abstractedly singing, and looked often into her larder for the pleasure of reviewing her jars and bottles, her olives and onions, her little choice cheeses, and the crumpling yellow crust on her basin of Devonshire cream. A tune heard at the Players' Club had resembled a well-known ballad, and she sang a mixture of the two.

> *Someone to wash the baby*
> *After the ball is O.*

If a dish fell short of expectation she was as downcast as a nocturnal versifier next morning. It was all for my judgement—yet no cook more keenly enjoyed her own cooking: consequently she learnt at speed, and became very good. The old-fashioned range suited her entirely.

"Some people like plain living," she observed, sipping her hock, "but I like luxury!" Not the remark of anyone accustomed to it. It meant the rare bottle of good wine—the special ham or pâté—the sudden extravagance in a good plain setting: things we called "necessary luxuries." You can have the same pleasure more permanently in architecture—the rich doorcase in a chaste façade. Enlarging on meagre rations with local eggs and cream, before this was ruled out, I must say we lived very well. At the beginning it had been "I'm learning to cook and slowly forgetting that I was ever an actress!" Within a week or so she was writing, "I have found in it my real métier."

If not plain living, it was simple enough, surely—with no electricity, no telephone, no water, no sink, no plumbing of any sort. Drinking-water was brought down in a bucket from the Halsdon well by our neighbour, whose wife came in to work, with her black cat Charlie Meek. For washing-up there was stream-water, or the stream itself, in a dipping-place beside a plank bridge. For a bath one must climb to Halsdon or use a hip-bath in front of the stove. The earth closet, of the bucket-type mercifully, was some way off across the weedy yard in a shed full of spiders, built against the bank of the wood, and overarched by the great oak that dominated Halsdon Mill. It was dusty and wholesome. It was dark and remote enough for the door to be left open, and it had a charming outlook. It was much pleasanter than modern closets—even at night, even when approached with a candle in the hand obscuring starlight, even with the pins of rain darting hither and thither round the lolling flame. A tranquil and civilized spot.

Simplicity of living, happiness, beauty of season and place, came together in extraordinary contrast with the anguish of the western world. We burned to give it answer, to say something positive, however small, in that context. It seemed as though the west had been suffocated by bad habits, an appalling accumulation of greeds and illusions, and thus driven mad—that it would disintegrate if it would not undergo a spring-cleaning to redis-cover the shape and purpose of life. To suppose that what is right for oneself must be right for others may be ridiculous. But later history does not convince me that these ideas, if ingenuous, were quite unsound, or that individuals ought not to attempt the good life as best they can, like Plotinus in rotting Rome, whatever the destiny of civilization may be—indeed careless of that destiny. Civilization is always the crust of foam revolving on a torrent.

A new book of verse appearing at this moment did not give me great pleasure, for the poems were old by the time they could be called new. I was now working on a lengthy Ode to the Sun in which I tried to distil these notions; but the result was too facile for a distillation. The model was the sun itself, which shone daily, and Akhenaten's *Hymn to the Sun*. We had been studying Egyptian art, and were excited by the whole el Amarna episode. In an isolated place, besieged by the desert and the dead-weight of convention and vested interest, the young Pharaoh had founded his brief holy city, and there lived in domestic peace with the lovely Nefertiti. Epileptic he might be, weak to defend frontiers, and unattractively womanish in figure. For all that, he had imagined the first universal religion of brotherhood and peace, to adore the one beneficent godhead manifest in the sun—from whose sculptured disc the long rays extended those little hands. The hands held a blessing to eye, mouth or brow. Sometimes they held the ankh, a cross with a loop for its head. I took this for our emblem; called it the healed cross; saw it as a symbol of the positive, of the self surrendered to love, and given back completed. Some verses of the *Hymn* seemed to speak for the simplicity of living we prized. We hoped that we were "Living in Truth"; thought any way that we were living, in truth.

Again she urged me to find my solitude, and took delight in it, always hoping to promote good works in me. "I'm so desperately anxious that you shouldn't feel me in the way or a drag on your writing," she had written in the winter. Through a sequence of bright days from April on into May, I wrote in the slants of bluebells just above us, or at the Top of the World, with Dartmoor, the holy hill, slightly detached in a heat-haze, or in the resinous warmth of a larch wood down-stream. Here she would come with the lunch-basket, sauntering in green skirt and sandals, lit or lost along the path through patches of unpierced shade; in reverie, yet observant. Sometimes we would go to the river, and there, as last year, I would build the fire and perhaps bathe; and then under a tuft of shade we would lay out supper. Sooner or later the required kingfisher passed—deiform, but also comic, as he nipped round the bend peeping the one note like a boy on a bicycle. At one time or another I have swum in all the pools of the Halsdon reach, downwards from the old mill, where one can lie on the tumbled stones of the weir with the water leaping like dolphins—by way of Golden Pool, ink-dark under sun-bright leaves. In the character of a log I have floated right under a perched kingfisher. I have watched his family. And I have seen him, unusual sight, leap for a fly and return to his perch like a flycatcher.

At last we would be strolling back along the marshes, in that enriched light of evening, with the outlined leafage of the trees particular as tapestry. And so we entered them, and climbed by hairpin bends through the palpable warmth of their shadow. On such an evening they would seem, when one paused for breath, uncannily rapt and attentive. All other birds gone mute, only the robins sang then. From far off came the sound of folded lambs, a blurred, warm, utterly consoling sound, like a long-drawn sigh for too great happiness. Friends, out walking, wish to fall in with one another's preferences. But what if simultaneously the votes are for different paths home through a wood? There followed a wild tussle in each other's interest, charging like bulls, enfeebled by laughter. I generally had her way in the end.

Sometimes the night pressed down on our obscurity with a close lid of stars. Sometimes the valley was so thick with rain it stood up like cold corn in the darkness. Sometimes she roused in the morning wide-awake, to sing quietly to herself as she pondered the dishes or ventures of the coming day.

When Nick and Theresa came to tea, the pleasure of being hosts made something indelible even out of paper boats dancing the stream. But when we left our own valley, the river drew us inevitably. To walk the opposite way into ordinary North Devon seemed dull by comparison; yet having reached the river there was no way across except by swimming. In any case the value put on privacy for one's own shore disinclined one to trespass on the other. This gave a special quality to the country beyond. A great sweep of pasture became the place for Jill where the morning stars sang together. As seen from the Top of the World the little church tower of Merton sat up like a long-eared owl above an unattainable hamlet. Distant telegraph-posts vanishing over a skyline seemed to hold the quintessence of endlessness, along a road one would never take: they lived in her unwritten Ode to Distance. The farthest clouds coming up, from a west still more remote, were throwing shadows on Rough Tor and Brown Willy, knobs of Bodmin Moor that lurked just below our horizon. Jill did not know the teasing transfluvial country at all well. She did not know, nor of course did I, that in Greatwood, the farm just opposite, there was a parlour with plaster swags and a panel for a painting like the one at Venton. We had walked through that country once, from bridge to bridge; she had ridden there in childhood. The venerable family Rover was only for long excursions, and had been silent for some time. The river was a frontier like the Channel, but with the opposite coast brought up near as in a telescope.

There would be no pleasure-motoring again. A car might be going into Bideford on business, or we would go there by bus. The steep streets crowded under summer awnings; the trite click of a shop-door; the chance remarks of West Country people; the scribble of copper wire in the dusky ironmongers; the overwhelming scent of dress material in the draper's—such things were, not foreign, but as if never met with before, although, and equally because, so endearingly familiar. Our journey through the town was like Leopold Bloom's through Dublin, in a different key. For now all the minutiae of sensation and thought, incidents of pause and advance, had significance. A flashing wind-screen was like hilarity. Shop dummies had glamour. An explaining or directing hand was benevolence. Whatever one could see at the moment— a pattern of brooms, bicycles, cheeses—looked utterly gratuitous and at the same time as if it ought not to be altered. For it was part of one thing, which had the new meaning just because it was unitary, and all our own.

Here the same river, our river, was so wide. Across from where we munched on the dusty quay, an engine moved away with a coach or two. Departure. But detached: across the water. Not a journey one was ever likely to take.

With bare walls to decorate, but with only five or ten shillings to spare, we presently made our way to the antique shop. It must be of the right kind, intermediate between junk and sophistication, and there was one kept by a couple in a side street, who did not press us to buy, spontaneously reduced a price, and shared our pleasure in a discovery. Unlikely as it may seem, we should encounter similar kindliness in other towns. Indeed it is curious that I cannot remember meeting, in her company, with any rudeness or ill-temper from strangers, for it seemed as though our happiness overflowed in such a way that others had a place in it and were essential to it; that the revealed being of a village or a town was itself a kind of being in love. Thus in Bideford we began to acquire, one at a time, objects that were made for humble parlours in late Georgian times—some crudely decorated mug or plate, with a pictured maxim or a Bible scene. In the evening I would wire the back of the plate and hang it on the wall, and we would view it and return to it, with a connoisseur's emotion, or a stronger feeling. Later we might be taken with a dark glass picture of the same period, printed and painted on the back of the glass; but of "back-painting" as a name we knew nothing, and of the technique only what the eye could discern. We saw that for the couple who illustrated, say, "The Affectionate Wife," the once-bright noon had darkened to mysterious twilight.

It was not that such simplicities were right for the cottage; though they were. It was not that they seemed to call, or whisper, from a world less threatened than our own; though they did. We found in them a touch of humble magic. It was as though the picture here and there said more than it should—as though the journeyman-artist, all unawares, had made a symbol where he meant a likeness. His primitive colours and bad perspective liberated a meaning. Clouds put in with the swirl of a brush were clouds for the imagination. Where the green of a hill crossed the frame of a window the view came alive. Mere cottage ornaments, for other eyes, had for us a correspondence with a way of living. Of course there was a relevant magic far transcending all this. There was Blake, both in pictures and words. There was Palmer, had we only known. Palmer spoke for our gratified twilights; the lineaments of our valley, like the shape of our living, would have won his approval, I think. There was Calvert, nearer than either, in his handful of tiny engravings; for the great star that throbs in his dawns and dusks is always the planet of love. Calvert knew the spirit in the warmth of the flesh. "Stay me with flagons, comfort me with apples, for I am sick, of love," we used to quote, unaware that he had illustrated this. It was all there in "The Chamber Idyll," with many a nuance—had we only known. Roses and raptures of virtue: incomparably more enjoyable than anything vice can afford.

By the oak in the Ram Meadow after tea, where the primroses were big as pennies along the mossed knobs of the stream, we saw the gnats make a parallel current, shooting endlessly over the dark water, to flow up again in a vague wheel as they tasted the rich warmth. Then we too would feel the light tangibly go out, when the sun dipped into the crowns high above. As still evening came on, the combe began to fill with shadow for the night, though it remained bright day on the hill and in the sky, where the swifts were wheeling very far up. So we would cross the stream and climb the hill into the blaze again, and sit with our backs to the earth-wall under the highest hedge. Of talk with its grateful digressions there could be no surfeit. The sun was now riding high above the opposite woods, with a good half-hour of warmth before it dropped behind them once again. Below, the trees around our island coming forward a little—ash, oak, and willow—we had them for a long time very tenderly modelled by light, as if affirmed in their young foliage against the massed shadow. The two houses looked more conspicuous now, moon-white on this background, with the tall feather of our smoke blurring out. It was like observing, from above, a later hour of the same day, though the cuckoo could be heard still haunting about down below, and though we might momently forget all time, seasons and their change. Once I recall her crying out there, in a kind of anguish, "*Why* did there have to be a war?" I wished she wouldn't. It seemed to put a point on what was just as well left blunt. But now the owls were astir beneath us. The sun was a few hairy stars in the wood-top; and a great hand of harmless shadow had reached up over the curve of turf. It was time to return—to a late supper; lights carried up to the big room, dangerous to moth and may-bug along the valley. And in darkness those owls far away like soft exclamations, the hush of the stream, and the occasional murmur of the window-fastening.

VI

Ironic clemency of faultless light. On May 10th we were lunching in the Ram Meadow, half-aware that the world had truly caught fire that morning, as the Germans flowed over Holland. High in the immaculate blue above our valley the flaming sword might almost have been seen to wink as it twirled, but the light was dazzling. A short figure appeared on the crest of Venstave—Mr Bater, the aged "telegraph-boy." Relieved to see us down below, he waved an orange envelope and shouted "Here I are!" I climbed up and opened a telegram from Christopher and Eve Hassall, announcing their arrival. We had plotted for this, wanting them to share with us, while time allowed, a life that "has quite outshone every period of life, and made a week of days, years of months."

The hour of registering approached for Christopher and myself, being just of an age, twenty-eight and a quarter. Some of my juniors in the parish, called first, had found themselves in the same regiment, and I wanted him to register with me in that uncertain hope. He wanted me to avoid the totally unknown by enlisting with friends in an anti-aircraft battery, then forming. This in fact he had now done: there was just time for me to follow him.

Up at Venton serious counsel was taken with my father-in-law. We ought to have been a serious party altogether in the valley, but fiesta prevailed by stream and river, until we saw them to bed in the room next the kitchen, long afterwards referred to as theirs. For they were the only guests, outside the family, that we had had together, or ever should have.

So Christopher sailed over the lip of the vortex—even as my brother did in the same week. Rex had got himself a commission in the Guards, who were the last regiments to grant them direct. He had not relished the idea of service in the ranks. Nor did I.

Yet in the end I had settled for the "totally unknown." Two futures, entirely different, hung on the choice, as we knew. But rightly or wrongly we never regretted the decision. Incidentally it gave us far more than we dared to envisage at the time: three extra months.

In the parlour at Venton stupefying news came from the uncleared throat of the dry-battery set. In the cottage there was no wireless; though sometimes we could just hear the Puddicombes' set, above the jamming of the stream and the interference of their fowls, spiralling out a very thin music, sweet and irrelevant as convolvulus. Spring matured and put on weight in the hollow. The cuckoo orbited ceaselessly. The bluebells overhead blanched into uncouth pods. Herb Robert, crushed between finger and thumb, gave the scent of a thicker season—and the stream was lost in that thickness. Red roses underlined the sill; and now they appeared with honeysuckle and pinks among the altar-furniture on her dressing-table. Soon it was foxgloves that rocketed from a jug in the corner of the Skull Room.

> So all these things and many more, deeper and indescribable, are stored against the darkness. I can't tell you what happiness we have, and what peace, in spite of everything. It would last a lifetime of war and tragedies. Once one has lived as fully as this, nothing that could happen to one's body or even to one's mind could do any damage.

This she wrote to her grandmother just before setting out for Bideford on the day of my registration. The loan of the car that I had driven to our wedding and honeymoon (half a lifetime ago) turned the duty into a spree; and as soon as I had taken, in some fly-blown office, the first inky step towards our separation, we made a day of it.

So we moved into the June of Dunkirk, when the world held its breath; until out through the sense of relief peeped the novel idea of invasion. One result was the hurried establishment of the Local Defence Volunteers, afterwards renamed the Home Guard.

My father-in-law, a distinguished cavalry soldier of the First World War, was given command of the Dolton platoon, and I was his first recruit. He never lost his air of serene, almost festive confidence, whatever he may have thought. Perhaps it increased at this time. I drove with him about our deep-cut lanes—and I heard him use a curious expression when referring to the possible arrival of an enemy column in our midst. "If the old gentleman does walk up the lane . . .", he would say. I also heard him declare, though not to his platoon, that he gave such a column, on butting its head against the defences of Dolton, a maximum of three minutes' delay.

North Devon might be far from the area of invasion, but there might be parachute-drops and diversions, and it all might occur rather soon, one supposed. Therefore about the middle of June it seemed unwise for us to remain where Jill could not be warned by telephone, nor I called to duty if the old gentleman did appear in the lane precipitately. She was very well, and as tranquil as she had said in that letter, but now growing heavier with child. We agreed that it would be best to dismantle our home and move up to Venton.

Before locking the door I engraved a rhyme on the window of the big room, for a memorial to our April, May, and June. There was a fancy that we might return there one day—when the war was over. Round the pane I put the Roman numerals of the clock-face and the signs of the zodiac, and in the centre the initials J and L, intertwined to form a heart.

On the day France surrendered, Jill and her mother buried the household silver and Celia's jewellery in a tin box behind the summerhouse at Venton, in a hole they had been worrying for some time. (Later it was retrieved full of water, with the pearl ear-rings reduced to half-size; for they had omitted to block the key-hole.) All that same grievous afternoon we made hay on the farm. Few words were spent on the news, but Tom Pickard, the Venton farmer, summed it up to me. "Ah, we've come to the sharp concern of it now!"

In the parlour Jill typed out her father's "Instructions for Patrol Leaders" again and again on to postcards. Each man on duty was to carry, "if he has one, Gun, with at least 4 cartridges, otherwise a Cudgel." There were not nearly enough rifles in Britain for the L.D.V. to be equipped, and rounds, too, were treasured. But we fired off a few at a local range, "to get the feel of the thing." This I got. For the first time—I had avoided the tedium of the Corps at school—I felt it leap excitingly in my controlling hands, as a buck-hare might leap at the shoulder to escape. I achieved a good card, and felt the appeal of marksmanship. Yet I never afterwards visited a range unless ordered to. The fact is that though I was by nature moderately good at physical activities, they did not hold my attention. It was the same at school. I played Rugger for my house at Stowe with much excitement, yet as soon as I reached Balliol and was free to play nothing, I played nothing; and have never since touched a ball in a properly organized game.

Besides, leisure was precious—how precious in the dwindling summer of 1940. This meant that when our shuffling band was dismissed from drill, I set off homewards and not to the pub in a proper corporate spirit. I think most of them did the same. They were pure civilians, like me, rooted in a way of life. I had married a local girl, one well-known and liked in the village, and they did not treat me as a foreigner. I find it hard to believe they would have done so anyway. West Countrymen are courteous and civilized, the younger men with a coltish, amused, slightly self-deprecating air. They were not bumpkins; they were thoughtful men, called to what nobody wished, and presenting a good heart to it. I liked especially Jim Woollacott, the young farmer with whom I had quiet conversations in the dead of the night.

The Torridge bridges were few, and miles apart, and if anything in our area had military significance, this fact could have. The bridge to the west of Dolton was approached by a long steep lane from a hill-top, where four lanes crossed beside a lonely chapel. Here my father-in-law established his outpost and potential road-block, to be manned every night as the countryside emptied. When my turn came round I would bicycle away after supper, into a warm evening full of the scent of clover and late hay, with a sporting gun at my back, some ammunition, and the thermos and sandwiches that Jill had prepared. We divided the night into long watches, two on, two off, and now and again I took pulls of hot coffee. Consequently I never slept for a second, but the reason did not occur to me at the time.

Still, it proved a worth-while experience, as well as a remarkably tedious one. Moving stealthily about, sitting silent under a hedge with gaze fixed on Vega, listening—the gun across my knees, and the lane dropping whitishly away to the invisible bridge—I found that my mind, and as it seemed my heart, would fall into a slower pace, and keep step with the entirely unhurriable movement and method of darkness; where a star might show and vanish at the edge of one particular leaf countless times with inexhaustible patience, before it finally withdrew from sight. Nothing happened; and this made the least happening momentous —an agitation of small night-animals in the bank beside me, no louder than the creak of a boot, yet convulsive—a dog barking in Petrockstow—a bat only known in a blink across the stars. More than this, the desultory whisper of the ash-tree over my head began to seem significant, its continual uneasy stirring deliberate, as if it were tracing out a pattern in time, and against the stars, of whose importance I had dimly become aware. I felt let in to a secret hardly relevant to a human being. I felt, through my boredom, the strong presence of living things, not as gods or spirits or anything anthropomorphic, but as the utterness of being so humbly and without ambition what they were and nothing else—that particular twisted branch I had come to know so well —this one unexchangeable blade of grass, nodding at my side. Everything was unique, patient, and valuable. I brooded on this landscape I had grown to love dearly, on England herself coasting or forging on through time to whatever apocalypse awaited, and I wondered what least contribution I could hope, such as I was, to make to her survival. I thought of the "old gentleman" in the lane. I could see him approaching with slow steps—not a ferocious old man at all, and oddly enough not specifically German. A stolid figure with a walking-stick I saw him, deeply lined in the face; impassive yet also ominous; not the figurehead of an enemy; more the ghost of the impartial misery of war, himself weighed down and sobered—that was the word—sobered by the desolation of which he was everywhere the silent announcer: such an apparition as might be seen coming up from below in the half-minute between the alert and the certainty, to be effaced by excitement.

As early as two the cocks began to crow, far off, close at hand, and measurelessly far—the merest filament of emotion along the horizon. The Crown slid away to the west, slowly tarnishing. And in the end, and sooner than had seemed likely, the objects round about assumed the altogether different ordinariness of daylight. The grasses waved on the banks in their day-long celebration of nothing. The yellow-hammers in the hedge struck up that reiterated phrase which, though an endless affirmation of high summer, is full of pathos for its passing. Some distant field in the dawn wind was crawling with barley; and far across other fields I could see the edge of Venton in a tree-clump, smokeless, with all its occupants still busily asleep—one of them awaiting her child. I rode home to breakfast, thoroughly jaded, and dumbly wondering how well I should stand up to the real thing.

I used to think of poems on night patrol, but with a bad verbal memory and so many alternatives rising through consciousness I could never compose without a pencil and paper—when awake. Asleep I could, and often did at this period. I wrote constantly, and in the evenings engraved against time. Although she never lost her looks, as women do who mentally turn inwards, absorbed in gestation, Jill was tired of being ugly in her own opinion, and ready for the birth. We would walk out to the top of Venstave, and sit against the bank as in the old days (a few weeks before), looking down on our smokeless home in the chiaroscuro of evening shine. "How little we need to make life worth living, so wonderfully worth living," she observed, "—and then there are wars!" But we had no sense of regret. It was achieved, it was garnered. And there was a sense of solidarity— all of us under one roof-tree in the growing danger. We were given the former guest-room, where I had engraved the family names on that decisive day, with Malmaison roses outside, and the view of Dartmoor—something the cottage had lacked. Here I hung up our plates and pictures. She slept badly now, but was still serene, and the days at this time began with more than normal merriment, at the inconveniences of childbirth, or at trifles. It was not a question of keeping up spirits: rather, it took more than the news to keep them down, and as always, any conversation could deviate into laughter and out again. This was not mockery; though it could have seemed like mockery to a rigid mind. At all times we laughed a great deal, and chiefly at each other. I am at a loss to understand what Bergson meant when he said that "laughter is incompatible with emotion." It seemed to us to go with, and in a special way to irradiate, deep affection. It was important to us, and we tried to think why.

Could one say that humour is fundamentally an enjoyable sense of the incongruous? I thought it was the only enjoyable sense. For the fact is that we all need a great amount of congruity in the conditions of life for our safety and sanity. This may explain why it is so much harder to imagine heaven than hell—if by imagining we mean the invention of unearthly imagery for it. The very word "unearthly" has a sinister note. If we think of a face worthy to exist in heaven it must be the most beautiful and spiritual we have known on earth: if changed—changed only to be more so. There are endless ways of altering a face that will make it seem hellish, by distortion, addition, etc.: only one that will make it seem heavenly, by appearing more completely what it should be—itself. Heaven must be infinite riches. Yet the picture we two tried to form of it could only be the best that we knew—the apotheosis of the familiar. As Milton said:

what if earth
Be but the shadow of heav'n, and things therein
Each to other like, more than on earth is thought?

Of course, heaven may be altogether different from earth, but if so, it must be altogether unimaginable. Hell very quickly comes on the scene when congruity is violated; which is why effects of horror are among the cheapest in art. In the general obnoxiousness of incongruity, laughter can work only between narrow limits. For if the comic is taken ever so little too far, it becomes the grotesque, and from there quickly slides into the horrible. A swollen lip may give a funny expression. One flopping open from a wound does not. The funny and the horrible are mortal enemies; though where exactly the frontier runs between them may be a matter of opinion, or taste. Hence the unrelieved solemnity of art when its business is horror. What is more humourless than surrealism? If Kafka's bad dreams ever strike one as near to the comic, they are perilously near. Francis Bacon's "Magdalene" ceases to shock if we describe her as a lady on all fours beneath a parasol, naked to the waist, and bellowing.

By contrast, Jill and I found no enmity at all between the funny and the heavenly (as I use the word). For humour was entirely at home with "the best we could imagine." In great art, humour and the tenderest pity can be mixed, as by Chaucer and Shakespeare. In life there are times when the mixture is extraordinarily subtle and elusive, when beauty itself seems to make one laugh for joy. Perhaps even then an incongruity is sensed. Perhaps it arises between effect and means—that such poetry could be made from such everyday words, and such a landscape out of common lights on common fields. But, if so, the sense of incongruity is lost in the impact of beauty, leaving only a touch of its laughter. We held, then, that humour essentially knows nothing of mockery.

Her humour was quick, subtle, Chaucerian, and never unkind.

Her gift for repartee was Elizabethan rather than American: what she enjoyed was the elaboration of the jest itself, erected with, more than against, another mind. And because her touch was sure, she could mix her moods—tender, bawdy, gay, and serious in a space of minutes.

Our reading this August included a study of Blake, and books by J. W. Dunne, *An Experiment with Time* and *The New Immortality*. According to Dunne's theory, it is not you but your attention that moves forward through time (as we ordinarily think of time) creating the illusion of transience. In reality the whole of your life-span is in existence—though the future can be altered—and after death it is all yours. Even now, in dreams, because the attention is relaxed, both past and future are available. His analogy is to a man playing on a piano a simple scale (waking life), breaking off to strike notes at random (dreams), making discords (nightmares), and returning with relief to the simple scale—never guessing the true capacity of the instrument. Yet even now "you can dream what you please, once you realise that you are dreaming and are the creator." A difficulty obtruded. Suppose a friend who is legless in your waking life becomes a champion runner in your dream of him. One view is as real as the other, according to Dunne. But if you can shape or "play" reality as you like, what proof of anyone else's participation in your music, and therefore of any genuine meeting with another person? I thought I smelt solipsism, and wrote to Dunne for elucidation. The courteous reply I received did not greatly help.

Dunne excited us. For one thing we were both accustomed to those dreams that afterwards appear to be previews. Later in the war Jill would dream of Stephen Haggard's sudden death; and know what was in the letter before she opened it. I saw both our children, before birth, as they would be at four or five—sex, looks, and "quality." Such evidence can always be discounted. But, more puzzling, I had had brief dreams that led up to, and were completed by, an event in the waking world. Someone interrupted a conversation: "Wait a minute—he's going to fire now!" The report awoke me in time to recognize the back-firing of a car in the street. Another time I dreamt that a friend was seized and flung through a window to fall on a conservatory roof below. I woke in horror to the crash of glass—leapt from bed, and saw that a hand-cart had been overturned in Charlotte Street, flooding milk across the road. Again I was in time to hear the sound with waking ears. How could such fancies follow after the events that caused them?

But the possibility of glimpsing the future had no charm in itself. Quite the reverse. We should have fled from so dangerous and impious a venture. What appealed was the evidence that reality was not confined to the "now," to the cruel flying-point of consciousness—that "everything which has established its existence remains in existence." Here Blake came in. He spoke of "seeing the Eternal which is always present to the wise," and said "if the doors of perception were cleansed, everything would appear as it is, infinite."

What we, then, had in mind was not the future but the past, and chiefly its latest acquisitions. For it is not true that the happy have no need of a past. On the contrary, they alone can fully use it as it should be used—to improve or enhance the present. It is unhappiness that has no history, shunning its own annals. We could not believe—with full allowance made for not wanting to believe—that the substance and actuality of high days had simply vanished. Sometimes, while "reliving" a passage of our *annus mirabilis*, as she had called it when scarcely begun, we felt that we were on the point of literally reliving it. We had that sensation, almost uncanny, that it was in some sense "there," and within reach, if we had but the knack to disengage from the moment. Such were our Goosewell days, now so distinct in their flavour. They became the subject of a poem written by me in antiphonal form, as though in the mind there were two voices, alternately lamenting the fugitive and celebrating the permanent—aspects of a single truth.

It may be asked if it was necessary to resort to Dunne's novel theory for reassurance that vanished time is not void. A Christian may believe that the past is taken care of, or if it is not, that he will have no need of it when tasting a happiness even more ravishing because unmixed. I am not sure how accurately the name Christian could be applied to us at this stage: to me most inaccurately, I think. With minds no more logical than ours, talk on the meaning of things, the great subject, was largely intuitive. I hardly know what "position" I had arrived at. I thought my "healed cross," as I interpreted the looped one, or ankh, to be an improvement on the cross itself, I believe, in the sense of an answer, a completion. Abandoning so foolish a claim, I thought it later a lovely symbol of affirmation, and still do. Even regular churchgoers can be unorthodox; and for the rest, it is possible to receive the sacrament "with a difference," accepting, not the teaching of the Church, but some notion of communion with the source of life or of goodness. I make no excuses.

At school I was confirmed, and soon came under the influence of a sceptical elder boy. From drinking tea in a silent group, blue-suited for Communion, I graduated to reading Schopenhauer in bed. A far more lasting influence was Shelley and the anticlerical Keats. At Oxford and for years afterwards I was an agnostic, sometimes an atheist, a thing Jill never was. But an Anglican atheist. And for those brought up in the Church from infancy, the door is left ajar, the book lies open on the lectern, the altar-candles are lit. She was always ahead of me without knowing it, and influenced me to go in without meaning to—even consenting to my divagations. Her faith had been far more constant than mine, though her private praying, she confessed, was childish and brief. It included "Jesu, tender shepherd" that our mothers had taught us. My religion at this time was chiefly one of gratitude. I had the sense of eternity before the sure belief in immortality.

And still one hungered for reassurance, for the certainty that "all shall be well," and was faced by that vast geological fault that has appeared in modern thinking. On one side there was the truth of what love and the imagination had been saying from the start of our lives, and were saying now with such emphasis, about the existence of a good beyond transience. On the other side there was the truth of science. Three great scientific advances— in cosmology, evolutionary theory, and psychology—had over-run one outpost of faith after another. It seemed as if the two modes of knowledge could never be reconciled. Then Dunne's books came to hand, and seemed to have done just this at one point: by establishing personal immortality in terms acceptable to science. Note that science had to be the arbiter: mark of its prestige among even the unscientific. Those books have not done so, in fact. But for the time being they threw a psychological bridge back to belief; and that was useful in the summer of 1940, with long, if not final, separation just ahead.

It was mid-August, and still I was at home, I could not think why. I found out when I went for my medical exam at Barnstaple. Glass-engraving, it appeared, had hitherto been a "reserved occupation," vital in the pursuit of war! Being hale, physically, I seemed destined for the infantry, yet when the dire little form at last arrived, it told me to report on the 29th to the Royal Corps of Signals at Ossett in Yorkshire. No one had heard of Ossett, and the maps were got out.

For the last fortnight of my civilian life I carried out Dunne's fatiguing experiment, recording my dreams immediately on waking, only to lapse on the last two mornings, just because they were the last—the very two that were likeliest to bring results, if he was right. My findings were positive, though not sensational. I had one recurring dream which meant nothing then, but oddly "foresaw" an unexpected aspect of life in the ranks.

A room had been booked at a Barnstaple nursing home, and Jill waited out her time, with apparent calm, dismayed at the thought of giving birth in the thick of an invasion. I should have gone about ten days before. She had one fear which greatly helped her, because it made her want me to be gone. The Home Guard had no uniforms as yet, and it was said that, if captured, they would be shot out of hand. For myself I was morally ready and in trim. I should make a poor soldier, but not poorer than some others. If they had managed, so could I.

Meanwhile the true life, after the amplitude of that great spring, had once more folded in on itself, as if shut into one small room, blacked out, and roofed by the wavy sound of enemy bombers—all else invisible beyond the range of a confiding flame. So said one of her poems. Though verse was not a mode for the full affirmation of her mind, it shows that in verse, too, she could turn from the old romantic sadness, and affirm.

> *This candle will not burn again*
> *While rain reveals the staring glass;*
> *This very wind will blow to rest,*
> *And passion from us too will pass.*
>
> *But though we move apart awhile,*
> *And walk in rooms of crowded night,*
> *All is but lost to be renewed.*
> *We have a candle in our sight.*
>
> *That is our symbol of desire—*
> *A tongue not faithless to the mind—*
> *Truth burning in a darkened room,*
> *Without whose light the world is blind.*

VII

Two swimmers advance to the front of parallel high-diving-boards. Hands part, down they go, and in the roar of waters each is alone, wondering about the other. I remember drowning in a crowd, a sensation not felt since my first term at boarding school. I remember the pungent clatter of a dining hall, with food in slabs at once too gross and not enough. I remember the door with the word "Ablutions" scribbled across it. So wags have some licence here, I thought. Hardly. Another door had the same word painted in brisk military capitals.

Then existence became exceedingly small and fretful, smaller and more fretful than it had been since infancy. We were right back in the nursery, struggling, helping one another with straps and buttons, brass buttons with sharp edges for which the button-holes had been issued a size too small. We slept in "cots" and were given "biscuits"—square sections of hard mattress to place together on the floor. By the second night I was growing desperate. A very light sleeper, I was again kept awake for hour after hour by the trumpeting throats, not to mention an ache in every bone. But marching about and drilling all day in the open air is a great cure for insomnia, and soon I could sleep through an air-raid.

Even quite little children are told what they are going to do next, but we, I say, were as infants. It was wonderfully restful in a way—if one wanted mental rest: I thought it would be ideal for an overwrought Cabinet Minister. We never saw an officer, and no N.C.O. referred to the war. The greatest peril since Hastings approached, and passed. All we knew of it was the writing on some news-vendor's board—"57 down"—meaning enemy planes. In the evening we were too tired to discuss it, or too engrossed in what really mattered—pimply leather, small bits of bright metal. The Signals badge displayed a naked Mercury; but gender is not easy to detect on that scale. "Polish up the little lady!" Sitting round the walls in a thick yellow light with the black-out boards put up, we were mostly young family-men, with snapshots of children in breast-pockets. I wrote my letters to Jill then, receiving as many in return. The prognosis was that she might be too narrow for a natural birth. Sometimes I felt the utter hopelessness of our position. Sometimes I indulged the illusion that our love was its own guarantee against disaster: it was too special to be broken. Her handwriting on a table each day, fluent, lucid and sure, was like a Roman mile-post, claiming a desert for a civilization. But all those letters would be destroyed on a fiery window-sill.

For a fortnight she had worked on my feet with methylated spirit, to good effect. My weeping blisters looked modest beside some in the platoon, and I did not go sick. Sweating it out in battledress, I recognized beloved September, the old honeymoon weather, but now as if unapproachable through glass. A fragile ardour in the light on hoardings and stubble—it made the texture of plain brickwork so sweet as to be almost edible. There was the old innocence in the blue, though tinged in that northern world with the blight of the great stacks. Below in a valley huge muscle-bound L.M.S. engines clanked smokily to and fro, making heavy weather with a line of trucks—very different from the cavalier dash of the South Western, or the lissom, popping agility of the G.W.R. But we did not always drill. Once we were marched to a vast, vacant mill; to the windowless upper storey. The machinery had gone, but the ballroom-sized floor was a quarter-inch thick in the packed grease of the Industrial Revolution. We were given safety-razor-blades and told to scrape it clean. Every scrape encountered submerged nails and bolts. It was like the legend of Tregeagle on Bodmin Moor, doomed to empty dark Dozmary Pool with a limpet-shell with a hole in it. I thought wryly of the first day at Halsdon Mill, when I got down with bucket and rags to some mess on the floor, and had to give in to Jill's earnest plea to take over, because she felt it undignified for a man. "If you could see me now, dear!", as my comrades never tired of saying. After dinner we marched to our mill a second time ("183 down!"), to Scrape for Victory with torn thumbs. But not again. No reason was given, either for starting or stopping; it seemed like the momentary whim of some invisible tyrant.

I knew of young men, not professional soldiers, who found a true self in the army and secretly rejoiced to be there—not, I mean, for the reason which supported everyone, but because it absolved them personally from the fear of failure outside. My case was not theirs. I should have been more lost in the army than ever I had been in the rush-hour tube to the office, but for the reality of that love which was the meaning of life, and had already absolved me from a failure of talent. I will not pretend that my first weeks "on the square," though tough, were ever the savage experience described by T. E. Lawrence in *The Mint.* All the same—and largely because of the infantile dependence, the surrender of adult manhood—there were moments when it gave the horrid sensation of a dream where you know you are dreaming and cannot wake up.

And yet again. . . . Not welded by danger, or great hardship, or familiarity—only by the oddity of the life—we, thrown together in amused companionship, did have something of value. Surely there was something Stanley Spencerish about us, and worthy of a panel in Burghclere Chapel. I believe it for this reason. Never listening to the wireless in Devon, I came new to the popular songs they all sang that summer. I have only to recall the nightingale in Berkeley Square, or "Somewhere, over the rainbow," or "When your smile is so delightful" (or whatever the words may have been), for my mind to be suffused with the very quality of those days, and not without a twinge of nostalgia.

Meanwhile the tension in the air was more keenly felt under Venton's remote thatch. The invasion might exactly coincide with a difficult birth. Hospitals might be full, doctors unavailable, roads chaotic. There could be parachutes in any sky. To provide Jill with a last ditch that was better than metaphorical, her father had made a hide in the top corner of a field just below the brow from Venton, under thick branches. The occupants would have to lie down, but it might serve for hours or even days while the farm was being visited, plundered, or burnt. From there one could slip down the hedge on either side to fetch water from the stream. Tins of food were buried, and a small stove. And in those days Jill's aged dog Val was put down, the lean chaperone of former hours in the bracken. She would not like gunfire.

On the evening of September 7th the Venton telephone-bell rang and the weighty word "Cromwell" was spoken. This code-word had never been given to platoon commanders, and my father-in-law had to break security and ask what it meant. It meant the invasion of England had begun. He called out the Home Guard, and it remained out for hours, in that false alarm. On the second evening they were out again, in readiness. On the third the pains began, and Jill and her mother drove into Barnstaple, where a great gale huffed at the nursing home all night. In the early afternoon of the 10th, after only seven hours' labour, a son was born, quite quickly and naturally, weighing seven pounds.

Relief and elation seem, in memory, to be one with the light of the afternoon of the telegram. I had also a slight sense of guilt that I had not worried enough, had left things to Providence for hours at a time—as though luck were deserved in proportion to anxiety felt. Ordinary leave was everywhere cancelled, and what the army called compassionate leave, with odd-sounding tender-ness, would have been granted only if mother or child had been seriously ill. Because she was sensible, and outwardly calm through the air-raid alerts, the nurses brightly called her the "perfect mother," and neglected her for the hysterical ones, in spite of her inexperience in feeding from the breast. One raid was so close that preparations were made for a general descent to the basement. Jill felt she would be better off at Venton, though her return was premature. It had all been highly successful, but physically not a good preface to the privations of the middle war.

When my father died, peacefully declining, compassionate leave was mine for the asking, but to the wrong county; and if I took it, I should begin the long wait all over again. The new life and the old were painfully competing. My mother had Rex on leave, and generously made it easy for me not to come. Suddenly I was given a week's normal leave and sped across England in two expresses. It seemed as if an era had ended: gone finally now was the tremendous summer, tremendous in all senses. But everything had turned out well—or what would pass for everything in the zest of the hour. The threat of invasion was withdrawn. Jill was safely at home, slim again, with this addition to our love in the folds of the cradle, remote-eyed. It was late October, the logs were spitting in the parlour, the wind rattled our casement, blotting out Dartmoor. With a candlestick she was bending over this mannikin—who sneezed—who was a third person and yet incredibly of our contriving—whose skin was so smooth as to be almost intangible, like solid air—who puffed and guzzled at her breast, looking up in the sensual trance. We called him Simon after the boy in de la Mare's preface to *Come Hither*. We had him christened in the hamlet-church of Dowland, whose owl-tower could be seen from our window. The old blind parson wrote the names in a register that began before Waterloo and still had not reached the seventieth page.

Thus continuity held. We had taken up living again just where it had been interrupted, quicker than I could change into jacket and corduroys. We had been given a chance to "regroup," as it were, and prepare at peace for whatever ordeals might follow. The swimmers, having swum a length under water, had broken surface simultaneously.

VIII

A private soldier on the way to a commission is never completely in the ranks. A crowded waiting-room would seem a different place if no train could be expected. For the element of hope alters all. The Company Sergeant-Major looked me over when I applied: "I suppose one of these days I shall be saluting you!" I thought not. I did not want a commission in the Signals.

I was now at Huddersfield, set to learn the trade of Electrician Signaller, the most advanced, on account of my honours degree. But I was soon envying the commercial artists who trained, so casually, to be Draughtsmen. The exam I cannot pass is even now my recurrent bad dream; and every day then I sank deeper beneath vectors and cos θ. Soon a stripe was awarded to those who were officer-postulants. I welcomed it as the first step towards escape, but hardly for its own sake, since it involved some small authority over former equals. Of my duties I remember only one. Handed a large key, I tramped through the town before dawn to open the sticky iron gate of a submerged public lavatory. At six o'clock on a wartime morning in November, already filling with black rain, Huddersfield was not congenial, the very name suggestive of a huddle, a shudder, and some forgotten Udda, whose field must have been a by-word for shards and infecundity. I stayed there, at the foot of the tachist steps, in the action-painted interior, until the lavatory-man arrived at a civilian hour.

Nevertheless, under much boredom, anxiety or loneliness, I found myself far happier, as I told a friend, "than ever I was at Balliol, crawling out of bed at nine." She, who had made it so, presently arrived. That this was possible we owed entirely to her mother, whose indulgence of Jill and fondness for me would multiply occasions when she consented to take charge of Simon. Jill had spent three hours in the train at Bristol, in and out of a raid, with the occasional time-bomb exploding. She had had broken nights with Simon. Common sense must have said that it was too soon for her to come. But then, I should soon be gone; and the sweetness of being together atoned for a bad nose and throat, and for the squalor of lodgings. For the first time she had to conduct a domestic row, several rows. However, the meanness of the landlady, the meagreness of the food and the sadness of the one old servant make a tale too conventional to be worth repeating. It was funny when it recalled the North Country lodging house in *Goodness, How Sad!*, with the voice of Mrs Priskin heard on the stair. We were too poor to do better. Consequently a few days passed before she could bring herself to confess that she had lost thirty shillings or so; though her little-girl act, with frowns and hesitations, and demands for advance forgiveness, was more to engage than in fear of rebuke. She could have done to perfection the scene where Juliet is teased by the procrastinating nurse. I had seen her play such a part, impromptu, with her mother.

Suddenly I was posted to the East Yorks at Beverley, for pre-O.C.T.U. training, and found myself in a hut of young infantrymen. It was a relief to be studying subjects within my mental range again, such as the maintenance of the touchy Bren gun. Now, if Ossett seemed a narrow existence, at least it had a wind blowing in from a hundred varied occupations only just relinquished and still proudly discussed. Here civilian life had been forgotten. We had zero of intelligent intercourse, quite below the level of a dirty story, which would have shone like a maxim of La Rochefoucauld's. There was no "blue" vocabulary. There was just the one epithet, heard in every phrase.

Life was in fragments: there was no escaping that. We two must live it now in pieces of a week-end, a fortnight, at very best a month at a time; but what made us far luckier than most was the number of pieces we accumulated, to the extent that we contrived to be together for some part of almost every month through the following three years, and thus to preserve the sense that togetherness was normal. Apart from that, they were not really separated fragments of living, but like intermittent stones in a long necklace, the intervening chain of our thoughts and letters being sound. A life made of frequent short "lives"—such was ours from now on. And as each "life" began we were back in a world that revolved more slowly—or if not more slowly, so much more significantly as to counterfeit slowness.

162 O.C.T.U. at Bulford on Salisbury Plain was reputed to be the most exacting of all. I make no complaint about the course itself, which was no more rigorous than it should be, no doubt; but for me it held a quite gratuitous unpleasantness. Rumour had it that no less than half of a previous intake had been "Returned to Unit"—rejected. Many of the cadets were anxious. The less sure they were of being "officer-material," the more they felt obliged to assert themselves, individually or as members of little hostile cliques. I thought we should all do much better by full mutual support; but then my own misgivings made me over-sensitive. I thought that I had no gift of leadership whatever. I paid now for escaping the duties of a prefect at school, while enjoying the privileges of a sixth-former. I did not recognize that the faculty grows with use, like any other, and that it is easier to command when authority is real than when it is fictional and momentary. In short, I was suffering an acute attack of unconfidence. I detested each day from the hour when little Sergeant Wolf appeared in the pitch-dark doorway and simply howled like a wolf, for a kind of *rebus* reveille, palpably lowering our spirits, and also making me like him. I even toyed with asking to be "R.T.U.d", and trained as a Draughtsman. And yet it was wretched to embrace defeat.

All this receded, or was made acceptable, when Jill arrived in Amesbury for the first of many visits. She knew the malady. "You've no idea what a torment I am to myself," she wrote to her mother, "in the way of panic about everything in life;" and

I remember an indicative slip of the tongue. The conversation was to build our morale. "When we're an officer . . ." she said. So much was she identified. We were more than of like mind, *homophroneonte*. At the core we felt like one person; which only made the distinction of gender at the rind more felicitous. Homage to the gay and convenient invention of gender.

Our "lives" were in a new setting, at once private and public, at once free of constraint and so much the opposite, in dining-room and lounge, as to enhance the freedom when regained. I mean the ambiguous setting of the country hotel. Here life centred on a room that was both uncommitted and our own from the first juggling with the lock; a room that was a number in a uniform series, and yet singular, attached to its neighbours, if at all, by a few enigmatic filaments of sound. Here she would be, with new dress or shoes, and conscious of the heightened attraction that child-bearing gives, as if an instrument should not forget that it had once been fully used. In walking pinched corridors, every creak of the boards a *sotto voce* acclamation, in observing paired shoes by skirtings, footnotes to unread lives, in brushing some other life in the rustle of a dress from a door, life was centri-petal towards that comic room. It was comic in its union of daintiness and nakedness, this room with a lace "runner" but no pictures—apart, of course, from the one random landscape behind glass, revealing the hotel yard, or an alley, or someone's potting-shed, all protected by muslin like a masterpiece.

Returning to Devon from her first Amesbury visit she went to bed with a fever and a painfully ulcerated mouth, caught on the journey; for the steady health of our summer together had gone. She lived too passionately. There was nothing feverish in her happiness itself, which filled a day only as the sun may fill a summer solstice hollow, but it consumed her in this unnatural existence, with its sharply alternating good and bad. So the pat-tern recurred. As against that, she was quickly ill and well, and her spirits rose when any chance was given them. On April 3rd, her birthday, there was a dance at Bulford. Above the blacked-out, throbbing gymnasium the night was fresh, with the Plain vaguely humped around it. The sirens sounded as we arrived, and soon a few enemy bombers passed north. For a moment the great sullen war itself seemed romantic to her—the cadets dancing, the very cool spring stars, and the bugles blowing far and small over the limitless barracks.

I had my commission, easily enough in the end, and now, undeservingly enough, I had the choice of two first-class regiments. A brother could get me into the Welsh Guards, a brother-in-law into the Rifle Brigade. Of the personal interview I was not unduly scared: I seldom am. I thought, perhaps wrongly, that I knew how to look more likely than I felt. For brothers so attached and intimate not to soldier together may seem unnatural, but I expect that in his disappointment Rex understood my decision. He was always Hyperion to my satyr. I had built with someone else a world quite different from his. In the closed order of a regiment I must be accepted for myself, if that could be managed, and not as my brother's brother. Jill strongly thought so. And besides the Guards would be too expensive, whatever he might say.

A leave hung suspended in the gap between course and commission, refreshing as a spider's web after rain. It opened with a visit to Dean Prior in South Devon, where a Furse ancestor had been the parishioner of parson Herrick. We engaged to give account of the ruined house to Jill's father, who had never seen it. Here then was Herrick's church, with his verse on the wall to another of his flock. But the ruin was elusive, the very name, Morshead, having faded from local memory. We struck out in the direction of Dartmoor, down a damp lane studded with enormous primroses, whose sudden scent was the distillation of last April. It led into quiet-coloured pastures, into that slightly tilted, uneasy kind of landscape that suggests the proximity or "presence" of great hills, invisible beyond. At length across a stream we could see it, the very long Tudor manor house of Robert Furse. Under the granite porch the door pushed wide, while ivy and elder, leaning out, made everywhere the gestures of forgetfulness. But the slate roof was on, and the carved beams still held the hall ceiling.

I come from here! I have felt it myself at Whistler's Farm, and elsewhere in the yew-dark hedges of Hampshire. Surely it is pure illusion that the whole landscape seems faintly familiar? Yet one would have this illusion, even if "here" were no more than a single little turret—than a mound in a field—as it might be at Morshead before the twentieth century was out. The sense of inexorable human oblivion filled our minds with melancholy—pleasing melancholy, because countered by the thought that we were there to feel it, indisputably actual and together on the lovely, leaping crest of modern time.

In a Salisbury shop, nervously, I buttoned on my black-button uniform and made my way out to the 2nd Motor Training Battalion at Tidworth. Arrival was alarming, but after the first moment remotely enjoyable—I suppose like arrival at a grand house-party already assembled on the lawn, where the new guest is, after all, intended to enjoy himself. That, wonderfully, seemed to be the notion here. One was on trial, but the assumption seemed to be that one would succeed; and it was deeply reviving to be treated as a person again. Spirited guidance, with character-sketches, I had from Pat Furse, who was thriving in the army to an enviable extent, and generally liked.

The Rifle Brigade was gay—proud of its great record and many V.C.s, and priding itself on dash and discipline without excessive formality. Among N.C.O.s and riflemen a great many Londoners made for cheerfulness. Among officers a constant influx of agreeable youth would give much charm to the Mess in my eyes. We, in our batch, were first set to unlearn the staccato Guards drill we had sought to perfect at our O.C.T.U.s, substituting the rapid legato rhythms of Rifle drill. In the R.S.M.'s approach, the polite, the strict and the paternal were nicely blended. "No, sir, we haven't time to recite Omar Khayyám between every movement like a bloody redcoat! Loaf of bread. Stamp! Jug of wine. Stamp! And thou." (Later in Aldershot's only bookshop I found the "poetry section" to consist of nothing but a long row of *The Rubáiyát* in a cheap edition, and it speaks well enough for an R.S.M.'s philosophy of life.) This drilling culminated in the ordeal of the first Adjutant's Parade, when we must command the companies. I see them, motionless, and, to one side, the band in dark green, with sunlight winking from their silver instruments. I am surprised to hear them playing waltzes out there, as they wait for us, for to me the waltz has feminine associations—swirling dresses in ballrooms ... at Osterley. ... But slumbrous and sugary the music waits, dreadfully heightens the sense of occasion, and at the same time gives one support; until, breaking into the regimental quick-step, it makes our few elementary movements an inevitability.

I was put to learn regimental signalling: morse, cable-laying, wireless. Twelve weeks at school again, in an airless hut, or out on those lion-coloured hills. An intellectual, and in my thirtieth year, I was no doubt predestined for technicalities that seemed suffocating to most of the "young officers," two-thirds my age. I well saw the psychological advantage they had, when from prefect to platoon commander was an obvious step. I simply could not give my whole self. I craved solitude, the hermit's cell where I could think and write; and this luxury, a single room, I actually got and held on to through many changes. We lived pretty well at that period. "After Bulford it's Claridges," I told a friend. "In fact we have Claridges' head-chef to concoct our frugal meals, which are such that I developed a liver in two days and have to go for a run before breakfast." In the dining-room, one day each week, the almost contiguous band fairly soused us in melody from soup to dessert.

Simon flourished, and our "lives" had new zest. Jill thought of him constantly when away, but without anxiety because of Celia, who was, she said, the perfect grandmother in her unpossessive love of our child. No great summer this, like the last, but if it cleared at the week-end we hired bicycles, Jill advancing by way of spurt and glide, which she held to be more enjoyable than steady pedalling—a symbol of her course through life. Or in country buses we ambled on to Salisbury and Marlborough, there to browse and shop and spend in some translated restaurant the middle-eternity of a Saturday afternoon. She danced in the Mess, helping to twine the two threads of my divided existence, the plain and the coloured.

In the crisis of 1940 we had said goodbye with no hope that the best was not over—unless hope were stretched thin as elastic to the unimaginable end of the war; yet now living together was not only more available than ever we had dared to suppose, it was positively better in quality, and the very intermittence made that plain; as if the action of a film should be replaced by a series of "stills." Often looking back, we seldom looked back to anything as rich as the present, and frankly wondered at the sense of improvement. It turned every adventure into two—as when we slid out of Exeter St David's in an unfamiliar direction, down the estuary to where the sea flips pebbles at expresses, and onward all day to the remotest west. For we wanted to explore that peninsula which is the outstretched hoof-tip of Britain, the beloved sitting unicorn. It proved to be a curious landscape, ancient and modern, stirring and trivial as a book of hymns: the landscape of allegory, rich south, ascetic north, and between them the metalled highway of illusion, speeding—towards what? A shack full of souvenirs. The Last Toilet in England.

The West Pole could never be discovered: that indeed was its point. It would be hopeless to look for it in the glasshouses of Scilly or in America. If it pulled us towards anywhere, in our years together, it was to certain islands that were sometimes to be seen after sundown, floating islands of the air, a little above the horizon, islands where as yet the sun had not set.

One day to the north, then, where the hills fall treeless, populated by flocks of stones, grazed by boulders. It was here that D. H. Lawrence pummelled the yeasty dough of his religion of mindlessness, tried to found a community hidden from a war by these metallic hills that curved around his pulpit. But the hills became a sounding-board to gong back his own anguish of spirit. There was a curious similarity to our first home at Goosewell, and we saw ourselves exchanging with that company, brilliant though it was. Enormity of war: the same German war all over again. A bit of house on the coast: the same coast farther along. Rumours, isolation, convoys creeping the horizon. And within-doors privacy, the insane world shut out for a while. But there the resemblance sharply ended; for we, like many couples in the grace of obscurity, untormented by the urge of genius to false prophesying, could have been no little content in that small tower. The episode from the other war seemed desolate—as desolate as a 1917 Crossley out in the rain. Also futile, and like a mocking pre-echo.

Another day it was the south, where the combes run down to the mackerel-crowded sea, through oak-woods old as Caractacus perhaps, and dense with life. Here a cove, to our eyes, lay virgin. The headlands on either side folded it in as we followed the descent of a stream which trickled from tussock to tussock, more heard than seen.

Over one headland a hawk trembled—slipped aside, and trembled—as if, so light, it could be lofted to the end of its thread of concentration by an upflow of warmth, and there sustained. The low sea beyond rocks was dancing blue to the top of its camber. Presently it was broken far out by several porpoises looping through the surface like momentary eyebrows.

I swam from the rocks, the water cold but very clear, the floorscape visible to a great depth. Jill had never learnt to swim because of childhood illnesses; but today she was well. She found a place between rocks, and with careful placing of toes and fingers dipped once to her chin. I watched her naked form, eager and absorbed, cut off from one of the joys of the flesh that she prized, even as the rocks of her bath cut her off from the fulness of the sea.

Dragonflies pin-pointed ideas. I began to work at a poem then under construction. Convolvulus strayed about the rocks, and from one rock a mane of some grass hung over in a long cool beard for exploratory fingers. It was too warm to dress. She wove herself a garland of the spear-shaped leaves and white trumpets, a lei for her shoulders. Then she moved away and sat down by the beard and began to sing quietly, looking out to sea. It was one of those occasions when time seems threadbare and ready to pull apart. What she sang I forget, but the sound that reached me was of something rare, I should imagine, in the second year of the war, the sound of pure felicity with no overtone of care. This is for ever and a day, it seemed to claim.

There had to be an operation in November to put right that displacement, made worse by the bearing of a child, and she chose to have it in Salisbury Infirmary, to be near me, and in the hands of a favourite doctor and nurse. Cheerful when I left her in the high bed, though mutely scared, she came round to extreme nausea. The pain through the night was more severe than had been promised, requiring several injections of morphia. Rising and sinking in the slow swell of it, she fixed her imagination on the green tussock, remote now in summer, making it a symbol of our truth, holding it before her like a talisman, caressing it as if it were the beard of a sage, serene and reassuring.

The pain went on for a week, but she recovered quickly, and began to think that she had turned some constitutional corner into sound health. Because I did not want her to resume broken nights with Simon too soon, there followed seventeen days of luxury, by our standards, in an Amesbury hotel, which brought us near bankruptcy. Really there was no cure for her troubles but the one which could never be applied: undivided, unthreatened, unemphasized living in a climate of peace.

But that autumn a major event had occurred. Regular leave had been extended from seven days to nine, with an extra day for travelling. It was as though the span of one life had been extended from fifty-six years to seventy.

IX

The Household Cavalry had asked for the loan of a signals officer to form their own training platoon, and I was to be sent. I shied, naturally, and suggested someone else; but that was brushed aside. Anyway the posting meant Christmas at home; and that is why I know how the wooden door-latches of Venton sounded at a time when America had entered the war, Simon slept with his bottom in the air, and two battleships had been sunk. All this together was voiced for once and always by an orchestrated record of "Greensleeves" which we were given. We should have preferred the simple air, that spoke of England as no other; yet the ripe setting soon saturated that Christmas, the last ever to be spent in the old house.

Windsor proved manageable, for no one outside the platoon took any interest in us. The best of it was the companionship of my young assistant, Henry Uxbridge, now Lord Anglesey, whose bellow of laughter made concentration difficult in the adjoining class-room. The worst of it was the life, if that is not too strong a word, of the Mess. Since I could not afford to dine in the West End, and since no one might rise from dinner before the colonel, I fumed in my leather-backed chair for an hour and a half of unintercourse, with the occasional feel of cut-glass in my hand as the port passed me by. It woke a response in my natural radicalism; for I was long-since impatient with the whole structure of the old class-ridden England. This was in the war's midwinter, a grim period which extended from Pearl Harbour through reverse after reverse, when it seemed that the only objective of the free world was a negative one: not to be beaten. Jill found a lack of spiritual leadership in Churchill, tonic though he was. "When he gets through his speeches I always feel something is missing."

Really we were simmering for the 1945 General Election—and a more profound revaluation.

She arrived in Windsor feeling "dangerous" and in peacocking mood. She was restless for the bright lights again—that is, for the naked bulbs round a theatre dressing-room mirror. Too long her spirit had been pinched in a clothes-peg. She was not happy alone, and Venton was bleak without the family: every "life" we spent there was like a house-warming, she said. Now there was one which we failed to make truly warm, except physically, in the great wood fires that flowed from my saw. Simon had been ill, and she was exhausted. It was lovely to see him in her arms while she sang to him in evening firelight. He divided his kisses punctiliously, but all night betrayed the small welcome he had in his heart for this imposing stranger, this brief comet in his universe, towards whom his very sun seemed to turn like a sunflower. Which little drama, re-enacted in numberless homes, was but a minor drawback to a war.

After four days I was recalled, to take charge of our signals platoon at Tidworth. My Windsor blues had become less depressing by the end, because I had sampled the creative pleasure of a small command, and was now the less frightened of a larger one—also a good testimonial had gone to my own colonel. For Sir Charles McGrigor I already felt something of that grateful affection that a very amateur soldier can feel for a professional who appears to believe in him, up to a point. He sometimes took me with him on military car-journeys for no special reason, or to his home on the Test. Moreover, he approved of my marriage. Only, did he know she was an actress?

"Inside I'm as bitter cold as the weather," she wrote. "What a philosopher you are becoming in your old age—quite grandfatherly! I wish I could acquire a little of it. I *must* get back to work—it's tormenting me that these years are being wasted." She threw herself into lifting twelve sackfuls of potatoes with the farmer's wife, who observed, "Us are very good workers!", and next day she felt none the worse for it. "You can't imagine what

this means. It gave me a sudden new surge of hope and confidence." She paid visits to her grandfather at Halsdon, the sculptor, crippled and now out of his mind. One day when she bent to
kiss him, he mistook her for his young wife, who had died in
childbirth, when Jill's father was born.

Coming up through the wood behind the cottage I nearly
trod on a small primrose leaf uncrumpling in a sunny patch.
It was like a finger plucking a string in my mind. Do you know
the feeling? It makes a note that one had forgotten hum somewhere inside.

She began to write a novel. And she sent me this poem.—The
woman lies awake beside the man, thinking of the two selves her
love had presented to him, both at this hour discarded, and leaving only that other, whom he has not met.

THE SMALL HOURS: WOMAN TO MAN

The angle of your arm is bare,
Like a niche without a saint.
The virgin and the courtesan
Sleep where the light is faint.
They leave a self you do not know.
One you have never loved—
A child crying in the dark
Because a curtain moved.

But now the farthest cock has made
His fading Amen cry to sins
The lost committed in their dreams,
And gradually the grey begins.
Has that cry driven in your rest
The sad blade of a name,
Someone you desired once in sleep,
Or loved before I came?

As always, to construct something helped her, and quickly she became more reconciled. But our child was the main recompense for our division.

> I've settled very happily into this solitary life. Simon is always coming to my knee for kisses, or to help me by covering my book or this letter with little offerings. He is an extraordinarily sweet-natured little boy. The evenings are very cosy, and I am in no hurry to go to bed—so you'll see how much better I am. He came and romped on the big bed yesterday evening, and suddenly got tired of laughing and crept up into my arms and wanted to be sung to. He cuddled there for some time, smiling up at me and then just went to sleep. And slept for twenty minutes. I think I have never loved him quite, as much.

And then, just when she had applied herself to this rewarding life, there came a call from her agent offering her "a marvellous part in a marvellous play." On the telephone she heard me confirm that I really did want her to act in the war. And she felt so well. But her mind was in turmoil. Was it wise, this summer— perhaps my last in England? Would her mother change places with her for the run of the play, looking after Simon in Devon while she companioned her father in London? We could then afford to pay board in both places, instead of in one, as at present. Her mother had misgivings, not unreasonably. "Some of your arguments are good," Jill wrote; "others make me furious! . . . You'll go on saying 'You must go back, but is this the moment?' until I'm in my grave. You'll also go on saying, 'This is such an important time for Simon' until he's at Oxford!" And there the matter stood when she went to bed at ten o'clock on the night of March 10th.

At lunch-time next day I was called to the Mess telephone, to hear her voice, small and weary with some disaster. "It's Venton . . . It's gone." There had been a fire in the night. Nobody was hurt, though dog and cat had vanished, but almost everything had been burnt—the house, and everything of ours. With such news the shock and the relief are simultaneous, putting the mind into a choppy riotous condition like water where contrary currents are butting. I said I would come at once; but she asked me not to do that. Her instinct was to place our "lives" where they would yield the best, not to fritter one away on the makeshift of a haunted aftermath. She was all right.

How can I begin to tell you anything? It is now pretty well certain that the fire was caused by a box of cartridges under the airing cupboard blowing up. This probably killed both Merry and Johnny [the cat, Vanbrugh] instantly. It may have been a beam smouldering for weeks which caused the cartridges to explode. I heard the noise but never doubted that Johnny had knocked something over. Simon was very sick and that was all I was thinking of. If he *hadn't* been ill we should quite probably all have died, suffocated by the poisonous smoke, because I should have been in bed and asleep.

I kept thinking of this, and ultimately was left with a feeling of buoyancy, viewing our life from that hour as more than ever a gift.

I opened the bedroom door in order to go and fetch a little hot water for Simon and was met by a cloud of choking smoke. I shut the door and snatched him up in a couple of blankets and tried to get down the parlour stairs—but the smoke seemed thicker. So I went back to the corridor. I shall never be able to tell you what that journey downstairs was like. The smoke snuffed the candle out instantly and I began to go down the passage screaming for Mrs Pickard [in the farmer's end of the house] because I thought they might be suffocated before I could reach them. Simon screamed once, and then choked and went completely unconscious—I thought he was dead. I fell into both trunks and staggered down the stairs. It seemed like years and the smoke was in my lungs choking me, but I went on screaming for Mrs P. They were all in bed and never answered for one instant. I remember standing in her kitchen and thinking "There's no one else alive in the house." Simon was in a dead faint, and the dark was like velvet.

I got the back door open and Simon revived instantly in the fresh air. I shouted under their window and at last they answered—but it was ages before they dressed (or it seemed that). Finally I got Mrs P to take Simon and Sylvia up to Mrs Roberts. That left Tom and me alone. I went back into the big kitchen to call Merry and see if I could reach either the phone or the stirrup pump. But it choked me and I had to come back. Tom *would* take so long doing up his boots! It was beyond the two of us, and I knew the only thing was to get the Fire Brigade. So I ran in pitch dark to Venstave and screamed (again!) for Puddicombe to telephone from Halsdon. I nearly collapsed on the hill afterwards—I was soaking wet and my mouth had dried from fear and smoke.

Then I don't remember much. I tried again, crouching down, to reach the stirrup pump. I was haunted by Merry and went back alone into the front of the house to call him. I crawled to the archway by the little hatch which was now blazing, but couldn't see or hear anything. Then men came and got ladders and buckets and for a moment or two they seemed to control it—but the thatch had caught and there was no hope. . . . Later on everything was saved from the parlour. We made a chain of buckets till the engine came, but when they did come the wells gave out.

Three times I went up the lane to see if Simon was all right. He never cried. He sat smiling away, his hair all matted and filthy, but his smile was heavenly. And your three goblets sat on the table in the firelight.

But I have one terrible confession—that I never thought of any of our things in my room. I can't explain. I just never thought until the thatch caught above and it was too late. With a ladder we might have got something from my room I suppose. I tell you this honestly because when I realized, I was *glad*. I stood in the garden and looked up at the window under the flaming thatch—blue flame it was—and felt a kind of triumphant sense of the conquest of spirit over material things: that you and I could lose nothing that mattered. It was only momentary. Since then I've nearly broken my heart over your letters, and all the presents you've ever given me, and our plates. The house looked wonderfully beautiful burning. The wind fanned it, and a cloud of sparks stormed across the yard and barns.

At 12.30 I left. All that could be done had been. But all that night I lay in a state worse than anything that had happened. It all came back over and over, the feeling that Simon was dead and that I was going to die in that black, reeking passage. . . . At last the light came through and I was sane again.

There was no emergency in which she would not have been good, she who could imagine many that would prove too much for her. She made her statement to the police, admitting to a fear that she might have done better, but was much complimented and felt less guilty.

Well, there it is. I can't bear to remember the house. I keep seeing the parlour on a sunny morning. But it's no good. It was a beautiful and happy house and it ended triumphantly— at least that is how I thought it looked at the end. I hope you will feel that I did right and that I wasn't unworthy of you.

I found that I grieved most for the house itself, and next to that for a box-full of her letters; since hers to me, alas, had been stored in the same place. As for other possessions, here was an invitation to practise the detachment we had preached. "Now we can have the fun of building up 'rugs, jugs and candlelights' again, and what's more we can't have any qualms about catching the collector's disease for quite a time." We thought that an interest in collecting very easily replaces an interest in the objects collected. It was best to have a little of this and that.

On the day after her fire-letter she rang up with a message so different and so thrilling that it seemed as though the inward April of her moods, dark and bright, had at last contrived to take control of outward circumstance. We could have our valley home again. We could return to Halsdon Mill for my leave.

But first could we meet in Exeter for shopping? "I shall look terrible, you know. No lipstick, no clothes, no nothing, and I feel *very* plain!" From an upper window in the station hotel I watched her crossing the wide yard in her mother's clothes, with the effect of two exposures of the same negative. She moved with her lissom, rather long step, and, waiting for the traffic, puckered eyes in a little frown against the dusty wind. Nevertheless I wondered if a sensitive passer-by could not have divined the lightness of her heart. She did not know I was there, and it was like seeing her when I was not. It underlined the thought that it was she who might easily not have been there. That evening we heard the wailing of the siren through the Brobdingnagian chatter of a film. Some of the audience went out; but that was not to be the night of the "Baedeker raid." We indulged the crass illusion that bombs were too clumsy to divide couples.

In a bye-street window we saw a little Chinese picture, only about two inches high, but set in a deep-splayed frame of dark wood. It showed a boy, head and shoulders only, wearing a vermilion cap, crowned with a large pearl on a gold finial. Something like the spirit of Simon, something in the face, and something gem-like in it all, filled us with agitation that we might not be able to afford this. It proved to be the eighteenth-century portrait of a boy-Mandarin, painted on the back of the glass. In plum-colour and blue he stood with his back to a tree and a polished blue river. There at anchor, far out, was a little high-prowed boat with a tall mast, riding its calm reflection, no one aboard.

It is hard to explain why the picture meant immediately so

much. A black ribbon beneath the chin isolated the pallor of the face. With those eyes, under very clear-cut lids, lifted a fraction above the level of one's own, the boy appeared to be musing deeply on life. Yet there was hidden laughter in the eyes, and in the corners of the mouth. He seemed to have the secret of inviolable gaiety beyond misfortune, to know of some good thing, indestructible and incorruptible, whatever disasters might befall, and however ephemeral happiness might prove. He became the symbol of our faith.

That day I also bought, for three and sixpence, a small leather-bound book called *Pia Desideria*, fourth edition, 1712. Until this moment we did not know that the humble magic we had found, and now lost, in certain plates, certain paintings on glass, had another source, in the emblem pictures of the seventeenth century. Here were two podgy barefoot children enamoured of one another, a girl and a winged cherub, and the engravings were so artlessly circumstantial as to rescue the figures from the coyness they certainly courted. This group were illustrations to *The Song of Songs*, understood as an allegory of the soul. "I am my Beloved's, and his desire is towards me" we read in the flowing calligraphy. The magnetic compass in the girl's hand not only pointed at the boy, but threw up a veritable ray at his face. "Stay me with flagons. . . ." Here they illustrated the very verse that had become a motto of good living at the cottage.

Next morning we were on our way to that house, and it must have been mood alone that made the country each side of the train look wholly unfamiliar, for we were certain that we had taken the Okehampton line. But presently the echoing woods of the Taw valley closed in, and there was Jury's car, and the smell of its upholstery, the unique smell of arrival and rebirth. Soon I was carrying our suitcases across a meadow. To reach Halsdon Mill from the road up at Halsdon you crossed this meadow to a white gate, and dropped steeply down a narrow path, slantwise, from top to bottom of the Eastern Wood, so that at first view the house down below was chiefly a thatched roof through branches.

The scroop of the door was like a password remembered just in time, and here were the other and intenser smells of rebirth: the smell of soot and wood-smoke in the kitchen, of milk and dampness in the larder; the old, bare, plastery smell upstairs. It was so extravagantly *there*, the past in the present. The upper window swung open to the sound of the stream, which instantly had never been lost; and a hand, hers or mine, clutching at a spider's web, retrieved out of the past the initials in the heart, at one stroke. (See plate three.)

That evening we found a place for the Mandarin on a shelf beside the door of the big room, cut into the huge chimneybreast. The boy's right arm was bent across his chest with the two middle fingers folded under, and the first and the fourth fingers projecting: a curious gesture. It looked as though the forefinger were pointing. It might be secretly pointing at an object beyond his left shoulder, as he faced us, but actually behind him—that is, at the waiting boat. It would not matter if, to other eyes, the hand was only resting on the plum-coloured robe. It was as though he were intent on conveying a message, but only to those who could read it, and in such a way that others would miss or even deny the intention. It was not enough to point at the boat through his body. Even that would be too unequivocal. The little finger must be outstretched also, to obscure the signal. Even so might one point, in order to be understood by one person among strangers; or in a game; or in a dream. This was like an encounter in a dream. The sense of unclouded morning, blue in sky and water. No speech. The lifted look, serene, but with sidelong laughter somewhere in the offing. The sense of a message too sweet and enormous to be remembered or even understood. What voyage did the Mandarin mean? To us it was one into felicity, whether a new life after the fire, or after the war. Or he meant that all evil is like a pledge that is somewhere, ultimately, to be redeemed.

As she went in and out of the room, Jill was constantly glancing at him, and she spent much time in waxing and "nourishing" the Georgian frame. With nothing now to hang on our bare walls, I cut nine of the pictures out of *Pia Desideria*, lightly coloured them, and had them framed in a traditional dark reeded moulding. These she grouped in the smaller rooms. "My life is waxen old with heaviness, and my years with mourning."—Here the girl has sunk beneath a fardel: "Alaſs" rises in a visible sigh from her head. Time flies above, scything the sunlight; yet his winged hour-glass also lies heavy on the ground. Each side of her, with backs turned, Night and Day stride apart, the one into darkness with a star-splashed robe and wearing the moon, the other with his head almost effaced by the glory of the sun that crowns him.

The emblem pictures were full of suns, moons, lamps, rainbows, stars, candles, and meteors, and this was stimulating to one who had an inkling, partly from these, that light in all its sources and effects might ultimately provide the best themes for engraving on glass. For it is only by portraying light that the stipple-engraver can make pictures, leaving the shadows to form in the unengraved places. Moreover, to be properly seen, a picture on glass must be lit from behind, when it will appear to be constructed of light, having light not on it but in it. Apart from this, the little pictures answered, however artlessly, to a view of life in which significant scenes and objects appeared to be symbols. Symbols of what? it will be asked. And I can only say, of themselves. That is, of their true selves, whether conceived as projected beyond time by our awareness, or as models of which we know only the fleeting copies. And we were quite content with this crude and indeed fondly humorous notation of symbols, valued in shillings. It was as well that we were, with all the essentials to be paid for.

Other than clothes bought in Exeter, Jill had only the trousers and jacket she was wearing on the night of the fire. Knowing that I did not as a rule think girls well designed for trousers, she had never allowed me to see the close green corduroys she constantly wore in the country. Now it could not be helped, and now I was sorry to see them already well-worn; for with her narrow hips under a trim russet jacket, she looked like Ginger in the Beatrix Potter shop, especially when she poked in and out of her larder, deep in the old reverie. The impression was somehow strengthened by her strange gilded boots—gumboots gilded by Theresa for a ballet at school, and now cut short. The larder was restocked. The furniture sufficed. Of a large double bed at Venton, only the box-spring had been rescued, but this looked much better at the cottage without head and foot, and larger still when flat on the boards. It was so low that one seemed to be lying on the floor, a sensation oddly refreshing in a very low room. It rose like a dais—yet casual as a French railway platform—and was the Great Bed of Here; or of Fair Wear and Tear; a bed to end dressing.

Going up to Venton we were out of phase inevitably; for seeing is grieving, in a special sense. It was all new to my eyes, and already ancient in hers. Gone over and over in obsessive recollection, it had sunk through her mind into the same landscape where Morshead was for ever patiently unbuilding. Only the farmer's end had been saved. Our room was a windowful of sky above a mound of rubbish, with the one dire smell. Climbing a ladder, I found her locked diary on the wide window-seat, charred round the edges and exposed to a fortnight's rain, but still quite readable; also the album of press notices for all her plays. Of our picture-plates only one survived—intact, but with an angry flush across the legend: "Prepare To Meet Thy God." Then with delight we found in the chaos the little Eros and Psyche out of Constable's House. We valued it now only second to the Mandarin. Palely painted, it was darker in tone from a brush with the blistering smoke. If we sent it to Rex to restore in camp, he would gladly consent, and would keep it for months, and would lose it. We did send it, all the same. And he did lose it.

Returning through Salisbury, to begin her jewellery I bought a cameo brooch in rococo silver. Meanwhile she was writing:

It's difficult to tell you how happy this time has been. Disasters can enrich one as much as ecstasies. You are all my world and the only arms I can rest in. If anything happened to you I should die—not perhaps in the body, but in the spirit—so you would never be alone wherever heaven may be. And if it was the other way round, all myself, the real self, would be inside you. This is what I believe and know to be true.

In fact the fire had not let her escape, for that night had introduced her to more trouble. It began on leave with pains in her wrists and legs, depressing after all her hopes, though more than momentary depression was not possible. "Shall I *ever* get a strong woman?" she would ask mournfully, massaging an ankle, her eyes on the light on Venstave. And later:

> *The room is as it was—but how*
> *The dust, minute and sad,*
> *Happens like tears or snow*
> *To blur the shapes of what we had;*
> *For you are gone, and pain*
> *Lies, my bed-fellow now,*
> *Closer to me than even you have lain.*

Yet we still thought cheerfully of her living near Tidworth, to keep house for Simon and me at once. For her life was more than ever a switch-back of dark combes and goat-giddy plateaus. Here was a difference between us. To me on the sunny uplands of physical good health serious illness never seemed likely. On the other hand I had been closer to a nervous breakdown, and was perhaps always closer to neurosis. Did she seek the other escape, she wondered, from the hard exam which is life—the escape into physical illness?

Why can't I conquer it? Do you think I could by some different attitude of mind? I sometimes really despair of growing out of it as everyone promised me I should when I was a child. Perhaps God has given it to me to keep some sort of balance with the overwhelming happiness which you have given me and do give me all the time. It's all this that makes the burning of a roomful of our things truly unimportant. We *have* our past in us, in our blood and our memory, and it is renewed every time we see each other and make love. And apart from us it is all there, going on somewhere just else in time.

Now I've got a fat poultice on my knee and it's eased the pain. It's wonderful how much one *appreciates* pain when it's over—relief is an exquisite sensation, and, like a storm, any kind of physical suffering leaves the air brilliant and washed, and one sees everything in a kind of radiance. That too is what I have felt since the fire. Somehow, going down so far into the shadow, this sunlight beyond is incredibly beautiful. I suppose heaven will be just a concentration of that brightness.

Her doctor told her that she had narrowly escaped six weeks in hospital. Twice she put off a projected visit to Amesbury, with a day or two in London first, to refill her wardrobe.

I'm so *sick* of my body. It's hard to lie here and *not* think about you, and God knows I've nothing else to do. But then perhaps if I hadn't always suffered physically my body wouldn't be so sensitive to ecstasy—these things are all compensating and balancing. The birds are singing across the stream and the long slanting light quivers in the wet leaves. My heart aches so terribly to be with you that I daren't write too much. I get crazy at times and terribly rebellious. There'll be no holding me when I do come, if I ever do. I've quite considered the idea of being a permanent cripple. What a fuss I make!

I happened to mention to the colonel that I had never seen Winchester, and he took me over to the Regimental Depot for the outing. It was hot. The huge tender perspective of the cathedral was kind to the sudden glance, like an avenue. But heat, under a glaze of well-being, only serves to accentuate anxiety, and I was anxious. Out of guilt, or telepathically, I had rheumatism in the leg. We did not believe in telepathy so much as take it for granted, so often did it seem to occur—in shared ideas when together, and in similar aches and ailments when apart. Above us both that day stretched the one blue sky, in beauty umblemished, yet only seen, not felt.

X

Next day a telegram whirled the possibilities like the snow in a glass souvenir. Hugh Beaumont wanted her for Mrs de Winter, the leading part in the revival of *Rebecca*, a dramatized version of the novel by Daphne du Maurier, which was to open at the Strand Theatre in May. "Nares Devine and ourselves very anxious as think you would be magnificent." This was not the play foretold in March. The fire had seen to that offer.

It's such a lovely part, and a salary of between £40 and £50 a week! George [Devine] producing, and a nice safe person like Owen Nares to play with. I should see you quite often and they'll let me go at the end of August and Simon is provided for. But I've developed another go of rheumatism . . . What it means to look up from this tangle and see you like the horizon flung round me, lasting and strong. I have two pictures in my mind—one of dolphins looping through the summer sea in Cornwall—and the other is a theatre with

OWEN NARES AND JILL FURSE

IN

REBECCA

on the front! I'm hopelessly uncertain which to choose. I couldn't bear to do anything which would make you feel deserted or worried. And would you like to be married to a star? Perhaps you wouldn't. At times I get wild with excitement— at other times it seems horrifying. I should like to do something that would show you what you have made me into. But I'm not sure the part is quite all that.

In the cinema, when the siren went, I had thought I could not bear her to live in any wartime city without me, yet I also wanted her to act again quickly. How the mind wastes energy on futile debate! It was obvious enough that only one decision would not seem like cowardice, when taken. Bertie Scott had founded a students' repertory theatre in Bideford, and by good luck he was there that week and in London the next: he would help her to get into form. "There never was a job so perfectly planned," as she said. That is, if one disregarded the main consideration—her health, now improving, but not fast enough.

I had given her £20 to buy clothes in London, and there followed a week in the Amesbury hotel for learning the part, and every week-end during rehearsals. Tranquillizing, in the midst of excitement, those expeditions by bus, to find Rex at Edith Olivier's, G. M. Young at Oare with the delightful young poet Jonathan Wilson, who would be killed in action. He was the son of Steuart Wilson, the singer, and originally a school-friend of Nicolas's. Jill had given him confidence personally, and helped him to write, with her gift, so useful to me also, of entering and criticizing as if from within. We trundled along, with pins-and-needles in the floor-boards of the bus. "I could live in that little house," she remarked of one passing the window. But on a closer view it proved to have been burnt out. "It looks as though you had," I said.

"Please pray for me to be strong—spiritually strong and serene," she wrote to her mother. "I think this disease is still in me." Both knees were swollen and her nerves bad when she took train to Bournemouth to meet the company, who were just finishing the provincial run. She found herself in a hotel that was partly an arms-factory, in a room that had recently been savaged by bomb-blast—a Kafka setting. Long strips of wood had been torn from the door as though by enormous maniac finger-nails; and the factory, which began just across the corridor, hummed all night and kept her awake. But the welcome of the company made up for this. It included old friends like Mary Merrall out of *Goodness, How Sad!*, and new ones rapidly made. Soon she was with them in London and describing progress to her mother:

Owen Nares rehearsed with me yesterday for the first time and was very complimentary. It's a good part—but I'm only off the stage for about five minutes in the entire evening and there's a lot of rushing up and down stairs, kneeling and fainting, etc., which has been painful, as you can imagine. I have the most exquisitely lovely white dress—a genuine Victorian one with a bustle and huge train all frothing in lace. It's only seen for five seconds which is sad!

It's odd to find how much I've changed—how much more casual I feel about it all, and how much more actual talent and power *seems* to have accumulated. But I *can't* feel any sort of ambition at all—just enjoyment at being worked off my very peculiar legs.

She told me how three members of the company had separately come up to her to say that she would be lovely in the part, one an old actor with tears in his eyes.

It's a terrific part in the way George produces it—very tiring and emotional—but exciting to do. I never cease to think about you and all our joys together. George said yesterday, "God, how I hate actors!" I laughed, and he said, "Oh not you, Jill—you're not an actress, you're a woman!" I pretended to look stuffy, and he got quite upset in case I should have taken it wrong. But I think it's a great compliment—in that way I hope I never become an actress. I shan't while I have you.

It was now that she had the photograph taken which appears as plate two here. Most of the others, if not dated, were taken in 1939. By then her looks had matured, and they had altered very little, if at all, in three years. Her mouth was more receptive to life and her jaw stronger than I remember it in 1937; for it is in the area of the mouth that immaturity shows. She had lost a certain air of doubtfulness which encouraged some women to speak, to her disgust, of an "elfin" quality and "a little face," though in fact her face was not particularly small. Her ankles, that had been slightly thicker than she could wish on well-shaped legs, had slimmed. Maturing late, she was now in her prime at twenty-seven and was more beautiful than when I first knew her. De la Mare said that her face was so attractive at first glance that one might fail to realize how unusual it was, yet I suppose he would have applied to her his theory, or conviction rather, that growing-up is always falling-off. Years later I remember arguing, against him, that the flower is more beautiful than the bud, or ought to be, or buds would be enough.

Beautiful women are apt to be self-regarding before the camera, sometimes with the total absorption of an act of self-worship, which can be alluring. Jill's beauty expressed her fundamental humility, and came of features and character in concord. She was aware of it, obviously. She took pleasure in it, not without vanity, which could, like all vanity, have soon been pricked; for she needed praise. She did not rate her endowments high beside other women's. "We're neither of us beautiful in feature," she told her sister. "It depends on where we are inside." She did not see herself romantically *as* someone of particular quality. Hence she mostly looks outwards from her photographs, and they are strikingly like her. Like her too in this, that they do not suggest recurrent illness. It might, at one time or another, be difficult to believe that she was dangerously ill.

I had leave for the first night, May 21st, and went to our room in a friend's house. There, strewn about, were her things in the disorder of leaving: she herself was at the theatre. Somewhere I learnt that she had missed the dress rehearsal—had been too ill. Thus I arrived at the stage door in real anxiety. I had brought her gardenias again, the secret emblem. I found her sitting at the bold mirror—no mirror stares like one in a theatre dressing-room —in front of the nude lights, the pinned-up votive telegrams, the spread of little make-up pots, immersed in the illusory alarming glitter and supported by it. Clearly it was an ordeal and she was scared. Making up her face, assuming for the stage that mask of a harder beauty than was hers by nature, she bent to the glass and suddenly turned with a sigh that was almost a gasp of apprehension, and begged me to say it would be all right. From the fine stars of her lashes and from the firm line of her mouth, her courageous spirit looked out. But her doctor was uneasy about his decision. He was there, I heard, and was going to keep watch throughout the play from the wings. It was all curiously like a Meggie Albanesi first night, had anyone thought of it.

She was better alone. So to my seat in the stalls, with more unease than I have ever felt in a theatre. The orchestra ended its flimsy tune from Offenbach, and the stage blossomed. The first five minutes' dialogue was virtually a build-up for her entry, and for me she made it between arrested heart-beats. It was an exciting play, and her part was one which could extend her. She played the second wife, shy and unconfident, who is nearly destroyed by a housekeeper's loyalty to her dead corrupt mistress, and she made the part convincing enough, and moving. In the first interval I found her weary but exhilarated. At the end she was acclaimed. Then she was back in her dressing-room, half-mazed with drugs and praise, with lights and flowers and faces. Her doctor would not hear of her staying for the stage-party, and I took her home in a taxi. Full of pleasure and relief, she was saying that she had a great deal more to give the part. Next day her notices were all enthusiastic. Darlington again found her acting memorable, while the *Daily Mail* critic described her as "a young actress of brilliance and great charm, and I hail her as a rising—if not a risen—star."

We spent this "life" in a friend's house, behaving rather badly, with snacks in the bedroom: not that she did not occasionally need sudden nourishment. She felt that her performance improved, but all the while her body rebelled against the strain of it. A small misadventure comes to mind. Nares had to pick her up in a dead faint and lay her on the couch. Her hair became entangled in his jacket button, and there was nothing he could do but rise, and tear out several hairs by the roots.

One day she had an unexplained dread of the future. One

Sunday we took a room at the Randolph Hotel in Oxford, a room high on the corner, with a view of both streets. It rained, and we had to stay in it because of her rheumatism. Up there, among the solemn assorted towers and loud hours of an Oxford night and morning, we seemed to be in a tower ourselves, almost in a captive balloon. She was sure she had conceived. Suddenly in the afternoon she felt deathly cold and faint. Curled up like an ammonite under the eiderdown, she let me feed her from our private bag of sugar, precious food in those days; but the sugar got into her smile and looked like a bracket of hoar-frost. Immediately afterwards she became violently hot, and stared about the room, unable to focus. I borrowed a thermometer from the hotel and found that her temperature was about 103. Then it returned to normal. It seemed as though every emotion had been lived through in that ugly room.

I took her to the theatre on Monday evening. In the taxi she almost fainted, and again in the dressing-room. I found her some brandy. Due back at camp, I was utterly in doubt. It needed only a telephone call for me to stay, but she revived and assured me that all was well. Never, never did she want to squander a single day's worth of life together, the very capital of our joy, on anything so profitless as being unwell.

Knocks along the corridor. "Overture and beginners, please!" Left in her dressing-room I scribbled a note to post on my way to the station. "You have gone down, and now are just about to go on, I think, since I have sharpened this pencil. I do think you have a stout heart." I was still scribbling when Betty, the dresser whom she loved, came back to report that she was doing well.

But next day she awoke feeling very ill, with a high temperature again. She got through the performance that evening, by dint of scratching her fingers to avoid fainting in the third act. This was the most emotional act, where she had to fall prone in that pretended faint, very painful to her knees. Waking at six on the following day in the same state, she saw that it was enough. Her courage had carried her through nearly four weeks in the

"The Touch of Day"
A glass engraved by the author

part. Blood-tests were taken, and her doctor had grave doubts about her returning. Anyway she had not conceived: that was one relief.

It's all like a nightmare which I can't wake out of and yet can't take quite seriously. If I have to get out it will about finish my career, I'm afraid. . . Oxford was a wonderful experience in so many different ways. Isn't there a saying in the Bible—"like the shadow of a rock in a weary land." You were that for me in all my moments of panic. Some of it is left with me still, and I'm not nearly as upset as I ought to be! If only I didn't feel so hideously ill at times I wouldn't mind. And it's a little alarming not knowing what's wrong.

But the verdict was harsh when it came, however likely it had been.

It's happened. Hale-White won't let me go back. The blood-test revealed that I'm very anaemic (such a charming Victorian complaint). My reputation will be very much damaged, and I shall—if I ever do—have to make a new come-back—as an old crone of about thirty. I keep hearing them shouting from the pit that night I was really and truly on top of my form—and it hurts agonizingly. It was such a good part and had so much more in it still unconquered. I feel I leave it unfinished and I mind that very much. What am I supposed to learn from this?
Poor Bertie—how sad he'll be—the pupil he said he could turn into a great actress. O dear—*what* a silly self-pitying letter.
Was I thin-blooded that afternoon at Oxford? My blood is mostly water now apparently. And yet what you said that evening is a charm against these nightmares.

In fact, she was not anaemic, but the complaint was very obscure, and remained so. The company were distressed: the old theatre-fireman was seen putting back in his pocket the stick of chocolate he had brought for her. Many of our friends and relations had never seen her in the part. But she did not lack company in her bedroom, and the skies were mercifully peaceful. She was staying with Margot Fonteyn, whose mother, Mrs Hookham, nursed her with devotion; thus many theatre and ballet people came to her bed. And she was encouraged to find that Beaumont, in his letter of sympathy, was already suggesting another part in the autumn.

So, back into Devon, to convalesce. I was at Salisbury station to see the green express glide in, and out again. I would have gone any distance for five minutes at the carriage door, above the delicate ferns of steam. She looked better than I had feared. This time I did not bring her a rose, but sugar and eggs for her sustenance. I had also engraved a glass with a picture of the cottage, and a great carboy, with "Halsdon Mill" round the top; for it was still a novelty to have our house to return to, as home. The carboy-glass came out of my wireless store, but its wicker jacket was commissioned from a sound craftsman we had found in Salisbury, in order to have a sample of his work. We thought craftsmen the most likable class of men; and surely they are the most contented. Seldom knowing either great success or great failure, which are both so difficult to deal with, they know the joy of the maker, in a tranquil mode, remote from the moods and torments of the artist.

She reached the cottage, and at once Simon took her into the garden, to fill her palm with a handful of its dark earth; and she acknowledged the symbol—gave herself utterly to the other way of good living, as its magic received her.

You would be crazily happy here today. It's a kind of blue cool dream, and the house set in its neat garden like a cottage in a fairy-tale, brilliant with roses, the hedge full of honeysuckle, great tosses of Canterbury bells and neat rows of beans and peas and carrots. And the stream whispering in a green wilderness, and purple steeples of foxgloves.

In the critical days she had exclaimed, "*God* what a lousy body I have!" Ironically; for now there was expostulation and dismay:

her hair was found to contain lice, picked up, presumably, from someone who had used the dressing-room couch, or the property couch on the stage. (Refined people only catch dirty diseases from coarse people—who simply have them.) It amused me to think of my lousy girl: the more so, because it brought relief. For it was supposed at the time that this was quite enough to account for the fever and the swollen glands.

So ended her return to the stage, and with it the hope of £1000, or more. After expenses like make-up and the nightly cars to the theatre, she had made £50. It was true that with greater pleasure in her art, she had less ambition, yet it is natural to envisage fame. When the offer first came, she had day-dreamed that in *Rebecca* she would become a true star. But for all its quality a shooting star is not that.

XI

My battalion was moving north, though no one knew where, and so, not to waste the south, Jill came to convalesce at Edith Olivier's. But would it be lawful—would it be possible—to "live out" at Wilton and arrive at Tidworth for Company Office? Enough that it was just possible, by catching workmen's buses. We were given the Porthole Room, through whose circular window nothing but a wall of trees could be seen, with the early sunlight shimmering deep through them. Edith had been awake since dawn, praying and keeping up her journal. From her window she always observed my stealthy departure—expostulating, urging, scratching her head with anxiety; and wrote an account of this in her *Night Thoughts*.

Jill slept again till the breakfast tray brought letters that hurt while they comforted. She read of the girl in her part, "chosen to be as like Miss Furse as possible, because she was the ideal Mrs de Winter." When she appeared, it was to lie on a day-bed, entertained by good talk with Rex, David Cecil, and the many friends who came and went in that convivial little house.

Warm days they were, and I was weary of battledress by the end of training. In a borrowed bath-chair, under protest, she would let me push her through the park to the weir-pool. It lay darkish under trees, but with those discs of velvety light floating over it. Here enjoyment was exchanged like the light between two mirrors; so that it did not matter greatly who was weak and who robust. Weak she was still, and her doctors dissatisfied, but she ate and slept well, and by the second week could mount with me to the ruined Temple, overgrown with saplings. The sensitive profiles of cornice and capital seemed lost in thought, and the afternoon sun flashed and balanced in the leaves. . . . Only the weaving and whining of planes from all the runways of wind-socked Wiltshire at all infringed the tranquillity of summer in the high-walled park.

She stayed at the Daye House for a while after I left, and one day, during talk of Rex, Edith virtually bequeathed him to her. Speaking of his essential loneliness, and of the unlikelihood that he would ever marry now, she asked her to live with him after the war. Jill hinted in some way, with inward amusement, that I might be doubtful of that. "I don't mean as lovers, of course, but you are the only person who can take care of him"—or words to that effect. She certainly meant no harm to a marriage she had brought about. But then, physical love was outside her reckoning—not very important perhaps. In the event she survived them both.

A motor battalion in column, mile after mile of it. A kitten I rescued from running-over, who played in the roadside barley when we halted, and became my store-cat. A tendency to drop fifteen miles behind in my fast Humber truck, for unauthorized sight-seeing. All this led eventually to Strensall Common near York, where we must camp for the time being. It rained. But I liked my solitary tent, which I soon fitted up with a long table and candles in bottles. On the new establishment I won promotion for three of my best lance-corporals, instead of seeing them reduced to the ranks, and I myself was made captain.

The better pay could be set against Jill's forfeited salary. Her career she had not forfeited, after all; for Beaumont now gave her a choice of *A Month in the Country* and *The Little Foxes*, with Emlyn Williams producing.

At times I feel the only solution would be permanent invalidism! You see I *can't* deal with the problem—which am I going to be—the right sort of mother and wife or a fine actress. And it's no good—*Rebecca* made everything a thousand times harder. I can't face giving up the stage and I don't think it right to. And yet I feel that our life will—or may—suffer.

Though of course less in peace-time. The strain is so much our separation.

I long to go on—to work with what I began to discover in *Rebecca*. And I have so much to learn—it's so exciting—so *pure* acting and not muddied with personal ambition—as it used to be. Now I could begin to do the stuff that mattered—and I *must*.

She added that she never felt the same for two days running, so much did she love her cottage-life, and asked me what I really thought. Anyway she could not work until October, if then. Meanwhile, she turned down the leading part in a film, playing opposite Clive Brook.

It seemed best to affect, for once, the decisiveness I hardly felt, and I said I did not want her to be in London that autumn. Air-raids aside—and they were likely to be worse than last winter—I did not think she could be strong enough so soon; and that was sound. "I do think it will be possible for us after the war, or at another time in the war, even." She took it with all, or nearly all, her customary grace. "But I can't begin to tell you how much I mind. However, that isn't interesting." I deserved that touch. I cared for her art, but so much more for herself. It was difficult, in separation, to feel as I had about her Emmy—difficult to have a right judgement in anything. Anyway she was told by Emlyn Williams that a decision need not be made as yet. This was during two days in London when she returned to the kind of life we never had together. She danced at the Savoy until one with an admirer, and was up at seven to catch the York express, none the worse for it.

After calling on fifteen farmers, parsons, and policemen, I had found rooms—not just a room—in the local manor house, and all for £2 a week the pair of us, including food. "There is cream for every meal and the most wonderful cakes," Jill told her mother. "We don't know the meaning of hospitality in the south. You would laugh at the Warnings here. For the Alert a little man rides round rather breathlessly blowing a whistle, and for the All-Clear he comes again with a dismal old dinner-bell."

Strensall in August brings back Swettipur in the rains. Jill said she felt like milk and flannel in a warm room; and when the sun emerged, the camp steamed like a pan of mushrooms. It was providential to have York close-by, for a northern Salisbury. There was a spaciousness in those three weeks, because living-out would not end in farewell, for once, but in the fuller life of ten days' leave. We toyed with the idea of the lakes; but there it would be raining too, and she must keep dry. Still it rained, ruling out for us the regimental dance this year. A city was the answer—a new city. Resonance of unknown skylines; fresh architraves and accents; a foreign dialect of bells before break-fast. In September, ready for anything but expecting nothing in particular, we took train for our city, clattering across the drama of Durham's front, gonged slowly over the great Tyne bridge, and at last craning forward in a taxi for a glimpse of remote gran-deurs, mediaeval and Grecian, while I practised useful phrases in the vernacular, like "Wull ye no ha'e a glass o' wa'er the noo?"

I think how little I remember of Edinburgh, after twenty years. In response, the whole grey image of the once passionate puritan city looms like a floating island out of Gulliver, with every ray, cry, smell, and texture that once mattered so much, not sensed of course, but as if held there conglomerate at fingertips, for the sensing. We found our hotel in Great King Street, dined, and walked back in late twilight to Princes Street, and stood for some time looking out over the hollow towards the Castle. Not for us the flood-lighting of festival. We saw the case-hardened old structure only as the night had long seen it, stark on dark, and with hardly a glimmer in the Old Town crowded against it.

We were mere tourists, but without the normal concomitant of other tourists. When we picnicked on the banks of Loch Lomond, there was no one else to mar the misty islands with tripper-music. We made our own bagpipe-music—Jill supplying the drone, and I the tune through my nose. As for the hum-drumming city, it attended to its own affairs, and no doubt thought itself quite plain, in that summer of the middle-war. So much the better. We were unmarshalled and unremarked, except by passing friendliness, in our slow odysseys, day after day. Only a cat asleep by a fountain seemed to have been waiting for this encounter, and like a caretaker preceded us round the stones of a graveyard, breaking off at last with a studied indifference, as if to show that these comings and goings are part of a pattern, a game, and nothing for disturbance of spirit.

In a high room of some bookshop there was silence and Egypt-ology, wind-sigh, dust, the voices of children sifting endlessly up. This has come to pass. This is! Moment of togetherness, verified beyond the power of oblivion to dispute. Moment of in-tense recognition—more intense for being shared—in a life so much composed of memory and anticipation.

There was a café on a bridge where we would go with the morning richly in two halves, and with an old brooch or pendant to unwrap again, or with just the illiterate guide-book we pored over and cursed. An engine pulled out with a few carriages below. "Little train, I don't mind your going away at all," she murmured. For trains were always emblematic of departures; and now that ache was allayed.

In short, living together had begun to be a habit. Meanwhile the battalion had moved to Ranby Camp near Retford, my assis-tant managing the Signals. Retford was somewhere in the ig-noble Midlands, but at least it would be nearer London. When our southbound express moved on without me, she left the com-partment and stood looking out at what seemed to her a "flat and rather sour landscape. But then I saw it through tears, which is unfair." An American officer gave her a bar of chocolate. Both giver and gift were rarities in England at the time.

The doctors wanted her in London for more tests: they had, she said, "'overlooked some aspects of my case' (i.e. all my symptoms!)." In truth one of them had diagnosed an incurable disease, but this fortunately was not revealed, and proved to be wrong—at least, in the form which had been postulated. She felt a great deal better after her month of unbroken living, and slipped into London ways again, sometimes dancing late, meeting many stage friends, and being told once more that she would have to play Juliet.

So I'm having *that* kind of a time, which is great fun for a few days but would pall pretty quickly. I think about you all the time—even in the midst of talking and laughter—as though you were really beside me. . . . I keep thinking of you and Edinburgh and it's *so* different that I can hardly believe two such different kinds of living can exist in the world.

But now she was eager for the cottage and Simon. But it was warming to be believed in by stage people. "You won't really want to take that away from me, will you?" I hoped that I should never be envious of her success. I did not disbelieve in my writing, but thought that it would need ample time to come to anything: a new book of verse, this autumn, was again not what I meant. Nor was I jealous of the admiration she knew how to handle so deftly, flirting but never teasing, though teasing me. A measure of waywardness engaged me. "I feel very unmarried and naughty," she would write. "It's a great pity you're so far away. . . . Someone asked me if I was sure of you! I said I wouldn't dream of discussing it. He said, 'Well, he can be very sure of you—can't he?'"

Christian marriage, we are told, was dull before it was exciting, and took centuries to assimilate romantic love; which began as adultery. So history relates. Even when no longer a mere arrangement or a mercenary bargain, it must always be dull when the bond is viewed negatively, as mere prohibition. She hated that view, and liked to see herself as my mistress, because the love of a mistress can be freely bestowed. She saw no contradiction between the marriage vow and this freedom, held simultaneously in mind, for the one was enhanced by the other. She had been free at the moment of making the vow—and she would always be making it. Faithfulness was an affirmation. She would have agreed with Héloise: "A holy error and a blessed fallacy among the married, that a perfect love should preserve their bond of matrimony unbroken, not so much by the continence of their bodies as by the purity of their hearts." Only she would not have seen why it was an error and a fallacy.

There was now a firm offer of *A Month in the Country*—and "I've had to refuse the first classic I've ever had the chance of playing in," she mourned, (forgetting the Shakespeare heroines, lost at the outset). Her doctors would not have considered it for a moment. Again she asked me what I thought of the future, and I could only encourage her to live with me in the present, though it was easier for me, with no equivalent success. "I never think of next year or next spring: only of our next meeting." That was true. I guess that we lived about equally in the present, but differently. She was vehemently this or that in mood, but with glances of misgiving far ahead. I never looked ahead, but was more detached through self-awareness, except in moments of abandon. She wondered how I managed to be happier in the army than any of our friends, instead of wretcheder, as she had feared. It was not the army that made me so. But I had to put a good gloss on necessity. To have surrendered, like her, to desolations, would have undone me. I loved the quick variety of her moods; for even the darkest could always be tempered for me by tenderness or humour. Really she preferred a greater evenness in mine, and knew that impetuosity came better from her. A friend had just had a dark-haired daughter. I said that I could not wait for a dark daughter. "At the moment you might have a daughter, but not keep me," she replied. It had been her kind of remark.

I lay on my bed the first evening at Ranby and saw the colourless breeze-block walls sweep up to a metal-framed roof, vaguely wondering what time held in store for me there, as one does in a new room. Outside, the country shuffled off to a thin chimneystack on the horizon, bleeding its black smudge like paint squeezed from a tube. With about a hundred men under command, including a staff of thirty, I could think myself a centurion, though not a very convincing one. I had a succession of delightful subalterns for my assistants. On Saturday afternoons in the months to come we might be skimming the roads at seventy or eighty, to Sheffield, Boston, Nottingham, York, or the Peak. Most of these flits were frankly for sight-seeing and pleasure, though a few resulted in the best wireless schemes. All that mattered was that we produced good signallers; and we did. No one inquired beyond that; for no one understood the "mystery." But now a small wireless set was issued, so simple that even senior officers could work it. It required no mouthpiece, picking up vibrations direct from the throat. The colonel's fancy was tickled, and I fitted him up for a two-way talk. In the middle he was rung up on the telephone by Whitehall. Instead of switching off, he began to broadcast his highly confidential remarks very loud to forty square miles of country, while I doubled across the square with trembling aerial, to knock on his window.

My storeman's radio droned for ever in the signals store. Always there was the utter wastage of days. How much time should we have? Perhaps enough, in the end.

I walked over the stubble and root fields yesterday, to where big transformers sizzle to themselves in a dry way, like a fly in a spider's web. It was mild and pearly grey and a warm wind: good weather for thinking. I wondered whether there would be anywhere for us to be alone after the war. If a new world is made, it may be juster, happier and more equal, but will it allow for those who do not want to be organized, though ever so well?

Yet we were not badly adjusted to face the post-war scene in Britain; at least there is little I now regret of the pre-war scene, except a comparatively unspoilt countryside. Modern Britain is fairer, and the West as a whole, in my view, less haunted by a sense of encroaching horror, notwithstanding the hydrogen bomb, notwithstanding the new numbness to brutality.

A brief life in London for my mother's remarriage set us off on a new course. Jill had new shoes—no novelty that. Her pleasure in shoes could have raised a psychiatric eyebrow. She would line them up on a bed and "have" them, the gold, the black, and the red. Yet she moved them about irreverently, and entering a train would attract glances, first to herself, never careless in appearance, and then to her unlikely luggage. It included a ply-wood suitcase with a small hole in it, and a string bag full of these twinkling shoes, under last-minute additions. She liked a corner-seat and a picnic meal, drinking direct from a lemonade-bottle with unconcern, while watching a swan tousled by the wind, or a heron loping backwards, left behind by speed. In the corner of an empty compartment I tucked a rug under her knees. "You look like an old tart on holiday."—"I *am!*" The tone of this autumn life lasted on until Christmas, like one of those October sunsets that seem to hang fire or even grow brighter after the sun's disappearance. "How strange it is that almost the greatest gift one's lover gives one is oneself. I suppose that sounds selfish. You have given me to myself —the true me with all the possibilities fulfilled." Even the brevity of lives could be viewed in a rich light. "They are the gift of the war, and meeting and parting are so intensely lovely in themselves."

Moreover, Theresa had been allowed to leave school at fifteen, to spend the autumn with Jill and Simon, so that suddenly, as children do who are born far apart, the two sisters discovered each other. "I always wanted a sister. She comes nearer to understanding our view of life than any of the family." Then for the three of them the shared days went on with rich contentment.

O it's such a lovely morning, bright gold and blue—and warm. I'm simply and plainly too happy here. Sometimes I get really silly with the earthy excitement of living so close down against the earth. You can't think what joys I have, finding sweet chestnuts, cooking—even washing the potatoes has a necessary beauty. *How* can people find the country dull—or want a hundred labour-saving devices to separate them from real life. To me it's gradually becoming clear that a woman's life is really this, and that education only makes it all *more* exciting because one has a more sensitive mind with which to work and enjoy simple things. . . . It's all such an art, living and loving and even cooking and being a mother.

The aesthetes of the 1890s had also seen life as an art, but as a fine art, an esoteric ideal that demanded the sacrifice of much ordinary living. For her the art was in the ordinariness. It flourished in concentric circles flowing out through her child, her sister, her family, the neighbours and people of the parish. Diminishingly, all came within its scope; for it was a life, not merely in, but of, the countryside, while always quietly in the centre there was growth.

"There *was* a difference in Edinburgh and after. And why shouldn't there be every time, if you come to think of it? I mean love has to go on or back—it can't stop anywhere for more than an hour or so." But what was the relationship of thieving time to eternity? "It comes up to the surface of my mind in bright secret bubbles. But they burst before I can find the words —or entirely understand them. And yet it is so important because they hold my beliefs in immortality somewhere in them." It was a speculation of deep content. And yet the words she did find, though affirmative in drift, had the old romantic note, because verse seldom came to her except in that key.

> *When the last landscape stiffens into cold,*
> *And all my days fall in like snow,*
> *Shall I remember the lost girl who now*
> *Learns that the corners of a bed can hold*

In candid beauties of desire
This universe of married light
Between the candles and the fire;
Or must the years deny tonight,
And must our story vanish on a breath?
Surely such rare intensity of love
Burns now the future's vision on this room,
Till neither time nor absence can remove
Our ghosts, whatever we in time become;
And all our beauties and our raptures grow—
Locked in that other kingdom, which is now,
Which is tomorrow, and beyond all death.

Do you think either of us could ever have been one-eighth as happy as this with anyone else? And do all lovers think that? It's a mistake, I suppose, to think oneself unique in any way. Perhaps it's a mistake even to dwell so much on one's happiness. And yet I do—and have to—because it lights each minute of the day and enriches all my most ordinary jobs. I think I have never been able till now to fully *enjoy* our happiness, because I have been ill, and scared so much and so often, that I was holding very tightly to every ecstasy, and every scrap of our time together, fearful of the ending or changing of things. You have long ago gone beyond that, I know, but I have suddenly achieved it. . . .

I have been sitting a long time staring into the daze of candles and wishing you were here to give me another child tonight. As the year withers and draws in to Christmas, that miracle of birth seems so very lovely and necessary. I want you to have a daughter very specially—to be beautiful when I am not, and to match Simon.

To us both he was always the Mandarin, come true. He seemed to know something of life that could never be expressed.

This house . . . I hope Simon will live in it long enough to remember it as his childhood—the innocent white rooms and the endless winter voice of the water "going by" as he says when he stands on the bridge. He says it in a kind of dream— "water going by"—and drops a leaf in and watches it twirl away.

It was not a whim of the moment, the idea of another child. She often returned to it; for the glow of this autumn reflected an awareness of health. It also reflected El Alamein and Stalingrad, those turning-points of the war. All the silent belfries, that once could break silence only to announce an invasion, now broke it for El Alamein, though in the Mess there was no outward response, and nothing came through but one spasm of clamour when somebody was searching for dance-music, a bare second of exaltation and nostalgia. Of course there was keen regimental interest in the progress of the 7th Armoured Division, and in Vic Turner's V.C. There was also some emotional conflict, above a certain rank. While the issue still hung in the balance, a senior officer ejected into the silence after the set was switched off, "I *should* like to see that man beaten!" A moment's uncertainty followed. "Rommel, you mean?" someone ventured. "No, no! Montgomery!"

But Monty stood high with the men—one sensed it in the periods for discussion of Current Affairs. Though authorized by the War Office, these periods were suspect, inevitably. For the first time in history young working-class men, with wonder and cynicism, were being positively invited by "the authorities" to weigh and solve problems themselves. When the Beveridge Report on social security appeared, someone in Whitehall had misgivings, and discussion was banned throughout the forces; but I broke the ban.

There is a hard and bitter cold moonlight about. The camp buildings look so sharp in the distance you could cut your fingers on the corners. The Square is a great sparkling lake. I have just come back from a crowded and smoky room where the men have been giving themselves a concert. I am always amazed by the skill—but then I have one or two London musicians. Out here they will need all the entertainment we can give them this winter. I am rather pleased to be first off the mark.

With patience and guile I was trying to contrive a Christmas at home for many of my staff, and myself. Those who see little in the festival anyway will hardly understand how eagerly we wanted to reveal it to Simon, to act and re-enact Christmas at the cottage, we three, for the first time a separate family. Paper decorations, discontinued in war, had never seemed so desirable. Jill found two red bells in Bideford, and I a small shopful at Retford, enough for the men's club and the cottage; also Christmas Tree candles. Then, after a long search, and on the very day she left, Theresa discovered a small fir-tree growing close to the garden. The hollies were well stippled with berries. And Simon entered with wonder into all those preparations that are part of the festival itself.

Holly and the moon are the height of poetry to him. And I don't really feel much older than that myself, do you? I never imagined I should feel equal with my child. I can't help thinking that a lot of that famous "maternal instinct" is really a cloak for appalling emotional self-indulgence. Not that I mean I'm unselfish—but I'm not tempted in that direction, which is lucky. I think many women lavish on their children the love they should be giving their husbands. And though I want to be a good mother, and adore Simon, I believe that our relationship is the foundation and capital of it all. . . . He makes me cry at times—the heartrending faith a child shows is so touching. I love him too much I'm afraid—it's agonizing to think of him being frightened or hurt.

Only if the centre of gravity was not heavy upon them could children be safe from the love that is secretly a claim. Only if they grew up aware of that inviolable unity could they feel both secure when young, and free when older, to disengage themselves.

It was nine months since I had entered the cottage, for our phoenix-spring, and now I found wreaths in every upstairs room, and a great wreath over the bed. From suitcase and drawer quantities of bells and balls rustled open into crimson, green or orange, with the sound of preening birds.

Each evening we talked late by the kitchen range, with the shutter slid back along the two polished rods, the kettle fuming away towards bedtime, and Jill in the position she preferred, on the hearth-rug between my knees. It was such talk as issues from a place beyond difference of sex, where two beings, like and equal, converse. To me the beauty of it always lay in her openness of mind to every idea or impression, for she was still the least opinionated person there could be, and the subtlest. Then one of us, with the point of the poker, might trace some notion along the letters of the old stove-builder's name, H. I. MEREDITH, BIDEFORD. Raised letters they were, of cast-iron; and held in their angles a dust or pollen of memory from the days of the first spring, which now seemed like a spring before the war.

The nights were broken or at least badly scratched by Simon's restlessness. . It was nearly a year since he and I had slept under the same roof, and he was again finding a father superfluous, though our greetings and games said quite the opposite. My adult emotions were more complex. Jill, who had seriously supposed that my love for her at last would be divided, now perceived that it was indivisible. And yet I had another love for him, as well as pride in our achievement. I needed him from the beginning—and did not need him yet. I was in conflict. And the natural resolution was denied, the easy resolution that the after-years so amply have provided: that of growing older together, father and son, day by day.

Her rest was made up in the afternoons when he was taken out by a girl, his pipe dwindling into the hollow woods. Thus on

Christmas Eve we lay and listened to the carols from King's, Cambridge. "O little town."—We were there in the Chapel where the Toccata had once burst for us, and here in the humble shadows, in the context of a war and our togetherness, toes nudging the one hot bottle. In the dead winter of the afternoon valley, hardly a bird crossed the window, and by the end of it the room was full of darkness, and cold. Yet there was a peculiarity about this festival. As far back as either of us could see, every Christmas had been measured against others—or against an archetypal Christmas that never existed. "We all seemed to prepare with increasing excitement," she wrote in her childhood recollections, "for a feast that was never entirely enjoyed. The indescribable greyness of Boxing Day dawned curiously soon after our stockings were opened." For me, with my uglier nature, the falling-short had been so acute that the day had sometimes ended in bitter weeping. Now here was a Christmas, traditional enough, and not retrospective. As we made it new for each other and our two-year-old child, it answered for itself, and was itself to become the lasting archetype.

In the dark of Christmas morning we woke to a house that seemed in waiting—the coronal above our heads, the red bell, almost black over the end window, held by a stub of pencil, the dark leaves thrusting from behind plates and pictures, the angular stockings. Ceremonies of innocence in the desolation of time. Every custom was valued. Only the Kissing Bough, that would have formed a centrepiece, was absent, because I had not yet read of it in certain old books, and described it for Joan Hassall to engrave. That would come after the war with a book on festivals; but it was in those days that we first talked of such a book. Everyone has trades or professions that he might have followed, and scholarly research was one of Jill's. In our earliest days the discovery of this gratified me, when my life with Vanbrugh seemed dim beside her more glamorous life. Recently I had seen in Edinburgh, when we began a little research for a play on Mary

Queen of Scots, how much she would enjoy working with me in library and museum.

The Day itself was arduous without the help of the little girl from down the valley. I took Simon for a walk in those damp and hairy woods, while Jill worked on turkey, plum pudding, and all the accessories. We had claret from the Mess, and finished with chestnuts in syrup. At tea her cake, ringed with candles, stirred the red bell pendant above it. Then Simon was let into the sitting-room, where under a tent of paper-chains the Tree glanced and wobbled with lights, burning its image in a mind that would put it away in some place beyond recall. "Church was my only failure," she wrote. Four miles on foot was too far. "I made mince pies instead. I think God will have understood."

Happiness can never be pursued like pleasure, the pursuit of it is always hopeless. As in work, so in love, it is at the same time inessential—both can go on without it—and the supreme reward. It is the crown. And the crown at a coronation is rightly bestowed: you must not presume to place it upon your own brow. Only Napoleon had sufficient effrontery for that—an ephemeral emperor. And David's painting of the act becomes the symbol of a modern error: the claiming of a bonus, a boon.

We seemed to have grown so fast in this week that looking back she would describe it as like dying. She had written a poem for Christmas, afterwards many times anthologized, read by Robert Donat on the air and included in his long-playing record.

CAROL

Beyond this room
Daylight is brief.
Frost with no harm
Burns in white flame
The green holly leaf.
Cold on the wind's arm
Is ermine of snow.

Child with the sad name,
Your time is come
Quiet as moss.
You journey now
For our belief
Between the rich womb
And the poor cross.

XII

Making early breakfast while I polished up shoes and Sam Browne belt, she sang to herself, she hardly knew why. We said goodbye in the kitchen, hugging each other in silent prayer; but she came out to the garden gate, the white of a fine daybreak just clarifying the top hedge of Venstave above us. Then, when I was quickly lost to sight among the night-bound oaks and hollies, we exchanged farewells all the way up through the steepness of the wood. It was exceedingly cold. But I was thumping warm with my suitcases by the time I reached the top meadow and the village car.

The dark woodland road finally emerged on high ground where Dartmoor stood up dead-ahead, sharp-edged, blue, and inexpressibly remote; supernatural; with the exact half of a moon to the right, and with the lid of yellow sunrise opening to the left, like one of our emblem pictures. There was a paper of ice all over the station platform as I stamped about, saying to myself of Christmas what she was then saying: "Now it's rounded the corner into that world where we have so much."

At Exeter I just missed a daylight raid, it seems. "How our Eden blossoms on the lip of the chasm," she wrote, when telling me of this, its magnitude probably enlarged by local rumour. "But I know utterly that there would be no end and no loss in the true sense whatever happened, as long as we still love each other. I could only lose you if you stopped loving me." Now perhaps she accepted that this would not happen, a truth that had been evident to me from the night when the picture caught fire.

You must see that at last I have fully and truly understood my own happiness. You always wanted me to—and for some reason I was often haunted and fearful. Now I am not—you do know that, don't you? No woman has ever been made so happy as you have made me. And I can only thank you and thank God for it and for our lovely, lovely life together. . . .

Dimly from that I know what heaven must be because then we are one—it is the real union of spirit through flesh, the body at last performing its greatest miracle and the thing it was created for. I would work till I dropped and dance till I died to give you the life you want. Your life is mine and your need is my need. Surely then we can do what we mean to do. I want us to build between us a fantastic varied and very brilliant cloud castle of love and adventure, on the solid and holy foundation of whatever it was that shone so in that wedding in the Cathedral.

She was well. It seemed a propitious moment to discuss something that would have been more prudently discussed before, the subject of my going abroad. Though always taken into account, I doubt if we had talked this out since the weeks before I put on uniform. I knew this to be unwise, and had been seeking a good opportunity for some while. Not that it was imminent: no low-rank officers over thirty were being sent to the Western Desert, and a request had been made in the regiment that none over twenty-six should be sent.

It is a happy time to discuss it. If I were single and not in love it would be unpalatable but not too intolerable, and with a certain spice of excitement about it. As it is, it will be cruel for us both, and we needn't be ashamed of that. But I think it will be *less* cruel if we have faced it beforehand. You once said that I needn't worry, you would behave all right; but that was a little thoughtless—I don't suppose you meant it—since it is not how you would behave, but how you would *feel*, that troubles me. The only thing that would torture me if I were told tomorrow that I was going—as might happen any day in the year—would be the effect on you. It is not a question of anything so trivial as controlling emotion, but of tempering it beforehand. I know that I should be true to you, that our love would not fail. We ought to think of it as an unavoidable journey abroad on business, lasting a year or possibly two, such as lovers have to endure. And we ought to think how Sophie [Devine] and others are able to endure it. At any rate we ought to think of it.

Now, don't wonder if I am trying to break some bad news to you gently. As I say, I see no reason why it should happen for some time. I hope this letter hasn't depressed you—in fact it *mustn't* depress you—that's just what I mean! . . .

. . . I do agree with all you say [she replied]. But apart from thinking of it quietly—which I often do—accepting it—there's nothing one can do. At least that's what I feel. I know I shall be able to make you feel that I shan't be too shocked or unhappy when it comes. But I can only assure you of that and hope you will understand. As long as you will tell me quickly and cleanly—I mean, making a nice clean cut—please do that. My fears are for the state of your mind in action and not for your body. The pain I can't bear you to have to suffer away from me is the strain and nerves. I don't know why, but I fear death or wounds much less. And absence is a little thing *really* between people like us. And I am a strong person inside though I don't always show it. I think I could be worthy of your love however far and long we were apart—just because of your love. And I *do* want you to go—if you have to—with a feeling of freedom and the excitement of something new and adventurous. Otherwise it will be hell for both of us.

Dismantling the garlanded house was depressing, and anyway a New Year always daunted her because it was no true festival, and affirmed nothing but transience. She had an equal distaste for August Bank Holiday. "I *hate* the day—its ugly, dusty, paper-bag air of dreary festivity—somehow the lack of even the name of a saint or religious feast makes it flat and material." But this was in the dark of the year.

Just a great wind outside, and the grey unknown steep of this year rising ahead. And I miss you so. You don't mind my saying that, do you? I only miss the sight and touch of you and the sound of your voice which I can never remember. To-day I accidentally turned on one of the carols we heard that afternoon and it hurt like a finger on a wound—only a beautiful and consoling hurt. All the bells have shut, and the wreaths are burned, and the house has rubbed its eyes and come out of its Christmas dream. Only the wreath above our bed remains because I just can't bear not to sleep under the holly for a little longer. Simon says "Daddy's balls all gone" continually, and I agree with him that it's very sad. And yet I don't feel that it's all over, because you're not really gone and the house retains you like a mirror you've once looked into.

So the Christmas Tree was replanted in the garden next the hedge to the Ram Meadow; and now the family was arriving, her mother to be given a much-needed rest in bed. I hoped Jill would not overwork; and at least she had unbroken nights with Simon, from the day his father disappeared. "We shall have to remember that your first months at home after the war may be very difficult to adjust—for all of us. But it is so simple really." Meanwhile our next meeting approached. It would be her first visit to those Midlands she had still only blinked at through tears from a train. A bicycle-ride away I had found an old coaching inn, as empty of guests as the road outside was of traffic. Now there were only a few days to go—and then the telegram came. She was ill.

She had been baking for the family, and a very fierce fire had scorched her face. She had gone to bed that night with a stiff neck, and awoken two days later as if with an appalling hangover. In the interval she had been delirious, crying out, and sometimes asking what house she was in and whether I was coming for Christmas. But of this she afterwards remembered nothing, except the benignly reassuring smile of her brother Nick as he sat by her bed. In pain, she had watched reality slide back into a room that seemed entirely strange. It had been curiously like some lines about Ophelia in one of her poems.

The water shining through an empty mind . . .
Your image gone, and the whole crystal blind.

"No one knows what's the matter with me. They seem to think it's rheumatism in the head!" But only news of a "feverish chill" had been telegraphed; for though, one night, the country doctor had privately thought she was dying, he was soon discounting any serious trouble, as he always would. So she was better before I could be anxious; and I knew that she was being nursed by her mother, as in all her illnesses. Soon she was thinking of the life postponed. "I weep into the mirror every time I look in. Never mind, I may have picked up by then. The thought is very beautifying, I find. O God how wonderful—my knees go weak at the bare idea! Please tell me what you would like—I mean *plans. . . .*" But it was no good. Again she was very sick, with an appalling headache, and partially blind. She was given morphia. A specialist came from Exeter (15 guineas), made numerous tests, and ordered an oculist, though her sight had always been phenomenally good. Relapse and recovery alternated, with pencilled letters in the sanguine intervals. "I get very afraid of going crazy. When things are as horrible as this, the only thing to do is to be interested." She also wrote, "I'm so thankful you weren't here;" and then in consecutive letters, but certainly without design—"If you came into this room I'd be cured!" When I read this the second time I did what she had not wanted, and applied for compassionate leave.

She looked surprised, and rather flattered, to see me, for the certainty of love had not devalued its courtesy. We spent a tranquil week, while her temperature rose less and less each night, and the painful glands in her throat subsided. The early February daylight slid over the face of the hill, and all day long the clouds grew differently out of its top. Or it rained the small prospect into a threadbare tapestry. With nothing else to see from the window, she saw it clearly: the importance of mere weather. With nothing else to hear, the muffled riddling of the stove underneath, the passing remark of a crow, or the gush of our neighbour's bucket going into the stream lower down seemed indispensable notes in the theme of contentment. She thought what a pity it was that it had seldom been the other way round; for it had been a rare enough pleasure, that other one, when she could look after me. The week closed with a night of Chaucerian merriment among the medicines. "I can hardly believe in our happiness," she wrote. "It dazzles me." But this had been the true lip of the chasm—closer than the crater of some random bomb.

"I always think after each illness, '*Surely* I've learnt enough now and God could let up on me.' But he doesn't appear to see things in that light yet." The health generated by a full month in the north had lasted on until January. She could find no explanation for this unlikely attack, claiming that she had not overworked, "though I was worried, at least I was unhappy for several days."

Anyway, within three weeks I saw her alight on Retford platform with attraction heightened by frailty, as it can be, and took her to that rambling, hot hotel, which whistled steam through some apoplectic vent all night, and offered remarkably good food and comfort. Prying about in York I had found what we most wanted for the cottage, and now for a surprise unboxed it in her room: a large old cuckoo-clock, dark-vine-wreathed, with a clear double call, and with the carved bird haunting slyly above. The limit of her walk at first was a near-by level-crossing, there to wait for the splendour of an Edinburgh express, while watching

The still cool parallels that run
Bright as a cry into the evening hills,

as she said in a poem.

She lay abed till lunch, sun on the eiderdown, a persistent, unidentified smell of hyacinths poking at her memories of childhood. "Sometimes I would give all I have to be able to convalesce at Netherhampton, and walk now in the wilderness among the early jonquils. There are moments when I feel lost—that there is nowhere I can go to be ill." But she dressed, and was soon hobnobbing with an old lady, who pushed her wig about engagingly and said that she had never made a friend so quickly. "My collection of old ladies is now too big to deal with, and I can't remember them or their names." She made friends as quickly with the staff, arousing affection because she felt it, and was sometimes moved by the narrowness of their lives. Expecting almost too little, she received a great many small extra attentions. Of course appearance counted: her delicacy stirred the bell-boy and the motherly chambermaid, if in different ways. She was clearly very young.—"So young, and such a good mother!" she would overhear in a train with Simon this spring, being just twenty-eight. In this hotel she was judged to be eighteen.

News came from Jerusalem of the sudden death of Stephen Haggard. They had played together in *Whiteoaks*, and "I loved him from the first moment I saw him on the stage, in a way that was quite removed from sex." His love for her was different, yet he was notably generous towards me, whose presence he must have deplored at the outset. It was his fancy, later, that we, the Christopher Hassalls, and Peggy Ashcroft and her husband should settle in the same countryside with his own family after the war. He sensed a general affinity; and it was certainly curious that of such a quadrilateral of intimacy as existed between Jill, me, Christopher and Stephen, each side or link should have come into being independently of the others.

Now a stranger was writing to her from Jerusalem. "You were an ideal for him. You know how much he suffered through this, but it had become peaceful and beautiful because of your own happiness, which was precious to him. He told me 'in her hands are wisdom, and gentleness, and passion, and also peace.'" Add the gaiety that Stephen's intense nature may not have evoked, and it may do for an abstract. Just before going abroad he had begged her to see him for half-an-hour. "I do so desperately need my sins to be forgiven me. . . . If only you could take this devil from me. No one but you can." She now recalled:

the last thing he said to me that evening in Ladbroke Square was "You are the only person who gives me peace." He was such a restless and tormented person. There was no kind of hope for him here. . . . How much one can learn in a short time. Do you find that? Life suddenly stretches all one's spiritual muscles. I feel immeasurably surer of some things than I ever have before. But it hurts to grow like that.

By now the war had accounted for Pen Tennyson, her young film director. "There are many people I've made friends with, but so few that I have loved. Stephen was one, Tenny another. Every wreck makes the living ship more lovely and more precious."

Now that she was much restored, we took train to explore Lincoln on a final day that seemed to be "the peak and crown of all sprees. Trains will never be quite the same to me again." It was a day when one could indulge an old, surely venial, illusion, if illusion it was, and see behind every event and trifling contrivance the deft, even humorous, finger of Providence. On the journey out we had wanted a compartment to ourselves; and there at Lincoln station it was, awaiting our return, an odd half-compartment tucked in at one end of a coach, as though the designer had been out in his measurements: confronting the comically close partition and running the full width across, a single felt-covered cushion, for long-felt want. Nor was there a sense of anticlimax when I returned by myself, soon afterwards, for something we could not buy in a Sabbath-tight window, and added "Connubial Happiness" to our glass pictures—white clouds of the simplest summer above a bridge. In fact I experienced a moment as of vision, "a moment of intense happiness, standing in a little churchyard near the Cathedral, hearing the clock strike three across the town like three gold shadows thrown out, and seeing our life together—seeing it almost as a shape, a gift, something put into one's hands." I jotted down the draft of a poem.

The life of "lives," I perceive, had by now developed a rhythm like the sea when it flows in a sequence of sunlit crests below sombre clouds. For after each crest felicity went glittering down a fair way into those cold-sober troughs where illness, loneliness and worry shifted about uneasily. The crest of one wave may be much like another's; yet if they were not all different, who would stare at the sea? It is the novelty within the known that absorbs. Besides, there was a current flowing on and on, or intermingling currents. Certainly there was an impetus given to the senses from this time forward.

Arriving at Gloucester station I found that she had scorned the taxi-rank, and engaged out of kindness an old man with a barrow to carry her suitcase; so it was behind him and slowly that hand in hand we passed to some blissful bower engaged at the New Inn. "Are there any theatres and cinemas in this dump?" she inquired over dinner, as if Beatrix Potter and the fan-vaulting were not the *raison d'être* of the place. We moved on to Cheltenham, and danced in the Town Hall. The expressionless appraisal of the Yankee soldiers, who appraised a woman without honouring her, was not really to her Francophile taste, though titillating in its masculinity. She wore a red velvet bolero over a flared silk skirt, black-and-white striped; and I had found her a white camellia. With hands to one side of her head, she inserted the flower, twirled and nodding, into her hair, and presently extemporized a fringe for the looking-glass, looping the curls at her temples. Her scent put all into italics. She was gay and darkling, flame-like, yet demure; and somehow contrived to be "dangerous" in two senses, her own and the mediaeval, simultaneously; for it was her nature to rejoice in the reconciling of opposites. I am sure that to some who would acknowledge her beauty she was not outstanding in sex-appeal. It did not ripple

out a constant welcome like a neon sign, it glowed to the occasion
like a transformation scene; and was enhanced by the involving
of the whole personality—those very qualities of spiritual and
intellectual that might seem to counteract it.

> *The days that forced our lives apart*
> *Are shut up like a fan.*
> *We shall not even speak of them,*
> *Because at last we can.*
>
> *There's nothing in between us now,*
> *Neither silk nor sheet.*
> *Our lives have come so close tonight,*
> *Even our graves meet.*

Again in her poetry the dying fall. David Tree heard it in her
voice on the stage, likening her to the young Duse.[1] But on the
stage she was mostly cast for pathetic parts, while knowing herself capable of passion. She fretted sometimes that she could not
prove it. In Stephen Haggard's long posthumous letter she had
just read "Your unique qualities are very delicate ones: they get
lost on the stage, or at least the stage as we know it mostly till
now. But one day we will write and put on a play in which they
will come into their own." Yet neo-Tchekov was not necessarily
the sort of play she would design for herself. There was the one
to be written about Mary Queen of Scots. Another might have
been on Nell Gwynn, whose warm and robust humour delighted
her. Such was her own humour, in one mood. She had a great
sense of timing, and would even have liked to try music-hall,
fantastic as that would seem to her audience. The actor who day-
dreams of rôles entirely beyond his range is a familiar and rather
pitiable character. It will never be known, and perhaps never
would have been known, to what extent she was doing just this,
even she, with her candid self-knowledge.

[1] 'The Gentle Art of Understatement'—an article on the acting of Jill
Furse in *Mandrake*, No. 3, May 1946, Oxford.

But verse always came from that solitude to which she had returned once more.

O what a waste that we should not be together at all. I saw with a shock of joy the first red in the apple-blossom buds today. The spring is moving and haunting and I feel young and lonely (that's an "n" not a "v"!); and I want to be told by you (and not others) that you love me and that I'm beautiful! What egotism. There's too much grass on this grass widow.

She stayed a few nights with Edith Olivier, who insisted on taking her up to the ruined temple.

I wonder what you were doing as the clock struck three. One of the most special prayers that can ever have been prayed for you started its journey then—out through clouds of white-thorn. Sometimes I love you too much altogether. For some reason the little temple and that half-carriage at Lincoln hold much the same mood. Odd that extremes of holy and pagan love are not even the breadth of a finger apart.

Without being influenced by him at all, or even aware of his beliefs, we were not far from Stanley Spencer's conception of physical love as the gateway to heavenly, through "the twined and unified soul of two persons." And it was this sense of completion, "a sense of the oneness of all life," as his biographer puts it, that the looped cross represented for me.

She had been reading a book about Katherine Mansfield, whose "deliberate cultivation of gaiety comes very near me," she said. Lawrence's persecution of the Murrys, at Zennor, stirred up in Jill feelings against him that were not allayed when she turned to his short stories. "I hate him. He was very badly needed but his work seems finished now, and I can only find him cruel and crude and unlovely." Cruelty nauseated her. Here, incidentally, was a feature of the modern world that she would never have come to terms with: the permissive indifference to it, and worse, the fascination. We have it in serious art, as on the screen and in the press, the same (highly lucrative) relish, masquerading as a salutary "facing of facts." She would have condemned that for the hypocrisy it is. But this is by the way, and not much to be blamed on Lawrence. "And yet D.H.L. had a kind of subtle crudity that adds to the faint scent of nightmare in all his writing," she went on. "No one has yet succeeded in writing of physical love in any way approaching the heights. I think it would be fascinating to attempt in some utterly simple way uniting the white-hot poetry with the earthy bawdiness."

Condemning the mental and spiritual for the sake of his "dark gods" in the blood, Lawrence rejected what is also human, and ended by diminishing what he hoped to enlarge, the stature of man. It was, of course, because he made much of physical love, because he came some distance towards saying, imaginatively, what we wanted to hear, that we roundly rejected him. No one is spurned like a failed master.

Always she was groping towards wholeness—ironically in one who was too often physically ill to be called "whole"—seeking a reconciliation of sacred and profane, of things good in contrary ways. This she hoped to express one day in her acting, and this is what she meant by her "finger's-breadth" remark: not, obviously, that she had experienced the extreme of holy joy, which could only mean the beatific vision, but that such extremes as lie within the compass of one nature can be very close, and in harmony.

To see life whole—but to *see* it, to taste and accept it in all its moving diversity.

I saw Grandfather this morning. He's as mad as anyone can be, without losing any of his odd charm, and told me the most extraordinary things. He was eating his lunch in the garden— mince and peas and a glass of beer—and Baker was whistling somewhere in the background. And I couldn't help feeling that it was all extraordinarily romantic and gay. I can't explain why. But it was like a detail in some great drama—*War and Peace*—

me and him and his madness and his lunch. And I felt a queer elation as I walked away and heard him bawling to some ghost he saw among the rosemary bushes. What a great variety of emotions there is just this side of fear.

Yeats in his *Autobiographies* regrets having failed to achieve "true Unity of Being, where all the nature murmurs in response if but a single note be touched." The whole passage curiously suggests a feminine kind of integration—the kind Jill notably possessed. Is unity, anyway, more natural to a woman than a man, or merely different? As she is to him, so may the pearl in its roundness be to the faceted diamond, where each facet is developed by an arbitrary choice. But where artists are concerned the subject is still more involved; for in the artist, whether great or small, there is much of the other sex. As for choice, she was confronted by such alternatives as even in time of peace would require all her reconciling. In war, longing for that unity of being, she was almost split apart by a life of bright facets—forced to be wholly one person this week, and quite another the next.

There is something wonderfully lovely about the simplest household day. It comes over me often in the middle of cooking and washing clothes. And one looks up and sees the hill and one or two cows doing illustrations—and a thrush singing in the rain. The meaning of humble, earthy tasks is always there behind the dirt or tiredness one may feel. Anyway I'm sure one *ought* to find those meanings, otherwise life is drudgery, and God never meant it to be that. . . . It must really be bed-time—but all I want to do is to curl up against you and murmur half the night. We must do more on summer nights— no, I don't mean what you mean, but we must go out late and walk under the stars and talk. My mind only wakes really at night, and then I become immortal. When it's bed-time for you, do you pray for us every night? Do please and I will always.

My job had suddenly become insecure. For two years I had seen many of my young officers and N.C.O.s return from a stiff and largely theoretical wireless course at Catterick, with the highest award, a "D" (for Distinguished). This was gratifying; but it did not make the course more attractive to me personally: obliged to do no less well—if I ever went. It now occurred to the colonel that his own signals officer ought to be Catterick-trained. But after the course, he added, I had perhaps better go on the staff somewhere, rather than return to my post. Military logic often escaped me. "For heaven's sake don't think I want to get rid of you. Of course the training of signallers here has been first-rate. There's no doubt about that. And that's entirely due to you." This was to sweeten another remark: "You haven't really got a military sort of mind, have you!" Perhaps not, but why take the course at all, if I was not to return to signalling? I should far sooner go straight away into Air Liaison, as Pat Furse was advocating. He was happy there, and brilliantly successful. Vehemently I wish now that the colonel had not scouted this request, but it only started him regretting that he had ever lost Pat to the regiment. . . . a damned good officer. There seemed to be a *non sequitur* here. He followed my argument, however, and finally decided on Catterick and a return to my job.

Such "theory" as I had was very rusty, and my self-respect could leave nothing to chance. Depressed, I began my homework at once. I now even found myself grudging the time I must devote to working out the design of a mural monument, commissioned by a friend in the regiment. "I beg you to put in a little variety of styles in the lettering," Rex wrote: "a little lower case or script . . . big and little intermixed"—in other words to make it a Georgian inscription. It exemplified an old difficulty of my discipleship. Rex was always right—granted his unacknowledged premise that the language of design was bequeathed to us intact and sufficient. (I speak here only of his work as a designer, chiefly architectural: not of his pure paintings and drawings.) With all his ingenuity and brio he never said anything, in design, that would not have been recognized as current idiom by one past generation or another. He submitted his inventions, unconsciously, to a high dead scrutiny. I thought of the past, rather, as a rich great-uncle whose views one did not engage to take over with a share of his wealth. But with less talent it was years before I had the temerity to move my own way. . . . However, back to the coils and resistances.

This was that epic May when the dams were bombed and half the Ruhr was set awash. I saw in it "a hint of future wars, when great and terrible gestures will be made, towns scraped out." Yet Dresden and Hiroshima were not so far ahead. Seen in that context, a posting to Catterick hardly signifies, and I mention it only to account for the long journey Jill made to the Dales. At the hour when the latening sun canted itself inexhaustibly into the hot top of our friend's villa, I threw myself on her bed to sing unprintable soldier-songs for her amusement. I hated the whole course, except for brief hours with a motor-bike, when I slept on some village green, and looked into little churches full of old-gold muskiness and clock-throb. "Why are the other boys quicker at learning? Am I getting old in mind?" Anxiety took charge of my very dreams. If only I had worked one half as hard at Oxford, I thought. Still, there was an evening at Richmond, where the lanes, cobbled and bloomed with grass, ran up into cumulus and down to the circling river, and after that she went south as if these interruptions to living were no matter at all. "Today I saw the first wild rose and nearly wept because it was there and June coming and it's four years of this incredibly lovely living. Everything all day turns towards you—everything I see or do, and I like to feel that I'm enriching myself for you." We looked only to the cottage at Whitsun, no farther.

So it was in the cottage doorway that she left me to speak first, telling her what she could not bring herself to ask. I had won my Catterick "D"; and unofficially I had been offered the command of the course, soon to fall vacant.

I was too ignorant. I had deceived them with stylish diagrams.

I was a dunce at mathematics, and had not really understood what I must teach. My training staff up there, technical fellows, would perceive it. I did not want a job that would absorb all my anxious leisure indefinitely. I craved a little leisure for writing. I had said no.

Jill did not demur, and thought well of the final reason. On the other hand, staff-pay would wonderfully offset the specialists' bills. I ought to have convinced myself that I could improve that course, even as I had improved our own course within the regiment. I ought to have said yes.

XIII

At this remove it is easy to discount the craving for leisure, but for months my mind had felt like an occupied city; and now I was liberated, for what seemed an inward Whitsun. As always, I was thoroughly dissatisfied with my verse. My early work in a vein of regret had won me her love, but the very winning had dissolved that romantic impulse. In two later books I had tried to find a language of affirmation, unsuccessfully. She encouraged me by saying that I should not write my best until after the war. "I never mean to worry you with domestic details. I don't want you to feel the responsibility of us weighing on you. I think these years of loneliness have taught me a great deal of self-reliance—more than I'd ever have had if you'd always been there." It was a generous impulse, but in fact our well-being itself would require a sharing of responsibility. During this leave I wrote a poem, later called "The Appointment," to express that instant of extreme awareness when the joy of being is suddenly and simply revealed in its glory to the mind. It was inexpressible, at least by me; but that perhaps was a beginning, though it hardly reduced the problem I was about to put to her.

I was now watching summer's arrival in the East Midlands, the top soil lifting off like a counterpane. It was always something to have soil at all, fields to vanish in; and outside my room a low field of rye was flowing shadows from one hedge to the other, until it seemed that fertility itself must pour away southwards into the hollow at the farther end, or into some thirsty vacuum beyond the horizon.

The problem was the problem of joy in minor lyrical verse, which has always been more at home with suffering; so that verse on this level untinged by melancholy, longing, or forlorn reflection, is a rarity. I wanted to make a poetry of fulfilment, I said ingenuously; and my letter was a rather grandiose introduction to the love poem I now sent her. Slight though it was, it pleased her more than any I had written in the war; and was the first of nine to be published under the title *Who Live in Unity*.

One cannot write a book, or even a letter, without assuming rough agreement on the meaning of words. But a word may be at once so important to a theme and so imprecise as to call for definition. Such is the word "romantic" in this book; of which the opposite has to be "classic." I define them in this way. The romantic is concerned with desire, and is a reaching-towards; the classic with the object of desire, and is a realization. The one has to do with disorder, and is in tension; the other with order, and is in repose. As great art shows, they may coexist. Dante is more classic than romantic, but both—desire for Beatrice subsumed in joy at her existence in the ultimate pattern. Classic Mozart, the mirror of divine order, has romantic overtones. Keats suggests a classic resignation for incurable romantic longing:

> *She cannot fade, though thou hast not thy bliss,*
> *For ever wilt thou love, and she be fair!*

With advanced romanticism the end can be lost in concentration on the means. Thus, though the proper end of desire is fulfilment, in the Wagner of *Tristan* desire is unappeasable; the will to love has rapturously been identified with the will to die; for, by the magic of art, satisfaction can be won from its denial. But if hunger were ever plenary and satisfaction at zero, we should have arrived in Hell, ultimate City of Romance.

The romantic position is always precarious—less or more so— a proud or delicious foothold in slipping shale; because it is not really concerned with satisfaction at all. When people are drawn to a West Pole (or equally to an East)—when "to travel hopefully is a better thing than to arrive"—when the garden in the looking-glass seems more alluring than the garden itself— whenever illusion surpasses reality just because it *is* illusion—we are caught by the romantic spell. Jill wrote, that autumn, on returning to Devon:

> I sat in a darkening carriage and came from station to station under the first few stars. There was a great range of black cloud low in a green sky, with a star here and there in a cleft like a light in a valley. It was very strange and made me aware once more of the power that a distant mountain shape can have over a flat plain. The fact that it was all illusion made it even lovelier.

According to this definition, then, the so-called Romantic Movement was not unique. Its period was merely one in which an attitude of mind predominated. Another was the Twelfth Century, with its revolutionary notion of sexual love as an ideal— love illicit and hopeless. The attitude itself is perennial.

Longing, nostalgia, dissatisfaction with life or self, and, in support of these, romantic poetry from the ballads down to de la Mare, had made both of us romantics from childhood. But this had changed imperceptibly. Romanticism had been expelled from the centre to the circumference, where it dealt with the tensions of war, frustration, and loneliness. Mouth to mouth in the whirlwind, Paolo and Francesca go by for ever, the very type of romantic lovers. Keats might envy them, but we did not. For us the whirlwind revolved; but at the centre, now, there was repose —the repose of the spinning top.

Heaven is presumably classic, whatever romantic overtones life on earth may have contributed; or perhaps it contrives to be fully both. Who, on a mountain-top, has ever looked at blue mountains far away and not wished to be there—even knowing that if he were there he would wish to be back? Suppose, then, one could stand on both viewpoints at once—and on neither— could simultaneously taste both wishing and having, in some simple unimaginable sense that was not, as it would be on earth, bewildering. But to return to solid ground. Earthly joy, in its brevities, may be classic. It does not crave: it is. And what is to be done with joy? Because to the born maker it is necessary to salute and use it in some way: otherwise one might buckle like an overcharged battery. And one may not have the opportunity, or the talent. And what if the charge should be earthed away before it has been put to full use? "I'm so happy, I simply don't know what to do about it!" I have heard her say, in a kind of exasperation.

It is a characteristic of advanced romanticism to stress, and indeed to relish, the mutual exclusiveness of two good things. Travelling hopefully and arriving, for example. Or consider Yeats:

> *The intellect of man is forced to choose*
> *Perfection of the life, or of the work.*

Before the war I used to tell her that having chosen the work I had missed both. Recollecting this now, she repudiated the obligation to choose—against likelihood in her own case. Bad things must be accepted, but good things must be viewed as reconcilable. Otherwise they ceased to reflect that ultimate good where there is no contradiction. "We shouldn't *be* happy unless we both secretly believed that, and lived for it." In short, we might be all in a tragedy, as she had said, but the "tragic view" of life was ruled out in a final reckoning. One observes that the supreme poem is a Comedy.

The old problem of mutual acceptance, father and son, was still there, and Whitsun posed it afresh. Rightly or wrongly I had thought Simon slightly spoilt, and after falling out with her over some triviality concerning him, we moved on to discuss the deeper theme of the relationship—with surprising effect. I used to flatter myself that I was too self-aware to perform a psychological somersault. But I did. I was released into full love of him. It seemed a miracle, complete in one evening. Conceivably it was more like a thunderstorm when people say, "This is clearing the air," and the sun comes out, and the air remains thick for a while. Yet in Simon's demands for my return throughout the months ahead there was the ring of sincerity, and that was like a confirmation. But with what unconscious sense of symmetry had we chosen the fourth anniversary of that evening which we knew to be our true beginning? I now owed another fresh start to this Whitsun—assuming that one had been made in my verse.

Of the need to cultivate acceptance in general—positive acceptance, which differs so much from martyred resignation—Jill once said, "I think rebellion is the only deadly sin." She thought it was in her blood and inheritance, to be deliberately countered. Of someone else's torment she wrote, "I am always desperately sorry for people whose own natures make their own hell. That in a way is true of everyone—I feel it specially true of me, and that only my incredible fortune in finding you and all we have together has saved me." Her escape was through conscious affirmation. "I have a passionate belief," she told Jonathan Wilson, "that to an artist (in the widest sense of the word) all experiences must be accepted and used to increase one's sympathy and understanding—to increase one's *stature* as an artist. It has often helped me through those awful valleys of drudgery and deadness." She also said, "I am not like M. who lives life from a sense of duty. I can't do that. I have to *make* it the only kind of life I can live, exciting and full of poetry." Consciously she meant to follow St Francis de Sales on her own level and to the extent of her power, saying "Yes, and always yes." Unconsciously she was helped by her nimbleness. "One rebels and is miserable one day, and the next the whole outlook is altered." That was putting it more coolly than she could, a few days later, when we were planning several weeks together.

Writing about this suddenly gave me such an acute and agonizing hunger for you that I had to rush out and dig frantically in the sun-hardened garden to keep myself under control. God how appalling it is sometimes—to be here doing nothing and all my love and all my acting bottled up. There's so much in me now sealed up that it frightens me at times. Perhaps it's only a kind of madness—but O God how it hurts.

And all we could do was exchange the two halves of a split summer.

Last night there was the fullest moon I ever saw, and our room was enormous with moonlight. This morning I walked back from Dolton, and I looked down at the cottage. The smoke went up blue and straight and the windows were all open, and the open door was like a mouth drawing in the long breath of summer with infinite contentment. It made me almost cry with richness and joy. . . . The day is blue-and-gold high summer and we lie under the oak tree and dream, and Simon says, "I *do* like you, Mummy, and I do like being in this place with you," and I feel as if a most special guest had conferred an honour on the house.

He was still like the boy in the picture. Only, where the Mandarin was reflective with implicit gaiety, he was the other way about, spontaneous yet sad, merry yet pensive—almost as if aware of some flaw in life, some grief, ineluctable but far and faint: farther than the sighing of the lambs folded into another valley, fainter than the questioning of final robins in the dark of the wood. "I must go up and read and sing to him. He is sitting in his cot contemplating the green opposite hill, stained with evening sunlight, and the plaintive little tune of the musical-box sounds through the house from time to time, small and lost as a mouse in the wall." The poetry in a child's mind seems arch or self-conscious only if the grown-ups make it so. He saw that the cottage was roughly the same shape as the musical-box. "Does this house make music too?" he asked Theresa once.

Over his evening bath there was wild hilarity. Such was his sense of humour that Jill began to wonder if she was too serious for us both—she who, among intimates, was the main instigator of mirth. Indeed, from another angle it was I who was the sober one. She had many varieties of laughter down to a minute whinny of amusement at the back of the nose, for which the musical notation would be double quotes above the stave. Perhaps one could laugh at anything if one was serious about everything. In the grate, or in a bonfire, a flame may appear to flicker just above its subject, as if detached and feeding on the air itself. Laughter was like that. Happy when the substance beneath is happiness. For laughter itself is not happiness. It may, as everyone knows, conceal a void like an ache.

There was still the mysterious pain in her head, seldom forgotten altogether for more than a week. She slept badly, alone. "I can't put out my hand and touch the one warmth in all the world that strengthens me and gives me peace. You do know, though, that however tired and unhappy things make me, nothing touches the core." Therefore her visits to the Midlands began and ended with doctoring in London—that visit, for example, when the Anglican sobrieties of Southwell were all but dissolved into a light like inebriation; with quiet talk in the crowded train home, talk tendentious, elliptical, proleptic, seated on the Pullman car table.

And so back to the little specialist. "Can it go on? I can hardly believe that the prosaic world can hold minutes and hours like that. The little man was very pleased when he saw me after I got back from you—most people would have been." Soon there was a new dentist who was reported to have described her as "like an old master."—"I thought I was like an old mistress—but not so *very* old." This only brought a new diagnosis, and a dread of false teeth, but the threat came to nothing.

The bills were becoming formidable. Resignedly I put in for the Catterick post, just now to be filled, while she, because it was no use waiting for ever to be really well, thought again of the stage. There were various propositions. A young dramatist, now famous, wanted her in his new play forthwith. "£50 a week is a great temptation, but it's just amusing drivel and I turned it down flat." She was encouraged in this by Beaumont, who offered her *The Last of Summer*, soon to be dramatized from Kate O'Brien's novel. And Gielgud might be producing. "Please believe in me and help me to fulfil myself as I've tried to help you since we married. I need your faith in me."

A life began with painful debates on the wisdom of this, in her present health, and ended with a resolution in Blyth church, on the fourth anniversary of our wedding. Afterwards it seemed as though I had dreamt of a country church called Blithe where we were left alone after early communion, repeating the marriage promises to one another. She was now making trial of an address in central London where she might live for the run of the play, rather than return home to Holland Park at night, held up by "Alerts." Vivacious people would be coming and going. But, for needed rest, there was rather too much activity around that diminutive room, with "endless dramas of sex and drunkenness which I don't mind in any moral way at all, but they are tiring. I suppose I have led a very sheltered life, in spite of the theatre. Here they all sleep with one another and think nothing of it. If it really troubles you I will go away. But I feel very blithe in spirit, and one can live anywhere."

Young Free Frenchmen, who any day might again be working at mortal risk in occupied France, took her to dine and dance in their clubs. I think she must have been intriguing to them, with her blend of responsiveness and reserve. She was attracted by Frenchmen, could talk their language, and liked to feel herself French, remembering her ancestry. As she had been a courtesan in a previous existence, apparently, and had more than once assured me that she had "all the makings of a thoroughly loose woman," I wondered if a "sudden Diomede" was not a risk.

They were charming—but became a liability, and I am wondering if my head is turned. They think me *very* beautiful! It's odd to sit at a table in a night-club and be told how much I am desired—by two men at once. The French are so different, and that kind of thing is so much gayer and lighter. This is not to make you feel jealous—only to show you that I can speak of everything to you. I wonder if you know how completely your strength is under me, holding me up? It's very important that you should approve of the life I am leading.

It proved too exhausting. And anyway the play was not yet even written. "Did I tell you that I went to the best and most expensive coiffeur in town, and have had an exquisite new style with a lovely fringe?"—as adumbrated in Cheltenham. "It went over so well with the French that I feel you will certainly like it. And O my scent. I must have a week-end in October—just to give you a taste of these new charms." Money for such things, however poor we might be, was never questioned. They were not even "necessary luxuries," they were necessities. One day, presumably, there would be an apex and a slow decline, but it seemed more remote than dying.

Returning to a pre-war haunt in Charlotte Street, sitting at the same table, brought home how inexpressibly different we were from the shadows whose remembered carafe of chianti stood overlapping ours. It was (privately speaking, and since the price had been fixed without consulting us) worth a war.

> Do you ever think what our life might be like after the war—cosiness and gaiety and work? Is it wrong to look so far forward and with such belief? Perhaps we shall regret the passionate brilliance of our short days together—but I don't feel the brilliance *need* dim, do you? . . . Sometimes in London I look up at the raw edge of masonry where a room has vanished from the other room, and I feel that I know that loss and incompleteness as well as I know anything in life. I'm not a whole person alone, and the edge of the tear hurts all the time. If there were no Simon it would be impossible.

The stream valley was pronounced too damp for her in autumn; so she brought him to the family home in Holland Park. There was nowhere else she could live for £3 a week—out of the £18 a month of my allowance. She made £20 by hawking jewellery down Bond Street, but "one thing struck me in conning over my sins, and that is that I have been harping so much on money lately, which is wrong in itself and very selfish towards you." My own chance of betterment had gone. Our new V.C. Colonel walked back with me from Church Parade. He had not entered me for the Catterick post. "The fact is, you are quite invaluable here, and I don't know how we could spare you." Fondly I reported this verbatim, even knowing it to be a guarantee of nothing. For change was in the air. Many superfluous officers were being "brass-buttoned"—transferred to other regiments. Could I rely more securely on my cherished black buttons of the Rifle Brigade, when a subaltern, prying in the Orderly Room one night, found a secret dossier and copied it out? "No good. Ought to go, and knows it." Such was the verdict on one elderly company commander. And on myself: "Very good at his job. Probably no good at anything else."

There was no certainty but what we gave each other, and that was always renewable. Her love was my only assurance in this world, which I hoped and thought that I should never take for granted. "I at least shall need reassurance as long as I live," she replied. "It is still as great a miracle—or even greater—that you should love me." It never ceased to be extraordinary that she should say what everyone else without exception, fully knowing us both, would agree was for me to have said.

Sleep was one of her needs in that makeshift, basement bedroom, and London was not prodigal of sleep. "Fright makes me stupid," she said. "It's a pity, isn't it, that I'm not more stable. And I wonder sometimes why at my age I'm such a coward. I pray about it but I still am one. Take care of me in your heart which is my only rest and heaven on this earth."

It was now October, and her plan was to conquer the unknown illness by the spring. "We have no future until that is done." Then she would act. Then she would give me a daughter. Meanwhile she would write her novel, and go into training with Bertie Scott, who was generously about to give her two lessons a week for no charge. "He still thinks I am the white hope of the theatre, bless his heart!" They were to study Juliet, Beatrice, I think Cleopatra, Miranda, all the great parts; and began with Juliet.

It was a horribly exciting moment standing in front of Bertie and feeling the rust on the works, and then *suddenly* the flow came back and the power from inside and my knees were shaking and my heart beating—it's extraordinary how ordinary life puts a calm layer over it all and how it goes on improving and deepening and broadening underneath. All our love and happiness and even my illnesses seem to feed it without my being aware—O if only you could care a little—and see how it's something you have a part in.

Alas, that I never concealed a half-heartedness that lived like a toad in the shadow of her inward and outward dangers, never convincingly showed her that I should care when the shadow was removed.

The lessons continued, and "even Lady Macbeth has some sort of effects!" Long afterward Scott gave me his own recollections of that.

She was doing the section of Lady Macbeth's opening scene, "Come, you spirits That tend on mortal thoughts, unsex me here. . . ." She looked and sounded to be in touch with the invisible; full of the mystery of the unseen. It was lovely beyond description. I expressed my admiration, but commented that it had been spoken by a "lovely woman rather than by a potential murderess. However," I went on, "we'll leave that till next time," as she had been going all out for an hour, and was growing tired. But she would have none of it, and insisted on getting what was needed there and then. She did, too, triumphantly, and then threw herself into a chair to recover from the tension of the effort. That was characteristic of her: she just wouldn't give in.

"I've done nothing all these four years," she wrote, "but drift from illness to illness—and in the interval live in a Paradise that beggars all description—which I don't deserve. O God how I hate my body—sometimes I feel like Ariel shut in his cloven pine. And then I remember. And what *fools* doctors are. I've just heard that when I was ill in *Rebecca* Dr —— diagnosed an incurable disease which would kill me in a few years!" Reading this in the Mess dining-room I was struck dumb, as if a fingertip of icy shadow had streaked at me from some post or tree on the horizon. But I reflected presently that it must have been discounted, for her to have been told at all. She was not herself disturbed by it. In fact she was feeling toned-up as a result of enduring heavy raids, when her nerves pleaded nightly for a return to Devon. In the street she bought violets that "smelled of next year and soft warm earthy days with weak February sunlight. Do you know—delicate gloomy little violets under their wet leaves?"

Last spring, on a visit to close friends of ours, she had felt envious of their lot: the soldier-husband affluent, and free to live at home. "They seemed so settled, right, and 'holy family,'" she had written. Now, it appeared, their marriage was on the rocks, though it would not be pounded to pieces for a number of years. "How specially grateful we ought to be to God for having found each other in such a crowd," she wrote. We had been discussing divorce in the light of C. S. Lewis's *Allegory of Love*, and the history of romantic passion from the Troubadours down to Hollywood. Surely one had to go on working for a relationship, she said, just as one worked at any art? And always the greatest was one that could never win fame. "I do think the crown of life is *living*, don't you?—above any doing or having, or not having."

XIV

Nineteen Forty-Four had a dark sound. "Another of these 'Howling Forties' and probably the grimmest of all."

I felt such despair last night, walking on Campden Hill under a cold and unforgiving moon. I lay awake and listened to the guns puncturing the stillness like someone sticking pins into balloons, and one of these awful waves of futility swept over me—the waste of years of our life and my own appalling waste of time in this war. I think I am ashamed, and yet there's an awful inertia that has settled inside me like a soft octopus. I think this war has gone on long enough, don't you? I sit up in bed, a little dingy with self-pity, and fill the room with inaudible screams of boredom. . . . I hate January and February: they're like going upstairs in a boarding house—long and steep and exceedingly ill-lit. Still, there's April in the attics, one must remember that.

Despairing words had a gusto that privately cocked a snook at their gist.

She had been invited to broadcast to the Empire on "Culture in London," but was there any? One play, *There Shall be No Night*, dealt seriously with the human problem of war. She thought it failed, but went home to analyse the performance of Lynn Fontanne, half-thinking to offer her critique to an editor:

It is not what is called restrained acting, for except for a brief scene one does not feel any great force of emotion being controlled. Usually a student of acting goes to see what a great artist does in a part. One could go again and again to see all the things she does not do. I missed three quarters of Mr

Lunt's microphone speech because I was watching Miss Fontanne sitting still. . . . It is as though she had considered and absorbed all the emotional possibilities of the character, and then discarded them to give a study in gaiety. She presents the rare spiritual gaiety that triumphs over grief, horror and disaster, and death itself. She convinces one that it is greater than courage—that it is the finest attitude a woman can have.

This was the gaiety of the final Yeats, "Gaiety transfiguring all that dread," but without the vitiating arrogance. However, it was not Yeats's "Lapis Lazuli" which sent her back to the Chinese poets at this moment, but de la Mare, who had just given us his new anthology *Love*—itself undertaken as one answer to the world's misery. In the Chinese she found a detachment that "makes one feel they have a more successful relationship with time than the West." One ought to be more relaxed about time than the nervous hurry of the age permitted; for the age had made a fetish of novelty, and taken the journalist, the news-hawk, for its hero—a figure unequal to the post. Hence the zeal to be "contemporary," as though it had intrinsic merit, and no judgement were needed to distinguish what is better, and what worse. I remember her saying, apropos of some prevalent taste or opinion, not shared by us, "but we're old-fashioned," and saying it simply, without defiance or apology. What did it matter? We did not, in consequence, stop being young. One should try to see a lifetime, even history itself, in the large—to relax and live along the line each way, noting growth and decay, echoes and pre-echoes, with a sense of the incompleted pattern. One should live in the moment, but in the moment mentally expanded, not contracted to its own desperate evanescent self. For the present was always what mattered, but the past and the future were aspects of it.

Separation can have its own high moments, or crests, and such a crest arose now, without contriving. We were writing simultaneously, and it was as though the news in one letter, though unguessed, evoked the affirmation in the other, which was mine.

You don't seem far away tonight, but I need you, and I am wondering how long I can bear to live without you. I have thought, too, of my supreme, unbelievable fortune in being a finder at last, not a seeker as I was all my first youth. I have known, I know now, the greatest joy that is possible to man. I can never cease to give praise, and to repeat to myself the truth of this good luck. You have given me all I need, and whatever is good in me finds its support in you. Perhaps I ought not to tell you this, it may be a proof of weakness, but I am always forced to tell you what is important to me.

We are young, you are beautiful, lovable, and responsive to love, and with a depth of laughing tenderness like a well that never begins to dry up. I want to share this youth with you. I want all the squalor and folly to be swept away. But I don't want you to think that I am oppressed by the ticking of a clock. I *know* I shall never cease to love you, and old age is not a horror to me. Love-making is the top and bottom of everything, the foundations of the crypt and the cross on the golden ball, but it's not the whole of the building, and there age has no horror. Can't you *see* that we shall lie together, considering the day behind and the day in front, when we are no longer young, when we are quite old? When I am making love to you, and you say "I love you" there is something infinitely moving in the simplicity of the words. What else can one say? Words can't say any more. But what else need be said but "I love you."

This letter brought tears—" but O I have walked about all day in a gold crown! Funnily enough I was lying in bed looking at the ceiling and thinking, 'Another day of my youth gone by. And we've lost four years that way. And *yet* it doesn't matter really.' And then came your letter. Sometimes I mind terribly, but I don't wish anything different when I look back." Her own letter of the previous night was to announce the hour of decision —a definite offer of *The Last of Summer*. Long delayed, it had come at the very time when her doctors had said she might consider working again.

> I don't believe I need tell you that this acting will *never* come between us, if you will help me. I see that you will never feel about it as I feel about your poetry. But it is our only compromise, and we could manage any compromise in the world. May I be your actress again for a bit? O I will be good whatever you say and whatever you want.

For some reason, which could only be subjective, I was free as hardly ever before from anxiety about her, so that the offer only brought me an increasing gladness; and to judge from the novel, the part should be exactly right.

In the same letter she had said this of her acting: "I know now that it can never be what I once wanted." Some weeks later, when rehearsals were about to begin, she received a copy of *The Craft of Comedy*, the little book that Athene Seyler and Stephen Haggard had written in the form of spirited letters to one another, about a fictional young man who wanted to act. She would read this:

> Does he aspire to be a power in the theatre, a leader, and, more vulgarly, a star? . . . [Then] he must breathe, eat and dream the theatre. I have never known a successful actor do less. This will limit him as a person and as a citizen. He must of necessity be an egoist, and will probably become a bore.
>
> If, however, he only aspires to filling some smaller place in the world of the theatre, and has less ambition and a humbler view of his contribution to his art, he may well lead a fairly normal life, with some leisure to cultivate interests outside his work.

And Stephen Haggard's reply:

> It is a problem that has vexed me considerably. I cannot feel, somehow, that acting could ever be my sole ambition.

. . . I resent the narrowing down of one's spiritual and mental development which seems to be the price of these things.

It is natural for anyone who has succeeded in a difficult enterprise to assume that others cannot do the same without superhuman effort. Also here again is the romantic notion, the perversely attractive notion, that good things have to be mutually exclusive. And of course there is an amusing exaggeration in Athene Seyler's words. Even so, Jill will have taken the point. One day she was describing her life to her charming new dentist. "You must love your husband very much," he murmured to his circular tray.·

A dentist's chair is an odd place to think how much I do. I suppose I am very proud of having "given up" things for you —but I don't ever remember thinking much about it before. One shouldn't, because it's a form of false pride—and the fact that I might have been a real star and very rich—if we'd not been married—seems a strangely unexciting possibility.

So, after all, "the intellect of man is forced to choose . . ."? Or is it only the intellect of woman? And yet I do not think she did accept the truth of Yeats's axiom, even for her sex. It was not a question of a mutually exclusive "life" and "work," but of two arts competing; and the competition was simply for time—there was no essential competition. On the contrary, the one would enormously enrich the other—given only time.

John Gielgud is producing—you wouldn't know just how exciting and strange this is. Twelve years ago I used to sit night after night in pit queues to see him. It's frightening to see this great opportunity ahead. It's the best part I've ever had. . . . Please go on thinking as you do. I could do anything if you believed in me. I am gay, gay all through as though all the dark branches within had burst into blossom. Come quickly and let me give you a taste of spring.

I came for a week-end, but it was not to be so simple. Because of her collapse in *Rebecca* she was uncertain, and being uncertain was peremptory, I thought, in predisposing of my next ten-days' leave. We must spend it in London with her family because her mother could only take Simon for one week, and that week she would need, later on, to be alone with her part. How easy to grant, if asked. As it was, we had to spoil one of three days with a quarrel about protocol or nothing; I even surmised that I might go to the Sassoons instead, for some quiet writing. Yet her plan was sensible, and afterwards I felt absurdly touchy. As for her,

> I had a bad lesson today with Bertie and came away convinced that I should never be an actress. So I went and blew 10/- on a picture for US (United State). Don't let's ever quarrel any more. It's horrible. I am so very sorry that I was so tactless and insensitive. I will tell you everything from now on. And it's wrong to say that my *ambition* gets between us. For I am not ambitious any more—that is absolutely true. Actually I never was enough in the old days. Ambition is a strong but not very pleasant quality and is very damaging in a woman. I only want to give the best I have. But money and fame are not what I want. If I had really been ambitious I should never have married. The thing that comes between us is my fear of failing. And you are the only person who can let the daylight into all my nightmares.

Quarrelling was horrible, and it need not be: some couples rather thrive on it. They must be individually more self-reliant than we were. It was like the killing of hostages when the armies have long since fraternized, and this was dangerous in that unnatural life, when the one refuge must not seem to be illusory. So we quarrelled sparingly, perhaps not as much as five times in five years, and in a mode that was mere wretched wrangling. I never felt furious with her at any time. It was the brief batting of hares.

Me it left contrite, serenely adjusted to the play, and with my own expectations now fastened to it; and of course we had been careful to return to "set fair" for the final day. She had woken that January morning to the song of a Ladbroke thrush, and secretly resolved that we must spend her one free week together in Devon, willy-nilly.

Jill lunched with Margot Fonteyn and went to her first night in *Le Spectre de la Rose*, redesigned by Rex.

> Margot was exquisite in the dance that she does in her sleep —like a feather lulling a little wind to rest. It has given me that strange elation which a piece of great artistry always fills me with. She is a very great artist—I think the most entirely satisfying one in the theatre at the moment.
>
> I wore my scarlet velvet blouse and was *much* fêted— —though I say this only to you to whom it all belongs. The wife of a brigadier took Theyre [Lee-Elliott] to one side and said I was the most wonderful thing she'd ever seen! It's not vanity, my love, but I can't help being femininely pleased.
>
> And a young man at least five years my junior, and playing his first West End part, said with great kindness that I needn't worry about working with Gielgud because he was always so good with young girls!

All this time the ground-bass of her life unobtrusively continued, with intermittent pain from throat or sinus; yet the specialist seemed to be content. "I am appallingly tired and nervy still," she wrote. The continuing raids terrified her when exhausted, thrilled her when spry, with the sheer pressure of rebuttal from the big guns. Early one dawn she and Theresa made a breakfast of fried bacon, then took the dog out into the half-light of a snow-storm by the Serpentine. "We ran and shouted like crazy things, the snow trimming our hair and a great wind hurrying us past astonished swans. There was a pile of boats upside down, strange and various-coloured by the way the wood took, under the water. After the guns at night this lashing snowy daybreak was extraordinarily exhilarating." But the war seeped in everywhere like London fog. "This house has grown tentacles to clutch at me. I still feel certain that somehow we'll manage the play. . . . Be gentle with me this time. You mustn't feel that that Saturday could have been avoided. But it left a bruise that took a long time to disappear. I want to rest on you more than ever."

We spent two nights in London, the second a noisy one. For the third we were nearly two hundred miles away, in the dark of the stream-valley, in rooms with that humble sweet plastery smell that seemed to emanate from the core of living itself, like the odour of sanctity from the undecayed heart of a saint. The mood of this life, unique as ever, was lambent with a quiet expectancy, both tip-toe and serene. We were anxious for Simon, but he would be leaving London with his grandmother when rehearsals began. Jill sang mischievously from her morning pillow the tune that had come into her head—as tunes often did—for a rhyme out of *Timmy Tiptoes*.

> *My little old man and I fell out,*
> *How shall we bring this matter about?*

She worked steadily at the play, but seldom talked of it. "It's funny that I never want to discuss acting much with anyone. Even Stephen [Haggard] and I—both in the theatre—always talked of poems and writing." The plot, briefly, was this. In August 1939 a young French actress, half Irish, calls unexpectedly on her cousins in Ireland, where she and the elder son fall in love with one another. At first the theatre is everything to her, but she will renounce it, and knows herself capable of lasting love. Then war is declared. The possessive mother (Fay Compton) works on the boy's simplicity and the girl's homesickness to break their engagement, and after an emotional scene the girl leaves for Paris. There were some nice correspondences here with Jill's own history, even to the French and Irish ancestry. Moreover, the Angèle of the play is subtly different from the girl of the novel, less sophisticated and tough, more gentle and spiritual. It seems that Jill herself had influenced the adaptation, and John Perry (who collaborated here with Kate O'Brien) has said that it may well have been so; for Jill was in mind from the first. Clearly it was full of scope for her. She was going to play Angèle with a French accent.

While she studied the part I engraved a three-verse poem on the narrow window of the Skull Room, one verse to each pane. My thoughts went back to that final day, four years before, when I scratched the initials in the heart on the window of the room where she was now lying, prone before the fire, lost to everything but her lines. But in engraving this poem for the house itself, as if summing up—rounding off—the good time we had known in it, I had no sense of finality.

On the top of Venstave I spoke casually, once, of a wish to leave my job and go abroad when the invasion of Europe took place; though I had no idea if I could, or in what capacity. I knew something about the training of signallers now—nothing at all about anything else in war. She did not take it as a retaliation for the play. "Pulling up his roots in all directions," she murmured thoughtfully, her eyes on the skyline, but with an expression of interest and quiet consent. The prospect of service abroad did not wake my own unconfidence as yet. I knew that if I went into action I should be frightened of being frightened, but I assumed that nearly everybody felt this—more or less. Perhaps it was the sense of sharing, being merged in, a general experience that made it seem practicable, or perhaps it was merely that the event was still not imminent. We bought a copper kettle in Bideford. Now there was prunus blossom and the first wild daffodils each side of it on the shelf. We were well primed for spring, and its varied excitements.

Yet when we climbed through the wood to say goodbye, snow was falling—light flakes but fairly thick, sinking through the leafless branches like grains through water, slowly and straight down, intensifying the dark height of the trees, falling on the thatch of the cottage like a benediction as we climbed above it; and with the birds singing volubly of spring all the time. We parted by the white gate at the top, out of sight of the lane across the meadow. I walked away with my luggage, put it down, and returned. Twice, laughing, three times perhaps, I had to return to her winter-red jacket and scarfed head, against the bushes that were breeding snow quite fast. We were, in fact, but unawares, now leaving the high peaks of happiness for ever—not of love, but of happiness. It was worth not breaking off too abruptly.

It's a wonderfully companionable solitude you have left me in. You cannot imagine what a different room my spirit has to live in now. Sunlight and peace come in just the touch of your hand in the middle of the night. I never cease to marvel. Bless you for this week and all my time with you. How one must give thanks for it. I so often find myself praying too much in petition and not nearly enough in gratitude. . . . Do you really believe that before *long* now we could live here for the summer—perhaps next summer? My life through *this* summer shall be a pilgrim's progress towards that.

There was news of lemons, almost unheard of, and she went to the village to inquire. This led to pancakes for a lonely supper— too many—and they to a nightmare air-raid from which she woke in alarm. That in turn tinctured her thoughts throughout the following day—or else telepathy was working again.

She went up to Venton, and found wild daffodils in the haunted orchard where once long ago we had played tenniquoits, still almost strangers in that archaic spring.

The lambs were crying in the last late sunlight and a crowd of plover rose from the green forehead of the hill like disturbed thoughts, as I came home. You are the only person in the world that steadies me—that has power over my evil spirits. It's tragic in a way that you are not always with me, because then I should never be ill or frightened. I know this now.

Just how well I was steadying her at this juncture can be shown. After travelling all day, with a deviation to see Simon, I reached camp at two in the morning, carrying my luggage out from Retford, discontented with an incipient cold, and other trouble. By luck I travelled north with Jonathan Wilson, but, having to suppress a nagging pain, was aware of seeming unfriendly to someone whose company would otherwise have been so welcome. Next day the Mess was fuller than usual of war-rumours. For some time Hitler had been boasting of his "secret weapon," and I now learnt that the local R.A.F. claimed to be bombing it—a wide arc of "rocket-guns" (so one understood), all centred on London at a radius of 170 miles. This angle on *The Last of Summer* was less attractive. At dinner, acting on a most rash impulse, I asked the colonel whether Jill should rehearse in London next month. I was fairly sure that he would minimize the threat, say something about the "chances of war," and thereby strengthen my resolve to think the same. "To my surprise he said 'No!' in his downright way. 'I wouldn't let her if you can *possibly* help it.' And this was echoed by the others who heard." Some officers were removing their families from London. "I simply don't know what to say. I long for you to be Angèle as much now as you, I really believe. It does seem utter folly to *come* into London just this month, and for Simon to stay there." And more in this vein.

The flying bombs and rockets have now dwindled somewhat in perspective. No one knew, then, what they were, or could do, in concentration on a city, though one had an idea of what conventional bombing had done to Hamburg. It was most repugnant to me that she should be in greater danger than before, while I remained safe. But when everything is said in extenuation, the fact remains that one must not obstruct a hard undertaking without offering a firm and honourable alternative. I did not ask her to withdraw. I was hoping that the play would be postponed (as would have been wholly to its advantage, in the outcome); but Jill could hardly bring that about. I was frankly unloading on to paper worries that could have been made acceptable in a morning's talk. If this was being "always forced to tell," it was certainly "a proof of weakness." Her answer still wounds, at the range of nineteen years:

Your letter utterly shattered for a morning all the lovely peace you gave me here. But I expect you had to write it. I went down to the river and sat in the sunshine in the little fishing-hut and prayed for a long time. And gradually the nightmare of anxiety faded. One's prayers *are* answered, I'm convinced. If I backed out now—at merely the threat of bombardment—I should never forgive either myself or you. If my health doesn't stand up to it—that is a different matter. I feel that any two people as deeply and brilliantly happy *must affirm,* as I think you said once. One day this will be over. One day we shall be glad of the things we've *attempted* to do. All our love is based on that, isn't it? Since that night at Charlotte Street. Our lives began that night, the ones—or the one that goes on here in this cottage, at Berrynarbor, at Porthguarnon. After all, look at the fire—safe in the country! Look at those dark haunted days when we expected invasion. Look at the fuss, once, whether I could or couldn't have a baby. All our decisions then were affirmative. My heart—let's be courageous and put this off our minds as a decision made. I *know* that God is with us and that underneath are the everlasting arms.

Out of tenderness she ended differently, reverting to that deep intuition of permanence.

Dear little house. Sometimes I get the strange instantaneous feeling—am I in the house or is the house in me? Do you know that half-comprehension of some immense truth? It sparks in a corner of the mind that you're not looking at—when you look it's gone. The words "intimations of immortality" mean that to me.

I recovered, and she travelled to London for rehearsals, saying to a friend, "I don't care if I never become a star or famous—but I must create those things that it's in me to create, however small they may be."

The first two days were an ordeal, "but today my nerves removed their clutching fingers from my diaphragm and everything was suddenly exciting and *free*. Kate O'Brien took my arm and said, 'You're going to give a lovely performance, child—I'm absolutely delighted!' So I felt happy. Fay is charming. I've completely lost my heart to Uncle Corney[1] already. He's superb." She liked the whole company a great deal, and the pay would be £50–60 a week, perhaps £80: a fortune to us.

But a daunting private worry increased with each day. . . . "I wish I were in your arms at the cottage coiled in that well of water and timeless night. It lies under all I do and say as Angèle, giving her truth."

All day my thoughts reverted to Angèle with pleasure and confidence, while at night I had anxiety-dreams about her. "You must be now beginning to realize what you are for me. Our leave is what I anchor to, when time was measured out like water in the harmless wooden spoons of the cuckoo-clock, and was cool, though fast, and not feverish." To assuage my misgiving for the present, I heard that she was going to the Rupert Thompsons and de la Mare at Penn, for the period of the "bomber's moon."

But alas that her own misgiving should be justified, and her guess confirmed by her doctor.

"You have won Daniel come to judgement," said her telegram. Daniel was to be the name, one day, of a second son. It did not feel like a victory, as I went to the telephone—aghast for Jill, and for myself deeply, if irrationally, disappointed.

This is the blackest Monday I ever remember. I feel sick with misery and disappointment. It was cruel of fate to let me get entangled again—to have a week of rehearsals and *then* this. I don't suppose Binkie will ever forget this—it's heartbreaking. And it was *such* a part. O God. I am taking Simon to the cottage. I know you will be relieved and happy and

[1] Fred O'Donovan. Others in the cast were her friend Hugh Burden, and Hazel Terry.

that is my one and only consolation. It is a very real one. The burden of your anxiety, which you did not minimise, has lain very heavy on me. It was a strain that I found very hard to bear. Anyway that's all one now.

Somewhere in me I feel glad—a kind of inevitableness and fitness that that leave should blossom like this. I thought Angèle would be its flower—but this is a greater creation, the finest flower of our art. I think I know now why I was so at peace and so sure of the rightness of what we did. I keep seeing you going from me in the snow—and unable to go—coming back because the little thread of sight and touch was too lovely to break. My dear I do love you. All this fret and disappointment are the foam on the deep and certain sea of our love.

I wish you had seen my exquisite French clothes—you would have had a grand time! Now I have that awful prospect of being clumsy and heavy and ugly again. God how I *hate* it! So will you. Let's manage to see each other before I get ungainly. O—if only I could feel that I was not missing my summer—*my* summer I mean. When this is over I shall be nearly thirty.

Now you will have to write me a really consoling letter, will you? I need it—though I must admit that I find the irony of the whole situation bloody funny. I am in bed with a shocking cold and feeling sick as a cat.

I did not write, but went the next day on compassionate leave. She met me in the dark hall, with a welcome compounded of despair, amusement, resignation, and excitement; also reproach; as if it were in some way my fault.

Throughout the autumn she had half-consciously hoped that a child might intervene, so much did she fear another, and final, collapse in a play. But if the wish for that honourable escape was still hers at the cottage in February, with who knows what fatal effect of interference in the chances of conception, it was by then an utterly unconscious wish. The timing was certainly cruel. Even knowing her as I did, I could not but wonder at her acceptance, as we lunched in Soho, rueful and merry. Nothing mattered, really. There is a level where nothing ought to matter; though one seldom reaches it. I thought: it needs only one good raid to make me glad about the baby; and that night there was a particularly good one, with the bombs falling nearer and nearer through a crescendo of gunfire. The family gathered in Jill's basement bedroom, sandbagged outside against blast. Side by side we wore it out, kept Simon as immune as we could, and were relieved to be together. Next morning I took them both, with Theresa, to Waterloo station, scene of many momentous arrivals and departures, not the last for me. The North Devon coaches, as ever, were at the tip of the Atlantic Coast Express, right up behind *Excalibur* perhaps, some splendid instance of the King Arthur class—and almost out into the country, as it seemed, because a bright skein of points gathered all feelings together in an affirmation, and sent them snaking out over insignificant London, down the one avenue of Dartmoor granite, chipped from below Yes Tor, all the way to the west, to the far landscape of the heart. I watched the green coaches sweep by, gaining speed; then turned, committing all I loved most to God and to the cottage stream, his local voice, the sound-track of our felicity.

XV

She was very sick, and the good health of four years before was manifestly absent. Out crept the horrors from a hole that could never be quite sealed off in a war. She dreamt there was a girl who was in love with me, and that I was attracted in return. We seemed to be discussing this, while we patrolled some hateful shopping-street; until, in despair, she saw in a jeweller's window a tray with little mounds of unset stones. One was of cornelians, bright like red drops of water. Suddenly the drops all ran together, and she knew that she was fainting. She sank slowly to the pavement, and was aware of numberless shoes all round her— shoes closing in. Someone said, "She's had a miscarriage!"

This sequence, like an extract from a film, she placed in its general context of revived insecurity.

I have not felt that for so long—partly because I've known this last year that I was more beautiful and that you found me so. That I'm afraid increases my self-confidence enormously. Maternity instead of glamour threw me back into one of my old pits of silly inferiority. I felt when you went back that I was left sick and altering—without you and with the theatre snatched away. Now you have plucked up my courage which Aunt Nausea had stolen.

She told herself that it was better to be pregnant now, in separation, than to begin the peace in that restricting state; also that a second child had been overdue. In the Dolton shop, and among her many other village friends, she was the centre of affectionate interest. As for the sickness, that only meant that she was "changing the sex," apparently. She herself thought that it would be a girl. For years she had favoured "Clare," the heroine of her suspended novel, but now she was tired of the name, and proposed "Gabriel." (There was a Gabriel Whistler far back.) "I like boyish names." Upon which I suggested "Robin," having wanted a son of that name since I was twelve. Unfortunately Rex had been the first to claim it; but now I had a letter from him which moved me, because he would evidently soon be abroad, and had renounced marriage as a likelihood. I felt that he would be pleased if we took the name. Jill had thought of it, too, before my letter arrived.

The prospect of a penniless confinement daunted her. I gave up alcohol altogether, and increased her allowance, grudging my twenty-five shillings towards the regimental dance, which meant nothing this year. Not that she was yet weary of dance and play, in her mind. "Tonight is the dance. O God please," she asked— with that same unconscious monism that had made her exclaim, "when we're an officer"—"please let's be beautiful and glamorous again after Robin, and make up for this." She used to say that she did not "know which of us is which, anyway."

Exasperated that I could not earn more, I did manage to place a couple of illustrated articles. One was about a working windmill I had discovered while visiting my wireless schemes. A recurrent scheme was to practise the young officers in observing and reporting complicated movements with accuracy and speed. A scene was enacted before them at half-a-mile's distance, and out of boredom I varied it from a burial party to the Rape of the Sabine Women in costume, and so to "Exercise Carmel." This required two altars, one non-inflammable. A little petrol and a smoke-canister made a great success of Jehovah's altar, after some preliminary invocations, and as the smoke cleared away the servants of Baal were smitten beneath the fifth rib. But half the subalterns did not know their Bible. Such an act I had the temerity to mount for a visiting general and his staff; and can it have been "work" of this kind that my sympathetic colonel referred to, when I revealed our poverty? He wished that he could promote me to major, seeing that I had "put such a hell of a lot of work into this place." Testimonial duly forwarded—to distract from nausea.

For another distraction she re-read the scorched diary I had found in the ruins. From the beginning it had been taken for granted that we never glanced at each other's letters and documents; but no doubt I could have read the diary at any time, had I asked. She saw no need to expunge that early passage where she had thought me untrustworthy: it had a place in the story. She then read on to our true beginning. "This June will be five years. I suppose we have had two actually together. But it sounds a long time, doesn't it, and somehow it's gone quick as light, as all happiness does." An occupation was to help me improve the eight new love-poems for *Who Live in Unity*. Thus in one she objected to the back-stage setting.

It's a feeling I have about theatre dressing-rooms. To me they are and must be essentially tawdry. It's not just because I'm untidy by nature. I *loathe* tawdriness elsewhere and am repelled by it. But I have an unreasonable conviction that it is part of the theatre, the old basis of roguery and vagabondage, tinsel and dust and a bunch of dingy masks on a string. Tidy concrete theatres and "star" dressing-rooms furnished like a hotel bedroom are horribly wrong. But though this is to me the essence of the theatre, it is still tawdry, and I cannot bear sex to come anywhere near tawdriness. Coarseness yes my God yes—but not the fading tinsel and the hungry unshaded lights. You may understand. . . . Subtleties of thought and atmosphere that are the joy and bane of both our lives.

This is not the language of impartial criticism, for indeed she was too "tied and tangled" into my work, as she said, to attempt that; yet she was right, as so often. The most useful critic is necessarily partial. He may well be wrong in his measure of achievement, but he is not there to measure, only to identify his vision with the writer's, and then to clarify and discriminate—a condition of helpfulness being sincerity. She now wanted a final poem, to give the dimension of "godly love" implied by the title; and this I had intended but not mentioned.

News came from time to time of the play, taken first to the provinces. Gielgud was reported to have been bitterly disappointed by her departure: she had the "most wonderful quality" and reminded him of Meggie Albanesi. Kate O'Brien "cursed our romantic love for each other," and said that they had a young French girl, but "she doesn't look like a Botticelli angel!"—as the text required.

> I know I should have made my name in that part. I'll never have a chance like that again. Perhaps I am meant to learn that I have really left the stage by marrying, and must forget it. I wish I knew. I am still entirely unsorry that we shall have Robin instead of Angèle. There are things that matter far more than success. At least I know that much. . . .O dear, how sad and far away it seems.

Partly to keep from fretting, she attacked her novel again. Before the war she had completed one, but not published it, and this was her third attempt, which might have proved marketable, although her fiction did not have the authenticity of her letters. She wrote fast, but found that it would go its own way, and thought this a proof of amateurishness. "Why is one so far behind one's ideals of everything?"

Quite abruptly the sickness ended, and she came into the spring overnight as into a delayed legacy. One sharp sinus headache— "and I am full of that Lazarus feeling which makes a blessing of pain—after it's gone." So said Socrates, rubbing his leg when the chain was removed.

> The day is a marvel and the taste of real happiness is in my mouth again. You know, a green leafy taste that makes me want to sing. . . .
>
> Such a spring it is—all lilac and apple-blow and bluebells—

and the green oak miraculously tender and round all over the woods. The rain moves along outside the window and the birds are growing sleepy. It's a lovely, lovely house this—so full of tranquillity and serene cosiness. . . .

This morning I have been making a big cream cheese. Just as I was squeezing the wet white bag, a blackbird sang deliriously in the rainy garden. I suddenly "saw" black and white—the milk and the blackbird's song, gay and black-shining like a jet necklace strung across the room.

For me this was not a description, but the thing itself—I cannot explain—exploding in my mind. I wondered if there were others to whom just these curious recognitions came. For all I know, the answer may be "many others." The fact remains that it did not seem as if she were communicating a congenial fancy so much as speaking through my own mind.

I had one of those rare dreams that seem to be a foretaste of heaven, with joy pure, joy classic, devoid of any sense of impermanence. I dreamt that we were near the oak by the stream, but also in a little wood, dark with a kind of whitish, primitive light striking through it; and we were talking and moving about, though what we said I have forgotten. Waking up beside her I described this dream, only to find that she had dreamt of the same wood, and in fact knew all that had happened! It seemed a dazzling proof of immortality, or at least of experience shared beyond this plane of life, and the emotion persisted after I woke "again," and literally this time, to my breeze-block cell in the Midlands.

There was something special about the oak, she said. "It was under that, one sunny evening after France fell, I had the strongest presentiment I've ever had that all was going to be well for us." But what is "all"? How much living together is enough to qualify as "all"?

They were good days that immediately followed—days to enjoy the world aright:

I went to Bideford—walking up Venstave in a thick mist. I was early, and waited some time leaning on the gate looking over to where Buckland should have been. A big bomber went snoring overhead invisibly. The birds sang and then suddenly the mist thinned like milk soaking into a green carpet and there was the white farm in its trees and the sheep like maggots in its fields and the woods boiling into the hot, almost metallic green of young oak. It almost made me cry it was so soon— and so beautiful! Then a woman with red hair came down the road, said good-morning and drew a little bottle out of the hedge near me and went down the lane. I don't know who she was or what she was doing but it seemed an amazingly appropriate thing to happen. Then the bus came and I trundled into Dolton—the houses looked so bright and innocent in the early sun, like houses on a plate. O it was such a day—one of those May days when summer is a state of the soul, as well as of the hedges and fields. I saw a crow land in a field beside another crow and they bowed formally to each other at least a dozen times and then flew away. And a hen was having a dust-bath where it had had dust-baths so often before that it had hollowed out a hole it disappeared into, and one saw only a dusty bunch of feathers squirming down inside. I don't know why these trivial things were such a part of the day's gaiety but they were—and you were there all the time, as you always are on that journey, and I murmured to you a great deal. I read your letter and felt happier than I have been for months, I think.

Such a day, could we have lived it together, would have seemed to stand from everlasting to everlasting. But we were fastened apart; for history was now coming to a head. All leave was cancelled throughout the army, and for no short while, one guessed. I tried to make the best of it.

How stoical you grow now that I am no longer slim and loose among the temptations of the town. You wait. I'll make up for this next year. I'll lead you a dance! . . . What a thing it is to be a grass widow. I shall be hay before long if no one walks in my meadow. Do you know that you and I are quite old-fashioned to have survived nearly five years of matrimony? During the last year three men have suggested to me, as if it was the most natural thing in the world, that I should be unfaithful to you. All three (only one was French incidentally!) knew I was happily married. I don't feel a bit smug about us— we have been quite amazingly lucky so far in every way. But it does seem to me that the more it goes on, the more holiness and depth there *can* be in marriage under all the gaiety and blissful fun. But I don't want to get all serious about marriage. Let's never get too serious about anything. I want our life to be always gay and precarious and unsettled on top of the fundamental rock of us. . . . If ever the theatre gets between us— or if I try and leave you—bring me here for a month! I am only the whole of myself here. I have just planted a blue passion flower under the window. It seems suitable . . .

I'm beginning to feel seventeenth century, the pregnant lady left at home, writing of cream cheese when the world is about to begin its greatest battles. But this lovely spring is very haunted for me. And what luck I have in not knowing that (yet) it means violence for you.

However, she would be ready for that, and inwardly provided. I spoke of her life in the valley and of what it would then signify to me:

If I had to go abroad, the strength it would give me to know that you and Simon were there, and our still-unknown, would be hard to express. I can hear the smallest sounds of the cottage—the scrape of the chair on the kitchen floor, the muffled creak of the stair, the blossoming of the stream as the bedroom window swings open. O how I hunger to hear the window murmur, like a friend who has not quite heard a question that has never quite been asked, but a question hanging in the white silence of the ceiling, which would explain everything, if it could be answered.

To be pregnant through two imminent invasions! Although the invading was now to be other-way-on, there had been far more peace for her in 1940. She felt this keenly between days of exaltation. Never had she swung so signally between the black moods and the white.

I have bought baby-wool and am like a bird on the verge of building its nest. But with none of a bird's serene confidence. Where do these things grow, when one isn't with the only person one really loves? In religion, I suppose. Mine falls apart into doubting and dismay so easily when you're not there. Not the fundamental faith, but the everyday kind that you and I seem to have together. Never mind. The sun hasn't shone and it's been very cold and I am a terrible barometer, like those donkeys on a card with a seaweed tail that used to hang in seaside lodgings when I was a child. Did you go there much? We did—sand in the food and a sort of uncertain horror that always pervades flat dunes and houses near the sea, something sordid and alarming in the grey fleshy leaves of sea poppies. O it makes me shudder still. Many things that children never forget happened to me on seaside holidays. Only this rocky coast of ours is fine and unhaunted for me by those half-memories.

It was no surprise by now that we corresponded, even to childhood. Could we have shared even then the unsayable significances? I think not. We needed all the years of our delayed maturing. For I had my own version of the scene: the flat white bungalows at angles, the screaming smell of burnt petrol at strange bed-time, the spanking hilarity of flag-poles. Such would be the seaboard of my hell, with sand for ever gaining on rubber grasses, and beyond it a half-inch of mindless sea. And all meant for pleasure—like the fixed smile of a lunatic. Of course mine were half-memories like hers, the genuine enjoyment for some reason forgotten; and of course she was dramatizing, in a murky mood. For my part, I could have added that, in childhood, coming on the blood and buckled wheels of a road-accident at the end of a day's journey to such a coast, I thought myself mad for a week, but kept mum. Yes, there was redemption in the cliffs of the west. Great breakers gnashed on great rocks are like Epic: terrible, but not horrible.

She knew now there were joys more dependable than those of childhood. Out flamed her dual suns again, the visible and invisible.

Yesterday morning there was a saturation of blue air in sunlight, and the cut pine-branches smelled of heaven. I became almost drunk with summer and happiness and sat on a tree-stump with more and deeper intimations of immortality than I have ever had. Many thoughts slide like fishes through my net, just perceived but never caught. O dear what a wonderful life it can be—as simple as bread and sunlight. . . . Sometimes now, looking round this house that our love has built, I am overcome to tears by the loveliness and rightness and peace of it all—of all we have and are. And then dimly I grope after the true immediate understanding of my fortune in finding you.

I had asked her to point the progress of summer in the Skull Room, and for a while lilac had lolled and sharpened there, sensuously Gothic. Returning one late May dusk she saw the first red rose beneath the end window, fetched a chair, and stood among the tight buds, regarding the symbol of what June meant to us. "So red it was that the white wall went dim and blue behind it. I couldn't resist snipping it off and putting it under the mirror in our room." She gardened with oblivious passion, tending

three rows of small but triumphant corn on the cob. They *spring* out of the ground with a kind of pagan hurry for harvest. They make me think of America when it was innocent and lost still

—Indians on sunny mornings bending over their corn patch as I do—and contemplating.

O another hot day is crouching at the foot of the hill—I can see it quite plainly—hot and striped like a tiger waiting to spring on the house and crush us into quiet. And tomorrow I'm cleaning out the kitchen, heaven help us. I wonder if June will really see you here. Couldn't you wait perhaps to write the last poem here? You could be alone and quiet in the garden or the woods. And this house is pressed down and running over with godly love. The windows shine with it, and the flowers look in at the windows, and Simon and I look out into God's holy hill. I breathe nothing but roses and innocence wherever I go.

But, with weariness, depression would return, and then, "sick with hope deferred," she would say "I don't want a kind of life. I just want you." But although she said "a few more roses bleed each day down the white wall," I never came; and for me there would be no more versifying in the shared valley. She wrote a little herself—this rough sketch for example, probably with Stephen Haggard in mind:

> Heat seals the valley up; the skein
> Of water hardly is unwound.
> From dry stone to stone
> There is small shadow to be found.
>
> Forget-me-nots at my feet have spread
> Their tearless blue over the dust.
> There is no answer to this thirst.
> And they remind me of the dead,
> For whom the sun had dried my grief.
> In time of drought I pray for rain:
> Dust so diminishes the green leaf.

Over a hundred square miles of the North Midlands my drivers and operators were playing "French and English." But though it gave admirable practice at the wireless sets and maps, there had to be orthodox exercises, like one when I took my senior men to the Peak, to work wireless by night. I bought three dozen eggs from a farm, a fire was built, and soon concertina, guitar, and clarinet were brought out.

A sadness hangs over the party. They are lying listening with immobile English faces. Do you know how the sound of two men carrying a heavy trunk downstairs sounds excessively like itself? This is one of those occasions. I suppose I ought to think it happy—the men certainly very much enjoy it—but all I can feel is the futility of their waiting to go to battle, which seems to me to be written in the sobriety of their faces more than they know, rather as a pond might not realise how the green of its surface looks from above, but merely feel that the light is obscured.

Perhaps they were playing "Lili Marlene." This she had just heard on the air. She wrote:

To me it has the sense of city streets in all the world, carrying the war over them like a great sad sky. There is some undertow of meaning in the fact that our enemy made it and probably still sings it. That moves me more than all our victories. That is the world and its tragedy and beauty, like earth under the soldiers' feet, no matter what country they fight for.

The well-being of those intermittent, radiant days was ebbing away. Perhaps I could have saved it for her had I been there. Perhaps it would have lasted had she escaped the gratuitous strains that were to come. By now she was deeply tired, and imagining a childish grace: "Thank God for my nice war may I get down now please amen."

It was hardly the moment for getting down. Full of excitement and sometimes in tears, she listened to the invasion news, knowing "it's a very English characteristic to romanticize France, but still I do. . . . I love France almost more than England, which is saying a great deal."

Poor *Last of Summer*! It opened in London the very next day. And now in the part designed for Jill there was an unknown Australian girl, Margaret Johnston. A week later the flying bombs swarmed into London, and after another week of increasingly empty houses the play was taken off. "How vindicated all your fussing has been."

But it was now too late for us, in a sense; for she was large and matronly and changed in mood. As she lay on her bed one day, thinking of a daughter, suddenly the baby kicked several times. "There's no way of describing to you the astonishment and holy wonder one feels at that moment. It's beyond words." This was just before our special anniversary—a lustrum—when she filled every room with flowers, "which is all I can do to celebrate my happiness, and honour you who gave it to me."

She began to feel deeply unwell, with fierce headaches and nose-bleeding the more obvious symptoms, and now concern for her brothers and for my brother was added—no less for her parents in London. Word came of some message for her at the station, and for half an hour she fancied that her father and mother had been killed. "How foolish one gets all alone." This was neurotic fear of a sort that she would have scorned in her right mind. "I fret so much for you, and uncertainty about leave is apt to get on my nerves." She proposed a compact, that we should never speak of leave again until Whitehall pronounced one way or the other; but of course we repeatedly did. Then she worried about poverty. Also "I can't find a doctor or even a bed in which to have the little bastard! (*I* think it is one). But you will only write poetically about 'the grass on the weir,' I suppose. *You* try having a baby in the grass on the weir!" To my surprise, I had saved £100.

For myself, I had nothing but my growing anxiety for her, to explain the lassitude I felt at this time. A brief camping in the Lakes did little to relieve it. The only good news for me was in a letter from our signals officer in the 1st Battalion in Normandy, describing my signallers as excellent and invaluable. As against that, one or two of them had already been killed.

She told me of a chance encounter with her grandfather, which was not "alarming or horrifying—just unbearably poignant. *What* happens to the true spirit," she protested "—where does it go in old age? *Why* must people one loves suffer these intolerable meaningless miseries. And yet even as I write I see a kind of beauty in it—a starved kind of light." It occurs to me that it might almost have been necessary for Christ to die in the prime of his beauty and vigour, for to have experienced old age without impoverishment would have been not to be fully human. Perhaps heaven exists for living in the prime, enriched in some simultaneous way by the other selves we have been between birth and death. Andrew Young suggests in *Out of the World and Back* that "a changing Proteus" will arise for each of us. Faintly I could taste the kind of pleasure this would be, when she adopted the character of little girl or schoolgirl, and very faintly could perceive how she would be, when old.

She became still worse, sleeping for only three hours of the night, lying awake with nerves that twitched in a pattern, she said, like the veins on a marrow-leaf.

> I would give all my few possessions for your company. How *can* I go on like this. I have never needed you so much, or been so frightened of life. I don't know what is wrong, quite. Sometimes I'm afraid—like someone walking up a long narrowing avenue towards that inevitable brick arch of pain on top of the hill. However, it's been done by quite a few women before.

And indeed by herself. After Simon's birth she had told Theresa to reject as nonsense what the novelists wrote about the anguish of childbirth. This natural pain she had never dreaded, and would not have been dreading now, but for an unnatural sapping of her strength. She was enduring all this time a relationship that brought her a great deal of exhaustion and misery, and there was nothing she could do but endure. "I have moved through a nightmare. This is not the life for a pregnant woman."

By now she was very sick, and our firm plan for the bigger separation, should it come, was dissolving. "I can guess dimly what I'd feel if you were there, and it makes me shake—just the idea of it." I began to be seriously alarmed at the effect on her, wondering in what way I could break the news by letter, or indeed face it cheerfully myself. When a little later she exclaimed, "They won't send you, will they? My whole life is torn apart and I live in anguish at it sometimes," then I knew the humiliation of fearing that they would. No doubt if my approach to war could have been more adventurous from the beginning, we should now be better off. But there it was. To prove equal to whatever was required of me was always the extent of my hope and resolve.

Four months had elapsed since we parted: by far the longest and most unluckily timed of all the gaps we had known. It seems now that I ought to have asked for compassionate leave, but I doubt if it would have been granted, then, for a state of disorder so little defined, and if I could have made any improvement that was lasting. Anyway it was never mentioned, and I had the conviction that all would be well in the end, if she could but hold on. Simon was her constant joy; and she loved and was loved by another little boy to whom she was giving a home, far from the raids. Her sense of humour often came to her rescue:

I laugh and sometimes I cry—but *where* is our valley and our quiet? Sometimes I don't know what to do—nothing seems familiar—a film of faint dust filters over it and makes me sick. I don't know what to do to keep myself quiet and under control. Can you tell me? Shall I think of Cornwall and Edinburgh? I do, but always it swims into tears in the end because our being together is like a dream from which I have woken alone. Perhaps you can imagine how healing in this pain and futility your poem is [the last for *Who Live in Unity*]. It is as near praying with you at night when our hands touch as anything I know. You must not say it's "flat." I expect you feel like a well full of leaves as I do. Sometimes I'm afraid I shall not hang on intact till you can come. But that is only when things go very badly. I pray often that Robin won't be neurotic. And I look at the Mandarin and wrap myself in the untouched shreds of real peace that hang like cobwebs in all the corners.

And later:

I no longer even hope that you may come. I suppose they'll give you compassionate leave in November, won't they?
O how very tired I am inside—sick of this heavy awkward body and stupid mind. I'd like to be someone else. But it would always be one who loved you more than anything.

And even as she wrote these words the faces I met in the camp were alive with the knowledge that leave had been restored. My first task was to contrive the best roster for my N.C.O.s and men, and this kept me in my office at nights. My own leave was quickly granted. "I am sometimes a little afraid of seeing you again," she had written. "You'll want slim pretty girls, and not this portly bus. You know, it may sound absurd but I really should feel a little afraid, if you came now, that you might not like me. We have been so long apart. O will you still love me?"
How if I had been four years in a prison camp? But it was illness that inspired the doubt. When we met, there was a reason why it was not very much in her mind.

XVI

At Waterloo station I found a corner seat and walked back to the barrier for a mid-day paper. Installed again, I began turning the pages.

"Londoner's Diary." The picture at the top was captioned "One of Rex Whistler's last sketches. Art and the stage suffer a considerable loss," etc. A wave of heat surged up from my chest to my scalp. The truth conveyed by small, detached, world-continuing print, the truth that something had utterly and finally occurred, hit me like a hot wave flying upwards. The next moment, such is my incurable self-consciousness, I was aware that there were people on the opposite seat, and that they had noticed nothing. It was not an Englishman's phlegm that made me not want them to know, nor was it hostility. I simply could not face their kindly, groping ventures in sympathy, and the meaningless rejoinders I should have to make. You have to be all oblivious spontaneity—or all reserve. I felt ashamed of my reserve. Then it occurred to me—all this in an instant—that Jill would feel the same, a criterion for me at that moment. She might perhaps faint or leave the compartment. But I should not faint, and I did not much want to cry until I reached home. A life-altering moment had passed, above a newspaper lowered, and after a while taken up again. A kind of exhaustion overtook me, and throughout the five-hour journey I dozed and woke to planless unprogressive thoughts that continually reverted in appalled questioning to my mother. Salisbury spire dawdled by. Through flying bushes there came a flicker of Wilton park wall—of the turning to the Daye House and Edith Olivier. In these objects, so relentlessly themselves and soberly persevering, I saw that it was accomplished, written off, left behind, a mere part of everything that had formerly existed, last week and ten millenniums ago in Ur.

I have been commiserated on the way in which I learnt of this, but really there is no better or worse way of receiving such news. The most sensitive breaking must give time for the mind's mute shout of apprehension—which I was spared. The crudest would seem insignificant beside the news that was broken. To be in the ambience of love: that is what one wishes. But it is a wish of the moment after, not the moment itself. And this ambience, for a marvel, I was now rapidly approaching, at the end of four months.

She had heard the news from someone that morning; and in the doorway I saw that she thought I had not heard. "Have you heard the news?" I asked with foolish lightness, shy of the emotion we must plunge into together. All day she had wished that she did not have to break it. Now she was wishing that she had. It was the old sleight of Providence, placing us together on two such occasions—when Stephen died, and even more importantly now. The pain merged into the infinite sweetness of being with her, and became indistinguishable. It gave me up to tears, broke over me time and again, the sharp dateless images, the old devotion, the debt I owed, and the remorse for never paying it—remorse for not soldiering with him, though I still did not think I should have done so. "Don't grieve," she said tenderly, not condemning, but as if somewhere the worst must be acceptable, a thing I remembered.

This "life" was now reduced to a week, so that I might spend some days with my mother. Nor were we alone as a family, for Jill was still looking after the other child. But anxiety was allayed, because she was tranquil now that I was there, and preening her hopes.

It was about midnight when I arrived at the Daye House, and opening the gate found Edith Olivier waiting in the leafy tunnel, silent, in zebra-striped moonlight. Next day the memorial service in blazing Salisbury. . . . Rex's death in action was one of the

most widely regretted of the war—to speak of personal regret—
so much was he liked both as artist and man. I feared the replace-
ment of the man by a myth, as with Rupert Brooke. For already
the fond legend-spinners were at work. But I was soon with our
mother, whose picture of him was to remain undistorted, wondering at the faith that enabled her to laugh at foolish jokes; to plan,
after a while, for the future; and to show no sign of self-pity in her
suffering.

Jill was not allowed to come to the service. "O these partings
—one should learn to bear it better, but I do not really seem to
improve." Instead, she had driven to a house where the harvest
had begun, with "those impersonal arms gathering corn and sunlight down the walls of wheat, and men in the shade of an oak
with a huge jar of cider—so like Rex's painting it brought tears."
For my part I should soon, on some military expedition, be looking at Fountains Abbey, and seeing it in a wash of sunlight,
neat as a Rex—the over-smooth grass, the branches gracefully
fronding from the stone, all the masonry more "understood" than
it would be in real life, one felt.

For a short time she was full of benison. "Simon in his little
cot hums faintly like a top before it sleeps." A day of great heat
had slid over once more into an evening of slow cumulus in
towering sunlight. "I feel rich—rich in peace and serenity again.
We ought to go up the hill in the sun, this evening. A bird cheeps
in the roses outside, and Simon has fallen quiet. I suppose I might
as well go to bed."

Such days were numbered, but they glowed. There was a
large picnic-party of neighbours at the Top of the World, with
Merton church far off across the invisible river, drowsy in
heat.

And through the conversation I looked at Merton and Merton looked at me and I felt one of those moments of radiant
closeness to you and to that strange third personality which
seems to me to grow, and which I can only call rather feebly us.

I think that in any perfect relationship there is something that becomes their trinity.

She went on to say that her Indian corn had suddenly swollen

under the female flower—an exquisite plume of pale blown silk that flushes pink at the tips. The male flower shakes its spiring heads and they rattle dimly and the pollen drifts down and fertilises the cob. It's so beautiful. That patch of corn has given me intense joy this summer, as you know. I'm sure that in some things far more than others the glass between us and reality suddenly thins and one sees through into heaven or truth or whatever it is that we are all painted on.

A confused image, but expressing three features of our speculation at once—things like symbols of their timeless selves; the timeless only just beyond reach; and mankind both constructing the timeless and aware of it.

Someone not unmoved by jealousy was reported to be "afraid" that our marriage would break up after the war. "How despicable it is to wish such a thing even on one's enemy, and how sad. I am getting weary. A moth flops across this candlelit page and an owl hoots in the wood. We *are* united, aren't we? That is all that matters."

But she wondered if it was good for the child to have so un-cowlike a mother. Even so, one or other of the little boys came often to embrace her ripening waist and to lean his head there, "as though some lovely natural impulse moved them. I've noticed that neither of them does exactly that to anyone else."

She looked into an old cottage newly and charmingly furnished, and felt envious. "We have none—or so little—of our own furniture." Yet I had told her about Rex's will: all the family furniture was ours now, some of it good, and enough to fill three or four such houses; also his big fast car; and the money from his life-insurance; and the leasehold of the house in the Close. We were paupers no longer. Not to have remembered this at all showed an inclination to make the worst of things because she was ill—pitiable in one so inclined the other way when well. "Yes, I had quite forgotten about Rex's furniture. But would much of it suit a cottage?" was her only comment. Possibilities of selecting or exchanging, which would once have put her imagination to work, were a burden now. Wanting and not wanting the peace, the unknown world, she clung to the simple world we had constructed, as if it were in danger. "I know I want to be poor."

Above everything she wanted a true home of our own. Loving-kindness of parents had left us alone in our cottage, when I came, and to this we largely owed, as I have said, the good living we had known through this war. Yet war and illness had deprived us of one pleasure, that of entertaining them in our own house, with the almost ritual relationship of host and guest. It was time we lived by ourselves. She had not forgotten her gratitude, when she wrote of a family debate that thickened about her. "It's so bad for me to be buried among them. If I don't get away soon from the Furse family (bless them) I shall go quite crazy!" This was what many a young married daughter has felt.

But how to prevent a falling-off into the peace?

Outside a lovely rain courses among the leaves and fills the room with its cool sound. Will one ever again be quite so aware of these things when they are no longer haunted by war and separation? Will everything be different once we feel secure? As you know, I have a horror of "settling down." Let's not—O let's always be happy and in love. We've done things that some people think impossible in our five years of marriage.

This was on a better day, when she could also write:

I can't find words for what I've learnt in all this strange and deep unhappy pregnancy. I feel and hope that I'm a better person than the one that began to rehearse Angèle. I think one of the strange facts of living is that the more one suffers the

211

more one's capacity for gaiety increases. Do you think that is true? Or is it just that I have always been so inclined to *imagined* fears that I am released by some real-life difficulties and grief?

It ought to have been obvious that she was now alarmingly unwell. There were days when she suffered acutely from sinus or antrum and her nose would bleed violently and clear away poison. There were nights when she could not sleep until four or five, "almost crazy with weariness and trying like a cork to get under water." Her limbs ached, and by the seventh month she was almost too crippled to walk. But she was far from the specialists—not that they had ever cured her—and her doctor put it all down to rheumatism, while reporting well of the baby. Then the extraneous troubles of the previous month returned, and wholly destroyed her peace of mind for a while. "I cling to you and all you are and stand for. God knows I lean on you. Loyalty to you and our kind of living is the only thing that matters." It was a relief when once again, as so many times before, her mother left home and husband to companion her.

I knew that if I missed altogether a more active part in the war I should long regret it, and yet the kind of separation we already had was enough for her to bear, in her adversity, relying as she did on a letter from me at least every other day. I had a fear that to go abroad at present, whether or not into action, might disastrously affect her, and had I then been sent I should certainly be thinking now that it had done so. I consulted my father-in-law, fine soldier of that other war. He said that, in this war, duty only required that one should do what one was told, and nothing to avoid danger. He thought that I might try to go abroad when Robin was born.

She kept casting about for a place to give birth in, and any seemed better than North Devon. She asked if she might take the Mandarin for a talisman by her bed. Her mother was troubled, rightly favouring London, but her doctor saw a risk of premature birth from shock—and now the flying bombs were giving way to rockets. Would that rain cease by October, by the time when she must not travel? The pain was very wearing, but she could still cook as a rule, sitting down, and laugh at her attempts to walk. Once she managed to creep up Venstave to shut a sky-line gate left open: symbolic act, maybe, though she saw it differently.

It was the old white and blue blowing weather of Goosewell days—loud and gay and the hill going up triumphantly to its green crown and the infinite promise of the gate ajar on to sky and adventure. And down in our garden a minute scarlet jersey scampering up and down and shouting encouragement in a preposterously big voice. We are so rich—far richer than we could imagine we would be on any of those lovely Goosewell days. . . . I love you now five years more than I did.

Correspondences with the past, more often ironical, were much in her thoughts. But now summer was gone, with the sun that could rally her, and rain was streaming into our hollow. "This sunflower is very weary of time," she sighed. There was a hint of real autumn:

I heard a sudden great wind hurling in the wood—and it was like the gale that blew all night when Simon was coming. Will you pray that everything may be all right? It's very lonely, you know, travelling alone just now. I want endlessly the bare touch of your hand—your warmth in the darkness. Now *there's* a difference I've never seen in words. What I have is reality—knowing all we have—but still one hungers for actuality. The Kit Wood horse goes neighing over the hill and treads away into darkness—the iron grey clouds blow over, ragged and thick with rain. It's twilight and the candle flares. It's beautiful—all gentle and sad and weary yet very contenting. What you wrote about receiving suffering with open arms is so true. I know it and believe it. I remember that in the pain of labour one must not resist—you go with it.

The rain made her sinus and joints more painful, and for a time she was crippled again. "Sometimes I feel as though I could never open the new book of days that this child will bring. I'm very weary somewhere inside—dangerously so at times, and I cannot bear yet to look at a new life—a peace life. It seems as strange and alarming as the war seemed five years ago." On that score at least I rightly had confidence, for I always knew then what I know now. Even if separated by years or by oceans, we should pick up living again like a conversation snapped by a flash of lightning—should pick it up simply and at once, with nothing but the dazzled question, "Where were we?"

"I feel like someone in the shadow of the valley," she replied in Blake mood, "seeing the sunlight brighten on the head of a watcher on the hills." Then the tossing branches outside would exert their reminiscent sway, and she would fall to thinking of "another Goosewell life, only with Simon and Robin. Happy—God, as only you and I can be happy." And then our notion of the parallel worlds recharged her spirits.

It's all there—just beyond the reach of my fingers—but *there*. You have never had the odd experience of living a different life in the same place. Sometimes I get a most funny sensation—a realisation that under the thin skin which is *now* is the true colour of *then*—not in the past but just below the surface of these days. So I look at our plates and pictures and hear the clock tick in two worlds at once.

Reading your poems this morning and seeing what our love is like, I was again overcome by the certainty that two people can look at the world from one window. It is still a miracle to me.

While proofs returned to Heinemann, Peter Newbolt, her cousin, and now my assistant, was setting up a very small, singular, and careful edition on his private press; so that *Who Live in Unity* became, I suppose, the only serious book of verse to be written and printed in the same military camp in time of war. But her novel was abandoned. "I know I could do nothing first-rate in writing. I still cherish the sad little thought that I *might* have, one day, in a performance, if things had gone differently."

A young officer came up to me in the Mess. He said that it was he who had found and buried my brother, without knowing who he was. I have told the story in *Rex Whistler, His Life and His Drawings*. "Don't you think that fitting things happen?" Jill said. "I believe less and less in coincidence, and more and more in some curious inevitable plan." This is easier to believe when things go well, or at least have obvious rightness. The plan may not always be to one's taste.

In the same anteroom another officer confided to me that he was about to take part in a drop behind enemy lines, which should end the war in October. He even named the place—Arnhem—and this was a week or so before it happened. I thought him perilously indiscreet, and told no one. Afterwards, in the disastrous outcome, I wondered if the enemy had been forewarned.

So the consequences flowed, even down to ourselves. Holland was not freed, the rockets continued to rise Londonwards, and the decision went by default: the baby would be born in Torrington. There was nowhere else to move to. It was soon too late for her to move.

She was described to me as looking beautiful. To give encouragement, I wrote dispassionately on this theme. "How can you be dispassionate, bless you," she replied. Then, modulating into the minor key of all this troubled summer and autumn: "And how can I face growing old, knowing you once thought what you write in this letter? Never mind—we have had that."

XVII

We could never share our miseries to the full, by coming together. Throughout one late October day they diminished with the distance between us. I found her cheerful, though weary, and amused by her further change of shape. She wore pregnancy well by accepting it like a part, if under protest; and here her un-suspected height was a help. For the evening she had a long black gown with a small white pointed collar of cambric, edged with white lace. Over this tumbled and gleamed her hair, darker brown in the candlelight, with red-gold glints in the last sun, for like her complexion it never seemed, when I was there, to have heard about the deep misgivings of her blood. Under this collar she might pin the little pendant with a painted cherub I bought for her in Edinburgh, or the cameo in heavy silver that was her first jewellery after the fire. She looked the Vandyke lady she had imagined, procreant in the wars, and her bulk and im-mobility seemed a foil to the animation of her glance. Though so full of aches, she did not seem to be in serious peril.

We were alone at last, our own family, and at peace. The exterior troubles were all at an end, the crisis seemed to be over, and in fact it was; for her course was determined, and now all moved forward by the light of nature. In the morning, when Mrs Puddicombe had come in to put on the coffee, I went down and returned with a loaded tray, Simon emerging eager from his room. It was a quiet life, with late rising, some cooking from a chair—and for myself the laying of a garden hedge, and a visit to the farm where she planned to convalesce with "the children"— strange-sounding words. Now also that minute particular laugh, which according to Jill she could never produce at all between "lives," was heard again in the rooms.

In the afternoon I lit a fire in the small basket grate upstairs. Viewed from the bed, the hollow underneath it, with angled sides and a sort of vague arch at the back, looked remarkably like a stage-set—one perhaps designed by Jill in her student note-book, after Gordon Craig—but very small and far away, as if seen from the back of a prodigious pit. Indistinct forms appeared on its walls. The fallen ash built up into dubious shapes— Titania's bank, was it, or Juliet's tomb? And the orange light, flowing down, brought back a conversation from the woods round Goosewell, in that now-almost-primitive life five Octobers before, when we had strolled and talked of stage-light-ing, with the last sun streaking the mosses of the ruined drive. How little she had acted since then, for all her hoping and fretting. Her voice on the air once or twice—four weeks in *Rebecca*.

It was growing late; a saucepan of rum, spice and lemon steamed on the coals. At twilight we had placed candles on any flat surfaces round about us, and in an odd assortment of candle-sticks, antique-brass and kitchen-tin, earthenware, and the two wooden ones from Charlotte Street. Now the flames composed a multiplicity of shadows over white wall and ceiling, pointed the green-and-white glass bottle I had engraved on our honeymoon for her wedding present, and seemed to darken into obscurity the glass-pictures we had collected: "Connubial Happiness"—"The Affectionate Departure"—"The Happy Return." Beside the door, as we went in or out, they showed always the Mandarin, his extended finger still secretly meaning a voyage.

Sometimes we dragged out her old heavy cabinet-gramophone, and listened to Flanagan and Allen in the tunes that meant, now, not so much the Palladium as our first winter in the Close. Their sentiment touched something that she prized, the more because it is generally eclipsed in popular music by inexpensive passion of one kind or another—in short, companionship. "Underneath the arch-es"—"Okay, let's be buddies." When they sang, or, rather, sang and talked simultaneously, we went with them all the way and were just comrades.

Good music had entered our lives very little, although I was potentially an ardent lover of music, after my ear had been awakened by a friend years before. But without application there can be no growth in enjoyment, and that I had lacked. Her love was better than potential, and she was better educated. She and Pat had built up together a collection of classical records, and with Stephen she had shared especially her enthusiasm for Sibelius. Before marriage she was often at the piano, to play ballet-music or romantic waltzes; and she could have played well. But it had soon turned to strumming. For though urged by her family, she had never persevered. Inwardly, perhaps, she had said "not this" to a skill there was no time for.

Outside-entertainment, for us two, had always meant the theatre, the ballroom, the cinema, never once the concert hall. At home we had seldom cared enough for the gramophone not to care more for talking, seriously or foolishly, but now there was abundant time to talk, so it seemed, and wishing me not to find the days monotonous, she proposed music at night. On the last evening but one we played her pre-war records of Brahms's Clarinet Quintet. This was new to me, and thus it came fresh to her. It quite exploded a silly prejudice I held against Brahms, but it existed for me in thrilling isolation, because I had enjoyed very little chamber music. I saw, with some wonder, that we had glimpsed a new kind of enjoyment in the years ahead. So the music in its tender darkness seemed to stain the last days we were together, and afterwards to have absorbed the very quality of that life. Other music might perhaps have done the same—the slow movement of Schubert's C Major Quintet; but this we did not have. In the slow movement of the Brahms there is a passage repeated, where the solo clarinet, high and rapt, falls singing through a phrase, and is softly answered by the strings, with indescribable pity. But the answer was more lovingly dwelt on by the Lener Quartet, playing with Charles Draper, than in later performances now known to me; so much so, that I should have to return to that recording to hear it. To me it seemed afterwards that the very heart of our meaning had been expressed in that passage, because, even beyond all that was rapturous and gay, the heart of the meaning lay in the field of pity and was compassion.

And thus we arrived at the end of another "life," I think the forty-second since I went to soldier. That night we talked on till the candles burnt down each side of the bed—talked of the way we would live, of acting and poetry, of our book on Festivals, of relationships hard and easy, of privacy and loyalty, of unselfishness and belief. All the problems were solved; or they were soluble, in one way or another. It was one o'clock when we turned to sleep, and heard for the last time together the low question of the window-latch, and from beyond, already amplified for the winter, the long whisper of the stream that was still time's audible voice, while time was still kind.

Another day looked in through the curtain with its vague steady gaze: every chink had one of its white eyes. To be awake was to be partly gone already. I dressed as a soldier, and got breakfast: soon it was time to be gone finally. Returning to the big room I was suddenly taken by a sort of giddiness or faintness, for some reason. Once in Salisbury Close I had had a curious turn when we were standing at the gates of the Old Deanery, looking at its gloomy front. So instantaneously did she respond with alarm, before the least sound or movement from me, that it seemed there must be something to respond to, something external to us both—in fact something malign in the building itself, with its huge disproportionate windows. Now I knelt by the bed and she took my head in her arms, reassuring. "No wish beyond a mortal sleep."

She said that she was very happy and confident, looking forward to the birth, and untroubled.

Then I was climbing the wood, once more, by the narrow path. It was very still and clear, but as yet hardly full daylight. The oaks and elongated cherries rose like motionless weeds in their deep water of silence, and the cottage seemed drowned in the half-light, as if dead in the bottom of the combe. By the white gate at the top I paused and looked down. She had come to the end window and she called to me. I could see her, but very sketchily, a whitish form at the open casement. I asked if she was all right, and she said yes. Up and down we called to one another for a while, holding on to sound and sight while we could. "I shall have to go now." "Yes, you must go now, my one. Goodbye."

Easier, I always thought, to greet the village car across the meadow, to compare watches and discuss the likelihood of rain, with emotion cut off like music by a closing door, than to be left with it till ordinariness supervened, the "different life in the same place." But her cheerfulness would last, I imagined.

> Even though the day became outwardly greyer and colder, nothing has altered the warmth and light you left me with this morning. It was lovely catching that last glimpse of you at the little top gate—that made me gay. I don't know how it is possible for any woman to be made as happy as I am by you. Today I have really looked forward with pleasure and excitement. The truth is that I am barely half a person without you. Together we are whole. I love and admire you more each day —and admiration is a beautiful thing for married people to keep between them. O I can't come within sight of the end of all the things I want to thank you for.

Admiration is right, however undeserved. We had always tried to temper it with the necessary criticism.

In the night's talk she had declared that she prized gaiety above everything else. An accepted idea has a different value when once it has been plainly framed in words; and I commented on this. She replied:

> I should never have been able to say that about gaiety, except from living with you. When I was small I was gay, but it has taken me nearly all the years in between to recover it, because no one allowed me to believe it until you gave it back to me. But it is true and so important.

There's such a lot to say—but I suppose we shall have enough time in our lives—other beds and other firesides. I need all eternity to love you in. It's when I think of that—often here alone by the bedside candle—that I find all this separation hard to bear, though with my reason I *know* it's not time that matters.

Yesterday I actually struggled up to Newcombe in one of those blue abstracted afternoons of late autumn when the sky seems intensely far away and absorbed in itself. . . . Beloved—the days go on. I do not miss you, for you have given me so much that I still feel I am with you. How inevitably one thing flowers out of another. I think we could not have had the harmony of this leave without the shared grief of the previous one. I still cannot quite get over God letting us be together just then. Something happened to our love then . . . I hope you won't think this probing too much. I love being *aware* of increase, and I can't bear to feel I might miss even one fraction of a detail.

With quiet work, and tranquilly, the days of waiting slipped by. She paid the year's coal bill and ordered six Madonna lilies. It was like the blackbird and the cream cheese again—black and white—the colours of gaiety, whether in a striped skirt, the outside of a Devon pub, or an Elizabethan coat-of-arms: the "colours" of her life, perhaps, with its intense contrasts. "Coal and lilies—O life is so right and exciting and beautiful. Sometimes silly things like that make me very nearly cry with awareness—the meaning, as you wrote, is rammed into them and I don't know what to do about it." Looking out clothes and shoes for the coming winter, her eyes fastened on a sheath of brilliant red satin and another of oyster-colour, quite forgotten.

It's wonderful to have come within a month or two of the end of this long pilgrimage. I wish one didn't have to go through it alone a second time. I should like more than anything in the world to turn from pain to see you by the bed—and to show you our child. There are many little things that the war has taken from us. But then there are equally lovely things that we'd not have had except for the war. How life balances itself quietly and incessantly if one is patient and watches what goes on.

I should like to walk with you out into the melancholy of this evening—to stand on the hills in the grey wind and hear our voices torn to shreds, and come home late, to children in cots asleep and firelight and gaiety. And talk—long talks that I'm so greedy of. Nothing—business, pleasure, or poverty—must jockey us into living too fast. We are not tuned to go at the modern pace of life—we want time like food and sunlight. Pace and crowds both make me shrivel up like a stalk in a wind.

It's Goosewell weather and a Goosewell evening. How far away and long ago. I see you as you were five, six years ago—standing at all the corners of my life. O God how happy we have been, you and I.

On a visit to the north I met some of her theatre-friends, including Michael Macowan, who said that she would have no difficulty in going back to the stage. She replied:

He was encouraging long, long before anyone else, except Norman [Marshall], and tried to work me up to playing Perdita at the Old Vic when I was twenty and still really at the student stage. It warmed me to think of you among those people. It's a lost world that might once have been mine, but never will be now, even if I do go back. I am shut out of that delusive shabby Eden—and I don't regret it in a way. I could still act —but never again belong—if I ever did.

Still the rain fell darkly each day into a hollow that had always been deemed too damp for her in autumn—until this autumn, when there was no alternative. But she relished a November so true to type.

I am dawdling in bed because it's raining so hard that the house is cold with falling water, and the stream seems to tug at the garden as though to sweep it all away. How lovely it would be to float in this cottage down past Woolridge and into the river, and then on and on past Lundy light and away to those fabulous western islands which is where you and I really belong.

O I'm weary this morning—pleasantly so. I could write a very good poem about this curious pause—this anteroom to birth—if I could write a very good poem. It's a beautiful moment, full of the greatest promises and intimations. I like to lie and think of Mary waiting for Christ to be born, and wondering if all women feel the same. I expect they do. Last time I was too afraid of invasion to have the peace of mind to appreciate all this. You know all these things without my trying to explain.

And so at long last she could say that. She had arrived where there was more peace for her than in 1940, instead of conspicuously less.

It was her last letter from the cottage. She had come to agree with me that it was folly to remain at the bottom of a steep hill where no car could reach her, particularly if the pains came on in the middle of the night. For her last week she would stay at Halsdon with her step-grandmother, whom she loved. "It's all very curious. I have found it suddenly easy to face Halsdon because I make myself think that I could cheer Evie up. When I thought of it from my point of view only, I was frightened." Nevertheless, to quit the little house which had been her ark made her apprehensive as the day approached, and more than she could well explain. Still "hating it, but quite resigned," she said farewell to Halsdon Mill with mind and eyes, all her senses, and slowly mounted the hill with her mother.

This minor birth accomplished, her mood was at once restored, and she was fired to finish her novel when the child was born. It was to be called *Before I Sleep* from the Frost poem. She asked for paper, then rationed and therefore semi-precious, and I sent her a ream of it, much more than she would need. "O don't you love *lots* of everything always! M. has said all my life, 'Jill *never* knows when she's had enough'—but I don't think one could ever have or give enough of the good things, do you?" Simon remained with his grandmother at the cottage while Jill was installed in the little room above the porch at Halsdon; and here he came to see her on the first morning, full of wonder at the translation, like a worker-bee whose hive has been moved in its absence. Straight in front was the huge Oriental Plane, among whose numerous dividing trunks she had in childhood planted a currant and a gooseberry, now grown to bushes. There was a sense of home-coming.

Last night I lay watching a troubled moon through the plane leaves, very peaceful and happy. There *is* something about a family house, ugly though it's been made outside. I like thinking of my ancestors back in the 17th Century lying in bed and waiting for their children to be born. And particularly in the autumn it has a shabby melancholy that's friendly and kind—great tawny drifts of leaves swirling in the weedy drive, and idiotic geese screaming in the wind from time to time. The leaves are beautiful, mobbing one's feet in the wind, and lying like footprints on the stones. So I'm glad you arranged this. I have all your serene confidence to lean on. It's stronger than anything else and makes me perfectly at rest.

Apart from my habitual sense, shared by her, that any journey may prove the last, I did have confidence by this time. And yet that constant need to reassure each other! The first birth had not disturbed in the same way.

The baby was to be born in the Cottage Hospital in Torrington, a little hill-top town a few miles down the river, where also her ancestors had lived in the eighteenth century. We had paused before their fine Georgian front on our way to an outing in Bideford or by the sea. At three in the night of November 14th the first pains woke her, and later she woke Evie Furse. By the time her mother arrived she had packed. There were big cups of tea. Then, towards four, "we departed under a crowd of cold stars and went darkly in and out that winding lane." Outside the drive gate she said once, "It *will* be all right, won't it?" but showed no other misgiving.

There was a letter awaiting her at the hospital:

> Remember our love and remember our joy in life. You are the centre and the meaning, and I can never thank you enough for what you give me, which can't be measured by me since it includes my true self. Be brave, and think of the Mandarin, and the serene silence which lies at the heart of things.

"Since then nothing has happened," she wrote to me, the next afternoon. Her ground-floor room, the friendly staff, even the food, were all to her liking. It was in every way better than for Simon's birth.

> Beyond the tiny marigolds in an oval bed on the lawn, and beyond a row of lavatory-brick villas, a hailstorm is lashing the grey country distance. It's all November, and very cosy— by implication I mean. I am here, warm and snug, and Robin —so warm and snug that she declines to leave her first nest and venture out in such cold weather.
>
> I'm idiotically happy, and, if I wasn't anyway, your letter coming this morning would have made me so. I don't deserve such love—it makes me cry—with the beauty of all this—even the coming pain—which after all is only another bit of work to be lived and accomplished in our way.

That day I was in York, seeing to the proofs of our new booklet, entirely practical, though ornamented: *The Officer on the "Air!"* (*Aether*), *Or, The Subaltern's Forget-Me-Not.* I returned at speed down a desolate Great North Road, the car-lights coming on and on through bleary darkness. There was a letter (still from Halsdon) but no later message. That night the pains began in earnest.

Soon after noon, next day, I was in company office when the telephone bell rang for a telegram. I had just seen a snowbow for the only time in my life: the sun came out yellow through the flakes, and there it was, very faint, two arcs of it up into a snow-filled sky. Looking over a shoulder, I followed the slow pencil: "Daughter arrived this morning both very well . . ."

I sent my reply, and went back to my room in an ecstasy of relief and gratitude. I went out to visit a wireless game, driving fast, as though the Snipe could take wing above the hedges. That night a few friends and I had a party in one of our rooms.

She was born at eleven and soon given to her mother, a very strong baby with a great deal of dark hair. After the second sleepless night, and the labour, Jill was tranquil but exhausted, and slept for the rest of the day.

The next morning she was radiant, and hungry for the roast beef and potatoes. She had her bed moved to the window, and wrote a short letter. "She gave me an awful time, but it's over now and forgotten, and I feel very well. O I'm so happy, so close to you and proud to have succeeded in giving you your daughter." All her anxiety that the baby must reflect the ordeal of the summer proved groundless. From the first she had the glow of good health, of well-being. By now, it seems, we thought of her as Caroline, perhaps Robin as well.

At the end of that day Jill suddenly fell into a shivering fit, but roundly affirmed that she was not going to develop a fever. The next morning she owned to having had a temperature; and that her sudden bouts of cold and heat had recalled the day in the Oxford hotel. Her temperature was now 102. She felt weary, though the milk was still coming. I learnt this when I rang up to ask if I could spend a few days with her. But as always she was resolved to save all our time for true living, and I never took the leave that was offered me.

226

She was given a drug, and for two days her temperature was normal; but the milk failed, to her great disappointment. Her doctor was unworried. I wrote to her each day, or twice a day. She replied, once, on a scrap of paper:

> The dragons forbid letter-writing. . . . They gave me M. and B. and it stopped the frightening pains. And now I'm quite normal again. I love you so—it's no good—it makes me cry and I can't write properly. I feel borne up on a great flood of loving and cherishing that blots out all the pain.

This pencilled note was her last writing. For one afternoon she fed the baby again, but abandoned that hope when she was worse at nightfall. Her mother had returned to the cottage with Simon, coming in by bus each day. Depressed now, with bad throat and sinus, unable to read, Jill asked her to stay in Torrington again. Once, after a silence, she quoted, misquoting, a line from a Frost poem—"She passed her daughter in a room upstairs."[1] Her mother said, to rally her, that such dangers were now safely in the past. She still did not want compassionate leave.

With nausea she could eat very little, but was very thirsty. She now accepted that it would be, like so many of her illnesses, a lengthy one, so that after all we should have to spend a "life" in Torrington—though not until she was better. Rivers of rain still fell. But there were glints and washes of sunlight now and again, and lying in the window she could see them. At the cottage, she heard, the plank bridge across our stream had been swept away.

Nine days after the birth she began to feel rheumatic pains in her hands, and for two nights was without sleep. On the following day it was believed that she had acute muscular rheumatism. Her legs were very painful and swollen, and she ached through all her body. Yet the headache had gone and her temperature was

[1] Your mother named you. You and she just saw
Each other in passing in the room upstairs.
        New Hampshire: "Maple".

falling to normal. It was not thought that a second opinion need be called. This trouble was so like the others she had mastered.

She could hardly move now, but was in good heart, and sang to herself. She said that she had been so happy all the week, in spite of the pain. For her sense of achievement in the birth of so beautiful and normal a child was great. She asked her mother to read, not from the Bible or Prayer Book this evening, as hitherto, but poetry; and from *The Spirit of Man* chose the first serene stanza from the Grecian Urn, and then part of Milton's Nativity Ode. But she fell asleep as the reading began and afterwards remembered none of this. She asked to be kissed all over her forehead.

That night a morphia injection gave her seven or eight hours' sleep, and she woke with a normal temperature. At the least sign of improvement she was ready to be cheerful. She had her letters and belongings sorted, and again sang to herself. "I sing to keep my spirits up." Her mother commented that she was better. But she said of the pain in her arms and legs, "it goes on getting worse." And once, after lying very quiet, she said, without further explanation, "I should hate them to be left." That evening her mother read to her the brief Psalm 67, "God be merciful unto us, and bless us," and, as before, the collect from the evening service on the perils of the night, "Lighten our darkness."

During the night she had only four or five hours' sleep, and those only with injections. The next morning her doctor was worried to find that all her joints were affected, with red patches where the poison showed. Too late now he called in a specialist from Barnstaple, suggesting that I should not be rung up until he made his report in the evening. She was very weary, and very thirsty.

Who Live in Unity, the first printed copy from the publisher, reached her this morning. She held it in her hands, and was pleased, but could not open it. My letter was read to her. And now at last she wanted me to come. "I do want to see him."

She had radiant heat on each leg, but said that it was too hot.

Tired and silent, she let herself be arranged. Her temperature was only 99—I suppose because the struggle was over. She refused tea, but sipped a little milk. Then she was very quiet, perhaps dozing, but all the while turning her head from side to side. Presently she said, "What time is it?" It was nearly four in the afternoon. "Isn't it very early?—It's all black and white."

Her mother sat in the window-sill, and left only when the doctors came in at ten to five. They were shocked. The specialist saw that she was dangerously ill, and her chances of recovery very slight. She was now unconscious, moving her head with eyes half-closed. Her mother decided to remain as night-nurse, and hurried to the inn to fetch bread and cheese. Returned, she began to ring me up, but was interrupted by the Matron who said she had better go to her: there had been a change. With her hand in her mother's she died quietly: breathed quickly once, and then no more.

XVIII

That evening, November 27th, a gale got up and blew round Torrington throughout the night; but in the East Midlands it was foggy and flat all day with a patient stillness. Soon after five I was called to the telephone by the Mess waiter. It was her mother's voice. "O my dear—she's gone." I went back to my room, knowing all privation in a moment, and as yet nearly nothing about it. It was like dying, I imagine—at once too strange and familiar to explain—and it was, in a way, dying. It seemed vaguely suitable to find somebody, and I went to find my closest friend, and returned with him. I remember the weight of my black top boots as I swung them up. I cried, and protested my love, and was chiefly aware of the extreme inadequacy of this or anything else I could be doing except physically dying. I was aware of his affection, and this was something positive though far away, and no doubt moderated the violence of it. But to say anything, or nothing, to be stretched on a bed, even to weep convulsively, all seemed merest convention, a meaningless formality to fill up a gap in personal continuance. I knew the converse of her sensation when she said, "I'm so happy, I simply don't know what to do about it!" Alone, I went on protesting my love to her or to nobody, or, if in prayers of a sort, without petition, merely affirming it over and over again, with the private name by which we knew one another. I felt no worse than I was to feel countless times afterwards, through the years ahead. There would be no worse and no better, only greater or lesser realization. There was nothing to learn, only consequences to explore. I was in the timeless present of deprivation. If I thought of a future it was of a brief one in which I could quickly be the same and die literally. No other prospect was tolerable. How could I live without her, who was the meaning, and my only certainty?

Compassionate leave was quickly got for me, and I left next morning. Outside the camp, in the landscape we had shared—the side-road to the hotel, Retford's shabby platform, the branch-line to Lincoln swerving away—there was not so much an anguishing reminder as an appalled and absolute recognition of never again. It seemed to be soaked into objects, into loud brickwork beside the train, and trifling grass along the top of a wall, this dreadfully indifferent yet helplessly passive quality of continuance. I hardly noticed that I had felt the sensation a few months before; for then the sweet core of life was intact, and, by comparison with this, not even that death really mattered.

Waterloo station again. Then Salisbury spire drizzling upwards, insulated for ever from the living charge it received as the fine point of her favourite city. Where, below, we had stood. Yet it was not the sights we had shared, but a new one that hurt most acutely. We had never travelled round to Torrington by train, up the estuary of the Torridge, with a view of Bideford across the river. Across the wide water that little town seemed pictured rather than actual, with its trim quay, its church tower and the hill behind, all rapt in its own fresh concerns and simple as a town in *Struwwelpeter*—as the "little town" in the carol. It looked like an epitome of all the rapturous days we had ever spent in it. From across the separating river I saw us there, and saw us too in glimpses of the twisting road that ran inland to Halsdon under the leafy crags.

Such was my approach to the Cottage Hospital. And there now was the oval bed of marigolds and the bit of distance that she had described and I was helpless not to recognize. Nothing we had seen together could have quite the forlorn desolation of this home she had made, these forever unshareable purlieus of her recent hopefulness. Tearless, I did whatever was suggested. One room was pungent with an unfamiliar brand of disinfectant, so that the clutching raw smell of it remained dreadful to me for years, and even today is at once disturbing. This was to be my strongest recollection, the uncouth smell of that most shocking and pitiable encounter, my first with a dead body—an encounter with something that bore her only a slight resemblance, such as a figurehead might bear, or an image carried in procession, small and stark. And of this small sad doll I was left alone with, to make some sort of farewell, I thought first that it was already too late for me to be there, and then how fiercely she would have minded that I minded that I was; and then I thought that wherever and whatever she was now, palpably and quite apart from any faith and any hope, she was not here and was not this. And in another room a bundle was brought to me with this other image, quick-breathing, dark-tufted, entirely healthy, not at all ugly, fresh-smelling, warm and warm; deep down inside the shawls; with one damp purplish papery frond that rhythmically unfolded and folded, like some tropical aquagrowth in its profound warm element. I sat with her on my knees for a very long while, motionless, not in a daze, but clear-minded in a kind of trance. It was momentous, this meeting of father and daughter. It was a moment for so many feelings; of love for one's own; of pity for a life-long motherlessness—all that she would lose and never remotely know that she was losing; of wonder that health could be amply given in the act of sacrificing it; of gratitude. I felt nothing at all.

I tried hard to feel these things, but I felt none of them at the time, I only thought them. I felt no antipathy or bitterness either: my will was entirely towards my daughter. Such feelings needed time to unfold. Only it was shocking to observe the immediate treason of my instincts, that so quickly, within twenty-four hours, could desert what they had cherished above everything created, and persuade me to remain where I was, not to go back, to prefer this other room with its brisk matronly note, with its active clock and cheery flowers, and the company of this milk-drugged breather, so fragrant, so warm, and so undisastrous.

Thus I entered the hemisphere of loss, which has, not a weather of its own, but a whole new climate of weathers flowing forward without end. They came over me by day and night, in flying fogs and lights of anguish, gratitude, unbearable or assuaging recollection. Within hours most of her family had arrived at the cottage, Theresa returning from Oxford; and in that primitive age or early church of grief it seemed so easy to be open to one another, to share and not exclude. The house was full of her: I do not know if in a supernatural sense. There are some who claim to be aware of the presence of the newly-dead. I am not sure if I know what is meant, but I lived all day in the certainty of our love, hers and mine, without need to differentiate sources, while I reconnoitred this novel hemisphere round the dark limb of the world of loving; while memory lacerated me; while knives flashed into me from her gold shoes in the cupboard, her few brooches in the box; while that passage in the Brahms quintet often fell through my mind like the very rune I ought to have deciphered; while her look was in the air, or on the hill, as if infinity were nothing but tenderness; while the night-window opened to the superficial solace of the stream. After the first return in the thick of that first evening, I was happy to be there, in our house. It is the places not quickly revisited that I should prefer never to revisit. Sleeping pills were pressed on me, but I hardly needed them; for tears were suddenly replaced by an emotionless and waterlogged calm. I slept because I was worn out, and because it is anxiety that keeps me awake. I had nothing now to worry about. Besides, I was accustomed to sleeping alone.

In the instant of waking it was there, with the impact of news. Perhaps I had been dreaming otherwise: I never remembered. Alas, I was to dream of her hardly at all in that last fringe of dreams that are recoverable, for then one seems to invoke chiefly those one is not at peace with, or those who have been guiltily left out of one's thoughtful day. In the instant of waking, in the moment of truth, it was there before words could present it: her notness.

There were times when it seemed an impossibility, suggesting delirium. I do not mean that I had utterly declined to reckon with the chance of it, nor do I mean that it ought not to have happened to *us*, that we thought ourselves privileged. I mean that long since, in some only just apprehensible way, we had dissolved in some area the primal isolation of the self. Fanciful as it will seem to many, I believe this to be possible, and the refutation of those who assert the absolute loneliness of man. Perhaps it is what is meant by being "members one of another." Rilke spoke of "love which consists in this, that two solitudes meet and greet and protect one another." This appealed to our romantic side, and she quoted it, sensing and believing also that love can go farther than that. The solitude is not sealed, somehow it is penetrable. Thus it had been: at times with mysterious effect. We did not merely love one another. We *were* each other. How could she not be there?

Then from this teasing contradiction would break the most grateful of the new weathers, with a sense of her nearness and our unity. Gratitude filled me, gratitude to God and to her. Praying was undisciplined and apt to be deflected from the creator to the creature, not because I thought of her as sanctified or changed, but because my mind was used to conversing with her in absence, and because I had experienced love itself in her image, and long since identified her with love. My prayers to God were a scribble of thanks and entreaties; of requests not only for her acceptance, but still for the safe-keeping of us all, as if she were still living— requests also that what had once been lived should not be cancelled. For myself, I asked to endure, if I must, in the knowledge of her. A friend assured me in his letter that though I could not see beyond the suffering I should in time come through it. I laughed, that his consolation should be so unconsoling; for I wanted nothing better than to live always in the immediacy of loss. In the sharpness of it I felt near to her. The worst was the best. What was unendurable was precisely the idea of "coming through." I distrusted my memory more than I need have, and dreaded the fading of her image if I lived very long. It troubled me that I could not remember her voice, though she had said the same of mine when we were apart; for they had seemed one voice discoursing with itself. She was too close to be heard clearly. But clarity was what I longed for now. If she faded altogether, I thought, that would be the real goodbye; whereas grieving was only loving in another key. For with my mind I might perceive it, but not with my heart—that the issue was removed from my mortal hands and evanescent brain-cells, that heaven could not conceivably depend on human memory, that we always believed the past to have the note of an architecture—and "God requireth that which is past." I clung to that terrific saying.

There is a kind of equity in bereavement: the joy lost is the measure of the pain, and the antidote for it. Lose little, need little, and find little. Still the best is the worst is the best. For the having of love must always be worth the losing it, when the loss is by separation, not by decay. The joy we had tasted together ruled out despair and any flavour of resentment towards God or "fate." That I never felt. Suicide crossed my mind, but only as every fancy crossed it like thistledown. It was repugnant to her thought for me and the children, and would only put some prodigious, if even then not finally uncloseable, distance between us. I had no choice but to try to be what she would want, her acceptance for my model. I must be what she would be if I had died. There was comfort in that pictured reversal, and the few words she had written from time to time about our separation by death made it more acceptably a part of our life. "And if it were the other way round. . . ." "If I ever had to go on without you. . . ." "I know completely there would be no end. . . ." I treasured them now like the fragments of a lost gospel. But if only we had even once talked of death right through, hers and mine. It was folly not to do this. Like most lovers we evaded the issue because we were happy; and then evaded it because we were not. This was a failure.

O yongè freshè folkès, he or she
In which that love upgroweth with your age—

my advice is to force that reluctance. Talk, once, while you may of each other's death. Decide together how it shall be.

The worst was not the fact of her death but the notion that she need not have died. In a forlorn attempt to exchange torturing doubt for a certainty no doctor will ever bestow, I asked that specialist, when paying his bill, if she could have been saved; but his reply was ambiguous. It seems now that from her so-called paratyphoid onwards she may have had only the one mysterious complaint, brought on again by the night of the fire; for two readers of this book with medical knowledge have independently seen it as Lupus Erythematosis, a disease very difficult to diagnose at the time, and still fatal. Clearly she had some chronic disorder of the blood, and at last had given all her strength to make a flawlessly healthy child; for such is the behest, and such the marvellous provision, of Nature. Whenever it seemed that but for the gratuitous strains of the summer, but for the lack of an antibiotic, she might have been alive, I suffered. She herself always maintained that, with me, she would never be seriously ill. I hoped it was illusion. I hoped she was incurable. Sometimes I thought so.

Next to this the worst pain lurked in a train of thought that de la Mare afterwards crystallized for me.

> *Never one came loving thee;*
> *Never loved thou one, now gone;*
> *But some hapless memory*
> *Was left—to live on.*

I would come, in her letters, to a place where I had failed her—as an actress perhaps. "O if only you could care a little!" That ghost, for one, was not laid. Then trifles might hurt. In our last days, anxious for me not to be bored, she had suggested my bicycling to the antique dealer in Hatherleigh. I did so, and returned with two chairs and a plate for her; but it took two or three hours. Some tiny uncomplaining comment then showed that she had minded the solitude, had thought it strange of me to leave her, after all the months apart. (I had some bovine superstition that time would be ample if one behaved as though it were.) I knew she would now say that it was nothing ... would take the blame herself. . . . But the stab of it went on.

And then round I swung to seeing that our love was a bonus from the beginning. How unlikely it was, as she said, that we should have found one another "in such a crowd." The war came, and there were still five years. Perhaps one should see life as a bonus always? If one deserves nothing, ought one to expect anything? It would certainly be gay if this notion could be sustained. Compared with some, we were patently unlucky. But compared with others?—those, for instance, who had travelled across Europe, waterless, in cattle-trucks. . . . All human comparisons are meaningless. There is only luck. And luck is always unique, with its never-repeated, its unrepeatable, challenge.

These thoughts had found a home in my mind by the day of her funeral and the christening of Caroline; which followed one another and made a single festival. She would have thought it strange, yet beautiful, that she should be christened and married and buried, and her daughter christened on the day of her burial, all by one man, her great-uncle. For it was again the bishop's voice—now imperatively uttering those words of an astringent consolation. *Who Live in Unity*, held by her hands but never read, had been put in her coffin. Controlled against the pity of the scene, I never thought she was in that box. Much of the poetry of death had become nonsense overnight. "And dreaming through the twilight. . . ." One never will be. "To lie in cold obstruction and to rot." A nursery nightmare—one can never experience it. I found the brass handles distasteful, with all the other fiction of permanence, and though I liked the box to appear with the old habit of flowers, I wished it were quite rough and makeshift, and the grave shallower—not such a plunge for root-fibres. Her father and I had chosen a place under great beech-trees on the south edge of Dolton churchyard. Here we planted an Irish yew, and another at the cottage. Here my body could be put next to hers—if my other idea came to nothing.

Any clue to her conception of what I ought to do, or probably would do, was important. "I should hate them to be left." Had she meant me and the children—or the children alone? The second I thought. She would not suppose that I should destroy myself, but I thought she thought that I should grasp at any honourable chance of dying. Thus, paradoxically, my own strong impulse was enforced by appearing to figure in her map of disaster.

I knew that the children would be blessed and happy with their grandparents, supposing they were orphaned. On leave I wrote simultaneously to my colonel and my company commander, asking to be sent to a fighting battalion. The former replied, "I will certainly go into the question of your going to France," and suggested that I might understudy a signals officer out there, who had been trained by me and was due for relief. The other promised support, while reminding me that the battalions had asked for no officers more than thirty years old to be sent.

I returned to Ranby to resume my duties for the time being. But a great apathy overcame me, and I moved like a ghost about the signals office, virtually handing over to my assistant. I mean that I felt like a ghost, only sketchily present. We joked a good deal, and the obscure technical and typographical quips thickened in *The Officer on the Air* with each edition. I developed a pre-dilection for a laugh at any price, but I did not take this for gaiety. A fling of small birds, making angles across the sky, meant un-happiness now, as plainly as once it would have meant happiness.

This job was finished. Yet to begin again as a platoon com-mander in an ordinary non-specialist company seemed to lead to the age-veto and was not advised. I must be patient. Sometimes I looked ahead to being in action, without pleasure but curiously without any concern at all. I had no day-dreams of reckless gallantry, but I was almost certain that, with self-preservation muted, and consequently fear, my courage was enough to meet the case. I really did long to be dead. This was a time when I most wanted help in contriving a means. But I had no friends in high places.

Three months wasted away, and the armies were already on the Rhine when I was suddenly posted to the Phantom Regiment. It existed, I learnt, to provide the command with direct information from the scene of fighting. Phantom had worked through every battle in Europe and the Middle East with great success and many casualties. Here was my chance. But when I reached Richmond Park it was back to school again for month after month, until the azaleas and bluebells were out round Pembroke Lodge in a sensuous daze. That is, I smelt them in a daze of remoteness, those hollow hot reflections of the brightness she had informed. I began then to see the beauty of the world like someone looking at a sunlit scene with one eye shut, aware of brightness and blindness simultaneously, the one not exactly diminished by the other but impregnated with it. The war was now ending in Europe, and in the Far East Phantom was not used. When I was offered the wireless training of cadets in my own regiment, I accepted. Perhaps if I had declined I could by some means have contrived to see something of "abroad"—after the fighting. It seemed immaterial. In short, it was too late.

In the following winter I travelled somewhere for my cardboard homburg hat and outsize mackintosh, on an afternoon that was the final reckoning for that other, four light-years away, when we drove into Bideford light-heartedly for me to sign on, and made light of it.

A civilian again, I went to live with my children and the Furses in London; afterwards in Devon. From the Top of the World I could see Torrington spire, like a thorn in the evening sky that glowed, far on, above Bideford. From a place not far away I could see the elms of Venton and the beeches over her grave. Between me and the one, the river; between me and the other, our hidden stream. With the beginning and the end of the story rounded into one countryside, the story seemed small, as it moved back irrevocably into the past.

Her death had been broken to Simon by Theresa, who more and more from this time took the place of his mother. In his desolation he received it like a grown-up, with a strange understanding. But the dead are so quickly locked up in each tongue-tied heart—drowned in the devoted silences of a Trappist brotherhood. I could not bear that this should happen to Jill. Yet what we two could have taught the children, by living it, I alone could never say. What could I say of her but trivialities to a four-year-old boy whose own disaster was all incommunicable? When we met after her death his one comment, before showing me some toy or picture, was far more poignant than loquacity: "I did like Mummy." Or what could I say, later, to a little girl who would unconsciously be dealing, not with a loss, but with an absence? Impossible to reveal the true material of my mind at all. The sheer density of it would repel. More hideous than silence, and more disfiguring to Jill's faint portrait in their minds, would be the imposition of an adult and unshareable grief. In any case "mourning," "widower," "bereavement"—how dismally Victorian it all sounded, smacking of the closed piano and the lowered blind. I wanted the thing itself, love-in-absence, without one particle of embalming convention.

I resumed glass-engraving and researched for my book on Festivals, missing also acutely at times that other companionship, my brother's. Poetry was finished, an abandoned working. Impenetrable rock lay between me and that seam of supposed promise. Also the sense of owning one's world, which is complementary to the sense of belonging, had evaporated. For the happy are like the successful in this, that they own whatever landscape they inhabit. The managing director, floated through the Midlands to lunch in some country hotel, is owner of each fleeting village. We had owned the Torridge valley, parts of London, and the view from every window we stood at. But the shabby man combing the newspaper in the reference library does not own even the grudged grain of its too-public table-top. In those first years of the peace that now seem to me, in my sanguine and extended summer, like one continuous winter, I felt nearer to him than to the other: of no account on the shiny pavements. The old nullity almost came back. I say almost, because I really knew that it could not come back, that in her love I had passed some point of no return. In bad hours I discounted this. I was back in the first nothing. We together were, and I alone was not. I needed her presence more than ever before, to bear so great a misfortune as her absence.

At those times I was glad when our love was remembered by others, and reflected from them; for a pleasure that had once been mere titillation had become a want. Anyone who mentioned us together gave an access of warmth; but few did, after quite a short while, for past relationships are tedious, and our marriage had been very private. Only her sister understood at all fully what had been, and what was.

Here I ask myself if I indulged in self-pity, and the only answer I can give in honesty is no, or seldom. The reader may have formed a different opinion. If so, it may be that I refuse to recognize in myself a failing I dislike in others. But I observe two things. First, when a young dog died of hard-pad, I felt exactly the same stuff of emotion, only less of it. My tears for that small rigid body were not tears for myself—in any sense that allows of a distinction between pity and self-pity; and without that distinction there is nothing to discuss. What, though, is pity for, in death, and to what directed? Obviously to the being which has relinquished all the sweetness of living—though also unreasonably; for either we are pitying a non-existence, which is absurd, or one who, still existing, may not call for pity. But surely pity is evoked by the mere and monstrous fact of death, that final outrage upon love, whose nature was at odds with transience even in its milder forms. It is "the pity of it" in abstract that we keenly feel. The second thing I observe is that I did not really think my case pitiable.

For all the while there was the knowledge of the truth of our love, which had meaning now—or had never had the meaning we supposed—and it did have that meaning. This I never disputed. Our sense of the eternal had not been an illusion. The truth still held. It was there always, through distraction or depression, now tentative and now insistent, withdrawing and emerging, like the three-note repetition in Vaughan Williams's Sixth Symphony, only never threatening; or like the noise of the stream as the window swung wider or was closed; or like spokes of light through some tumbling, chaotic sky, all the while stalking and scanning a cloud-dim horizon. In society I held our oneness like a talisman, secret in the hand. In crowds I cherished her.

> Too many people, none of whom are you,
> Pour through the station barrier; the swing-door
> Shudders and gives me the wrong face.

So wrote Christopher Hassall of Stephen. I knew that desolation, and the warmth it generated. The brevity of her achievement moved me to compassion, as if protectively; for though I never went now to the play because I shunned the stuffy fragrance of an auditorium, and anyway had to work until bed-time, I knew enough of the theatre to know that she would quickly be effaced from its shallow memory—far more quickly than Meggie Albanesi of the early death. And who recalls her?[1] There was a striking similarity between their careers, in fact, and this was remarked on for a time.

Given time and health she could have done in her art what I could never do in mine, for all her wishing: justice to love. "There can be no doubt that Jill would have reached the top," wrote Bertie. Scott. "Even as it was, her terrific spirit triumphed over her body. Her Juliet would have been ideal." I asked Norman Marshall why, in his opinion, she had never got to Shakespeare after all. Shakespeare mostly meant repertory, and repertory was arduous: perhaps she was not deemed to be robust enough. He also had the interesting notion that beauty is suspect on the English stage. A French producer had pointed out to him that in England if a girl has real beauty we seem to think that she ought not to have real talent. (The romantic abnegation again.) Marshall says:

[1] Died in 1923, aged twenty-four.

I know that as a producer I shall never again meet an actress of her peculiar quality—that combination of exquisite beauty and ability to portray emotion with absolute purity and clarity. It was the simplicity of her acting which was so remarkable, the result of utter sincerity, I suppose.

Against insincerity I took a vow. I would not exaggerate, or falsely simplify. If I forgot her, dreadful as it was to contemplate, I would forget. I would never pretend to feel what I did not feel, knowing that to do so would be to lose her more quickly. I would grieve for her when I grieved, rejoice when I rejoiced, and apart from her I would enjoy life as much as I could. Enjoyed it I have, in this second summer of my middle age.

Nor, I vowed at once, would I strain after illusory contacts. A spiritualistic lady soon offered to "put us in touch," delivering, by way of sample, a "message" from Jill so banal as to suggest that her personality had been dissolved rather than preserved. It repelled me; but I accepted that this person was innocent. There are others who are not—who wait about for the newly-dead like specks in an Indian sky. Direct communication with the dead, if feasible, ought to have some importance in the shape of things. Is it conceivably left in the hands of a few dubious women, operating for money, and by a method not acknowledged by Christ, a method which never seems to lead anyone nearer to God? To prepare towards her, I preferred channels that were less meretricious, and applied myself to waiting.

It might be for a long time. I had once dreamt of a painted plate—a picture plate for us to hang at the cottage. Under a blob of blue sky it showed the Prince bending over the Sleeping Beauty in the very moment of awakening her with an embrace. But the moment was arrested. Both figures were wound about and thickly scribbled over with green briars.

Waiting could be long, certainly; yet when the future seemed a patchy road across a landscape, to some flashing window-pane on the horizon, I reminded myself that it was more nearly a plank without a hand-rail from which one could step off sideways by accident. This gave a touch of excitement. I am frightened of the act, not at all of the fact, of dying.

And time had its curious repetitions and mutations. She died at the dead point of the year, a few days before Advent, which is the spiritual beginning. On every 27th of November it seemed as if events were taking place again, almost as if they were branded on a portion of space which the earth passes through at that period. As the short day closed in, often with the same damp inertia, I felt that she was dying again, and again might be saved, and I was not at peace until a little after five in the evening. On the other hand the whole background was changing. For us love and war had been so commingled that for some years afterwards the war itself seemed a great happiness. Really they had been like oil and vinegar whirled together: as they settled apart the war seemed increasingly dismal and depriving. And yet love and war are traditionally linked, and those lovers are lucky whose adventures fall in a time of long truce, though wise not to take it for a birthright. We live now under a threat more terrible than any; but the terror lies in the suffering, and in the will to inflict the suffering, not in the destruction. For things must end, and to pin one's hope on the perpetuation of the race is a vanity. If the threat can never be withdrawn, now the secret is out, I personally should like it to be heightened, with the discovery of a means to detonate all matter in the globe instantaneously by chain-reaction. Probably the public knowledge of it would have a disintegrating effect on society. I think it ought to have a tonic one: to know that life might end any day without pain and without grief. For every illusion of permanence would be exposed, every new day would be a gift and a matter for congratulation, as it ought to be now. Great art could be created for the only sound reason—even architecture or epic, needing years to accomplish. Nothing would be worth doing unless it were worth doing for its own sake.

Also it would sharpen the issue which is increasingly blurred in our time, and fundamentally there is no other—the issue being whether there is meaning or not. There is or there isn't. In the past I have sometimes doubted if there is, to my cost, but never since her death have I supposed that the meaning could be other than the truth of Christianity. If that were not true it ought to be true. If it were not true it would always be unique, and the best that could ever be imagined to the end of time. If it were not true, if even *that* were not true, meaninglessness to me would be proven. It seems that such an amalgam of perfection and unlikelihood would have to be true to have been thought of at all.

Still, lovers do not see themselves as due for obliteration, however painless, but fulfilment. Were we tempted, after all, to claim it as of right? "Happy as only you and I can be happy. . . ." Though not so foolish as to think ourselves unique, we thought that we personally had not encountered this love in others well known to us. Llewellyn Powys says that one should "sacrifice everything to it," thereby betraying an ignorance of the nature of love, which cannot adopt selfishness as a policy, but has to use it on the sly, like a secret agent, never "recognized." Our fault was, of course, repeatedly this—and generally to be too private and apprehensive. We might have been otherwise, but the timing was unlucky. No sooner had we found our truth than we must guard it against the huge disturbances of war, that always threatened to efface it, and did. So it was four cupped hands around a resolute wick in a gale.

"This candle will not burn again. . . ."

Yet there was one place where no fear existed: in the centre. There we were beyond fear of one another, and at peace. Poets and other romantics love to distinguish two types of feminine excellence, contrasting women who are good all through, but commonplace, with those who are rare in quality, but true only to themselves—the romantic point being that what you really want must be teasingly unattainable. For who wants either a self-centred woman or a woman who is merely wholesome? If the two kinds of merit are united, as they can be, the one enhances the other. You must do without the "mysterious," it is true; but in exchange you may enjoy for always the infinite novelty of the familiar. I never tired of her company at any time. She was no saint, I suppose—not that I should recognize a saint—except that towards me she may have been one. In great things as in small she put my good constantly before hers. Being also "rare," she deserved her match, a Troilus for a lover, or someone equally heroic and less silly—as Criseyde did not. For while she resembled that "rare" one in many ways,

> *eek simple and wys withal,*
> *Charitable, estatliche, lusty and free,*
> *Ne never mo ne lakkede in pitee,*

she was not sliding of coráge. She would have kept faith even when captive in the Greekes ost, even in a concentracioun camp. So indeed would I, in some filament of shredded self.

Her death, Kate O'Brien had written, was a blow of the kind that "only poetry can answer." This to encourage. The remark, or rather my perception of its truth, made doubly hard the silence in which I was locked. In my failure as a poet I was failing her, but if the muse became incarnate the muse could die; and I was not orientated to make a thing out of the absence of a thing.

Then one day, years later, I was on the island of the cottage stream in the noise and light that were above all her awareness. I began, with caution, surreptitiously almost, to try out words on the simple theme of her notness—as if the open window required her to look or listen, and received no answer. The dead weight of disuse had to be lifted with effort, but other verses came, if only in response to a few moods, a few weathers out of the whole climate. The present book was planned much earlier; for though I had failed as a poet I was still a maker. Since I could not share in her death, I had to make answer to it; and to make, in one way or another, and to the utmost of my power, however disappointing the result, became more than ever the necessity of my life. This book is not, to me, backward-looking; and I do not, myself, consider that I have been living in the past: it is a case rather of "I think so once, and I thought so still." Nevertheless it is also her memorial. And, yet again, it is partly worked by herself, a book by two authors written in the absence of one. For we were of those that have intelligence of love; and my heart is inditing a good matter.

Sometimes, in the right context, but by chance and never if sought, there comes for a moment actuality of the past, the very quality of some day or hour; for the lost joy is now like the scent of a flower which cannot be savoured for more than a moment. Sometimes there comes, like sun-bud over the horizon, a clear recognition that all shall be well. Then for a while the day is transformed: I would not have missed this suffering if I could. For if all shall be well from the temporal standpoint, all *is* well from the eternal. The restitution is a fact as well as a promise. Then any suffering must be accepted as a feature, rewarding and perhaps indispensable, of what truly is. But of "what truly is" one can guess very little: only that it is established out of love, and for it. At such a time it appears that this is what may have been meant by that rune often found on walls and windows, if it could be induced to mean anything at all: "God is love." Whatever else he may be, he is that of which one has had, still has, a pinch, on the palate, in the hand, like a particle of stellar dust. This is a fragment of the fabric of what is, and any genuine piece of it belongs to the whole.

It is. Not it was and will be. Love does not ask to be perpetuated. It supposes the timeless and tries every moment to extend in it as into another dimension.

But one must talk the language of time. There is the hope that it will be conspicuously different, without the gross alloy of selfishness and fear and ill-health—with no shadow to stay the fulness of her coming. After fourteen years I dreamt that she had returned. She came running out of a white house on a hill, with lifted hair, spontaneous and strong, transformed into brilliant health—running fast and shouting her lines in some play, her voice raised as if in some big theatre. A little boy was there, enchanted and impressed at the sight of her—perhaps Simon as she last had known him, or perhaps his half-brother, they were so alike. "It isn't any good for us to be apart, you see," she said so tenderly and lovingly, yet as if reprovingly, I felt. I was astonished again by her instant understanding of my mind. She was entirely known, and I was blessed, but too much moved. "I want to talk to you," I whispered. Her sister was with me, serene, and wholly involved. We linked arms and fingers, all three, and moved away somewhere. A dream may be a nothing, and still signify to the awakened dreamer.

There is the hope that it will never be different—that however bad the intervening events, however long the separation (but length is nothing) the same energies would greet one another— the very same. To look and to recognize. If I had forgotten, I should remember. I might forget, but I could not remember and unlove her for a quarter of a minute. To look well and to know, eye to eye, mind to mind, reflecting a truth to infinity like mirrors.

I know that her love existed and was good to me, and does not now exclude another love, but enables and participates in it. If her love was not good I do not know what good is; but I do know. If it is part of what is real I do not mind how small a part it may be. To have the smallest is to have enough, and in a way, through the essential vicariousness of love, to have it all. Envy more than momentary I never feel; for I would not exchange with anyone who has lived, or will live. And to have enjoyed rather more than a smile in the street is worth even Dante's genius. Stronger than all misery, with its harrowing sense of short measure, is the perception I always have—have now, as I had it then—of an unexpected, measureless, laughably undeserved, good fortune.

ADDITIONAL POEMS
by Jill Furse

POEMS

RETURN TO YESTERDAY

Here on the kindly and familiar hills,
The valley small under my idle foot,
Why should the heart be grieving any more,
What worm is groping at the happy root?

Because the crying of the sheep recalled
The ache of Spring into this barren field—
That cry of birth so very near our own—
A voice of childhood that is never stilled.

But there is grief at all nativities.
The birth of love is anguished and obscure,
And its hot flame in growing travail burns
All our first dreams, our childish furniture.

Till we come naked to the brilliant hour
Of earthly beauty, when in passion's name
Flesh too must fall and be consumed with fire,
Like a white tree of thorn in flame.

From that loved sacrifice, the child I was
Comes back into these country hills, a ghost;
And in this evening of an adult world
Cries for some early joy that has been lost.

[1939]

A DREAM OF OBLIVION

I dreamed you shut the door in anger
  Upon our loving for the endless years,
And I went out across the burning land
  Haunted with passion and the death of tears.

And like Ophelia, very cool with flowers,
  Laid this wild sorrow on the dreaming tide,
And in my slow, drowned heart the river
  Washed out Tomorrow from my aching side.

Until I floated in a strange oblivion,
  The water shining through an empty mind,
Knowing no past, nor any time to come,
  Your image gone, and the whole crystal blind.

PERFECT STRANGERS

He could not see beyond the pillow's edge
To where Time sheltered her, his rose to come,
Shut in the calyx of unopen days,
And all her warm dream innocent of him—
Yet like an angel in a country nave
Waiting to break her silence on his name.

[1944]

I KNELT IN STARLIGHT

I knelt in starlight after you were gone,
Knelt in the wind that closed about me
Like the petals of a flower
Veiling all nakedness of love and pain,
Wishing no longer that I had your arms again,
Content to give the wind his hour.

THE RAIN FALLS SILENT

The rain falls silent in the garden,
Of other tears compassionate.
Ashes of the declining fire
Whiten a little in the cooling grate.

And you have shut the door and left me
Walled up in silence, like a ghost
Nor book nor candle exorcises,
To haunt one room and think of what is lost.

I cannot read the page you wrote
In the brief hour that was mine.
In present tears the meaning dies,
The words run dark into the candleshine.

TRANSITION

The world, in whose enchanted arms
A child lay and dreamed of this,
Never betrayed how much is lost
In the betrayal of a kiss.

For love that now has captured me
In the snare of moving hours
Sets a thorn of ivory
In every gentle wreath of flowers.

With every rapture that I sing
The childish tears will blind me.
In every room I look into
A door has closed behind me.

GLORIA IN EXCELSIS

Fold your impetuous hands and kneel
On crowding daisies furred in dew,
And with their innocence look up
Between the tall flames of the yew
To where the white, imperial clouds
Sojourn awhile, divinely slow,
Like swans that sleep upon illustrious water
Breasting the warm air with a shield of snow.

THE HARE IS VANISHED

The hare is vanished from the darkening hill,
Colour from beauty, and the heart is still.
The lark no longer from his spiral stair
Exhorts the shepherd in the sunlit air.
Now along silent lanes a shower is born
In unlit diamonds on the margin thorn,
And on the mournful gate a fringe of tears
Delays to weep until the moon appears.
Now one by one within the valley's fold
Infrequent windows open eyes of gold,
And pause unwinking in the falling rain,
Or edge in envy round the patient train
That through the small and fading landscape plies
Like a bright needle in old tapestries.

ON A SUNDIAL

There is no future for us, and no past;
For though the hours still keep their ancient race
On a great wheel confined in little space,
Their numbers crumble into air at last.
Look now upon this fading dial and trace
The few slant capitals that hardly spell
How swift time's finger travels to efface
That very doom his journey would compel.
Here is a state divided, on whose breast
Time upon Time makes war: the figures steal
Out of the sun, like men, to find their rest.
And we, no longer broken on the wheel,
   Confess in quiet that we are set free—
   Time never was, and never more shall be.

THE TOMB

Here the dark answer of decay
Has closed all argument; the eager mind
However long it may delay
Must in this end conclusion find.
Beauty is dead; ashes of her perfection cloud
Forgotten hollows in the pitiful shroud.

The scattered gold from lilies blown
Into the shadows of her lovely name,
A little cipher carved in stone,
Gilds for a windless hour her vanished fame.
No sound can reach her, but the envious rust
Of lichen creeping, and the desolate hush of dust.

THE STATUE OF A NYMPH

Forgive me that my lips are cold
Beneath the amorous sun,
And in the quiet hand you hold
All tenderness is done.

Sweet warmth and I are parted,
Long absent to remain,
And I run stony-hearted
Through weeping summer rain.

Time's dark and groping fingers bind
Me here, with ivy stayed,
To run unceasing till I find
Love's golden accolade.

But what love is I do forget,
So know not what I seek,
And all the summer's tears are wet
On my deserted cheek.

[1937]

AIR FOR A THUNDERSTORM

O let the weeping flute complain
The summer storm's inclemency;
The lilies now are crowned with rain,
The rose relinquishes the bee.
The fountains with dishevelled hair
Disdain the pools that gave them birth,
And through the dark and hurried air
Are flung upon an alien earth.